PENGUIN BOOKS

SIMPLE COOKING

Although born in Quincy, Massachusetts, and now living in
Castine, Maine, John Thorne is no Yankee cook. An Army
brat, he spent his childhood sampling the many flavors of
regional American cooking and several foreign countries. He
taught himself to cook as an impoverished college dropout
living in New York's Lower East Side, where hunger sent
him exploring that city's many ethnic foodways for cheap but
exciting fare, and his later career as a low-paid private school
teacher and editorial assistant at Harvard kept those early-
acquired culinary skills honed. Since 1983, he has devoted
his time to writing and publishing a series of culinary pamphlets and the food letter *Simple Cooking*.

SIMPLE COOKING

John Thorne

PENGUIN BOOKS

PENGUIN BOOKS
Published by the Penguin Group
Viking Penguin Inc., 40 West 23rd Street, New York, New York 10010, U.S.A.
Penguin Books Ltd, 27 Wrights Lane, London W8 5TZ, England
Penguin Books Australia Ltd, Ringwood, Victoria, Australia
Penguin Books Canada Ltd, 2801 John Street, Markham, Ontario, Canada L3R 1B4
Penguin Books (N.Z.) Ltd, 182–190 Wairau Road, Auckland 10, New Zealand

Penguin Books Ltd, Registered Offices:
Harmondsworth, Middlesex, England

First published in the United States of America by
Viking Penguin Inc. 1987
Published in Penguin Books 1989

1 3 5 7 9 10 8 6 4 2

Portions of this book first appeared, some in different form,
in the author's *Simple Cooking* newsletters.

LIBRARY OF CONGRESS CATALOGING IN PUBLICATION DATA
Thorne, John.
Simple cooking/John Thorne.
p. cm.
Bibliography: p.   Includes index.
ISBN 0 14 01.1737 7 (pbk.)
1. Cookery.   I. Title.
TX652.T458   1989
641.5—dc19   88–22428

Printed in the United States of America by
Arcata Graphics, Fairfield, Pennsylvania
Set in Caslon 540

Grateful acknowledgment is made for permission to reprint the following copyrighted material:
Recipe for "Rice and Peas" and excerpt from *The Gentle Art of Cookery* by Mrs. C. F. Leyel
and Miss Olga Hartley. By permission of Chatto & Windus/The Hogarth Press and the Estates
of Mrs. C. F. Leyel and Olga Hartley. Excerpt from *The Autobiography of Edwin Muir*. By
permission of Gavin Muir and The Hogarth Press. Excerpt from *The New England Yankee Cookbook*
by Imogene Wolcott. By permission. Excerpt from *Good Cheap Food* by Miriam Ungerer.
Copyright © 1973 by Miriam Ungerer. First published in 1973 by Viking Penguin Inc. A
Wallace Cole Book. Reprinted by permission of the Schaffner Agency. Excerpt from *Pearl's
Kitchen* by Pearl Bailey. Copyright © 1973 by Pearl Bailey. Reprinted by permission of Harcourt
Brace Jovanovich, Inc. Excerpt from *Greek Food* by Rena Salaman. By permission of William
Collins Sons & Co. Excerpt from *The Fine Art of Italian Cooking* by Giuliano Bugialli. Copyright
© 1977 by Giuliano Bugialli. Reprinted by permission of Times Books, a division of Random
House, Inc. Excerpt from *Cucina e Nostalgia* by Alfredo Viazzi. Copyright © 1979, 1983 by
Alfredo Viazzi. Reprinted by permission of Random House, Inc. Excerpt from *The Mediterranean*

for Joan

Contents

✸

List of Recipes

Acknowledgments

❋

Almost everything in this book appeared in its original form in *Simple Cooking*, the quarterly food letter I've been writing and publishing out of my own kitchen and living room for the past seven years. I started it—along with an accompanying set of small pamphlets—with no special training either as a writer or a cook, just the desire to share my passion for seeking out the modest, delicious dishes that I was then (and still am) convinced that a home cook could use as the ground for genuinely personal cuisine. That belief is the true subject of *Simple Cooking*—both the food letter and this book, which examples the very best of it.

I plunged into this proselytizing mission with no thought of making it a career . . . and so was as much terrified as delighted when a success beyond my wildest dreams forced me to choose between *Simple Cooking* and my "real" job. The choice seemed obvious at the time, but looking back now, I can see what a risky midlife-career move it really was—and what a debt of thanks I owe my early readers, whose encouragement (and renewals) saw me through. Earning a living writing a food letter, even when its subscription base is doubling every year, is to lead a very interesting life.

A lift of the glass, then, to my first readers (and to a few especially, whose tireless and selfless effort on my behalf is owed what no word of appreciation can hope to express). Thanks, too, are due to my parents for their unflagging support, and to Joan, for reasons she knows well. This book is for her . . . and in memory of Mick, who tasted happily and without criticism, for he gnawed every bone, save that of contention.

John Thorne
Simple Cooking
Box 58
Castine, Maine 04421

Rice and Peas:
A Preface with Recipes

❋

Like most people nowadays, I learned to cook from reading cookbooks. Not only has most of what I know been culled from them, but, day in and day out, the culinary company I keep comes from the written word, not from personal experience or oral tradition. My grandmother was proud of a rich ethnic heritage, but her cooking was Fannie Farmer with a vengeance. She abhorred all seasoning, and the spice canisters in her kitchen looked as though they had been purchased one fine day many years ago and then set on the back of the kitchen shelf to wait a call that never came. However, she did have (or rather, since by the time I paid attention she was laid up by arthritis, the ladies who did for her had) a set of dishes that were rotated through the family week, requiring no recipes.

My mother, although by far the better cook, learned most of her repertoire from cookbooks and food pages. In her kitchen, the cupboard doors are covered with favorite recipes for quick reference, and if one falls and slips under the refrigerator, she, like you or me, finds her mind suddenly, stubbornly blank, no matter how many times that dish has been made before.

I cook like this, too, but I'm not happy about it. Cookbooks can be wonderfully entertaining and informative, but I don't like having to bring them with me to the stove. My goal as a cook has always been not so much to attain some specific sense of mastery as to be able to just go into the kitchen, take up what I find there, and make a meal of it.

If you're in sympathy with this notion, you'll know from your own experience that such simple cooking isn't easy cooking, or the supermarkets wouldn't be as stuffed as they are with convenience foods. You may also have discovered that an impromptu, impulsive, and ever-adaptive cooking style is not one that the cookbook—of whatever sort, it seems—is by nature equipped to explain.

That's because cookbooks are, almost always, compilations of recipes, and the simplest recipe, no matter how good and easily understood, can offer only an act of re-creation. Whether you follow the directions exactly or vary them to your taste, you still can't step back behind them into the sensibility that existed before it did—to that moment in the kitchen when the cook really *did not know* what she was going to do with all that stuff before her on the table (or before *him*, of course—I mean to make no distinction of sex here or anywhere in these pages, so far as they concern the cook).

In this regard, creativity is a one-way street: very few cooks are willing or even able to afterward evoke the ferment, the confusion, the groping before the moment that shaped the dish. What we get instead is a rationale that works backward from the finished dish, a rationale that makes everything seem as if it had all been clear and obvious from the start.

The argument for this approach is that anything else would confuse the reader, who really only wants to get the dish done and onto the table as quickly as possible. But even if this is so, it still seems strange to me that there is hardly a single cookbook in existence in which the author encourages us to share the muddle and mistakes and wrong turns—and to consult other cookbooks besides their own—in order to make the experience of cooking a real one. For it is exactly those hesitations, confusions, moments of panic—and then the growing sense of confidence—that shapes the experience of the real cook. The rest is only recipes, and while some of them do require skills somewhat greater than merely knowing how to follow directions, what they offer as *experience* is very limiting.

At first, this does not seem so, for a large part of any cookbook's intrinsic appeal is an enticing fantasy: when we cook from Paula Wolfert or Craig Claiborne or James Beard, we can pretend that we are, if not them exactly, at least just *like* them. And since most food writers don't actively discourage this sense of identity, it comes as a rude shock when we finally realize that when those cooks go into their own kitchens, they don't cook out of their own cookbooks—or, as far as they let on, out of anyone else's, either.

Of the many strange things about cooking as one finds it portrayed in cookbooks, one of the strangest of all is the almost complete absence of cookbooks themselves, especially other people's cookbooks. In all of Marcella Hazan's Italy there is no whisper of Giuliano Bugialli; in his Italy there is no hint of her—nor of Ada Boni, Elizabeth David, or Pellegrino Artusi. (And as Italy goes, so goes everywhere else except for such notable exceptions as Elizabeth David herself, Alan Davidson, Diana Kennedy, and a few others. We know them by their bibliographies.)

Generally, what these writers are saying to us is not "here is Italian cooking as I have experienced it" (since part of that experience must have included the reading of cookbooks), but the very different statement of "I am Italian cuisine"—as if it had just welled up inside of them in some kind of spontaneous generation.

Once I began to admit to myself the necessary place that cookbooks had in my own cooking—that, for example, Italian cuisine was never going to spontaneously generate in *me*, no matter what—I started to think about my use of them in a new and different light. In my kitchen there was more than one Italian cookbook . . . and, consequently, there was no reason not to introduce them all to each other. When that happened, the magically seamless world of those isolated Italian cuisines dissolved into five, six, seven Italian cooks all fruitfully squabbling with each other—which is just the way Italians experience their cooking. Except here, at last, I too could listen in.

I don't mean to pick specifically on Italian cuisine. This would be just as true for any congregation of cooks and almost any ordinary dish whose making is shared among them. I just happen to be drawn to Italian—indeed to all Mediterranean—cooking, and so I had that many cookbooks to rub against each other. And when I did, what had previously seemed the most ordinary of dishes sprang suddenly, vividly to life.

Take rice and peas. Almost every general Italian cookbook gives a recipe for it or something like it. Indeed, it is a combination favored all over that country, pasta replacing rice in areas where the former is the customary (and less expensive) starch. But there is a particular version that is very much a Venetian specialty, and is said to have been served to the Doges of Venice at banquets celebrating the feast of St. Mark on April 25. (What the connection between the dish and

St. Mark is, I don't know, unless it's that the colors of both city and dish are green and white.)

The dish has remained popular over the years, however, not because of its historical associations but because it is *good*. Cooked in broth, flavored with one or two aromatics (usually onion and parsley) and—sometimes—a little bit of meat, and served with a generous grating of Parmesan, the two major ingredients not only wear this preparation as if tailor-made but complement each other wonderfully well, in taste and nutrition both.

Rice and peas together fit into that category of dishes where two ordinary foods, combined together, ignite a pleasure far beyond the capacity of either of its parts alone. Like rhubarb and strawberries, apple pie and cheese, roast pork and sage, the two tastes and textures meld together into the sort of subtle transcendental oneness that we once fantasized would be our experience when we finally found the ideal mate.

Even if you have never heard of this dish before, you probably have some idea as to how you would go about making it. And surely the simplest way would be to proceed along the lines set out by Mrs. Leyel in *The Gentle Art of Cookery*, a delightful and very British cookbook first published in 1925. She gives her recipe with typical brevity and directness:

> *Cupful of boiled rice, cupful of young peas (boiled), one onion, parsley. Chop the onion and parsley and fry them together. Have the rice and peas ready, each boiled separately and well drained. Stir the rice and peas into the pan with the onion, cook them and serve them hot.*

Simple? Yes. Good? Yes. Correct? No. I quote Mrs. Leyel's recipe because it is probably the one thing on which every other writer on this dish will agree: this is *not* the way to make rice and peas. Waverley Root might have been glowering at that very page when he wrote in *The Food of Italy*, "Rice and peas may not sound like a particularly inspiring combination, and it is not as it is so often made outside of Veneto, where boiled peas are simply poured over boiled rice."

Well, then, how *should* we make it? Jane Grigson, in her estimable *Vegetable Book*, describes the dish as "made by adding [cooked] young peas . . . to a risotto." This is nearly all she says, too, but it's enough

to contradict Marcella Hazan, who states firmly in her equally estimable *Classic Italian Cook Book*, "Rice and peas is not a risotto with
peas. It is a soup."

Risotto versus soup: this is the core of the argument. But these
two factions immediately break down into splinter groups disputing
fork versus spoon (that is, how *soupy* the dish should be, irrespective
of whether it is properly classified as a soup). So, Ada Boni (soup
faction) and Elizabeth David (risotto faction) both agree that rice and
peas should be firm enough to eat with a fork, while Marcella Hazan
(soup faction) insists it be wet enough to require a spoon.

Putting aside this question of relative firmness for the moment,
let's return to the central bone of contention, that of soup versus
risotto. As you know, a risotto is made by first sautéing rice in olive
oil and flavorings until it turns translucent and absorbs a little of the
oil, and then adding hot water or broth in small splashes, stirring
constantly but gently, until the rice is tender and glossy. The anti-
risotto faction claims that peas can't be cooked in the rice if the dish
is made this way, since the constant stirring would break them apart.
They could only be added toward the end of cooking, thus inhibiting
a full merging of flavor.

True, says the risotto faction, but immaterial. What you want in
the dish is a *contrast* of flavors, not a blend: let rice and pea each
speak for itself and let the mouth do the harmonizing—although they
hedge this by working the (cooked) peas into the rice during the last
several minutes, when the rice has softened to the point where it
must be stirred with the lightest possible touch or the grains would
disintegrate.

The important thing to note here is that rice prepared as a risotto
undergoes a change of texture since the starch is cooked in the hot
oil before it begins to absorb water: the rice is thick and glossy instead
of fluffy and light. Making rice and peas as a risotto or as a simply
boiled dish is to conceive two good but distinctly different prepara-
tions, and this without having said a word yet about ingredients.

Happily, our authorities are mostly in agreement about them. Rice,
of course, and nice, plump Italian Arborio rice, too, if you can afford
it. The peas, if possible, should be young, sweet, and freshly podded—a nice spring dish. Moreover, according to Waverley Root, purists insist that the peas should come from the "vegetable farms between

Chioggia and Burano, which means those which border the lagoon of Venice itself." We won't worry too much about that—those farms by now have probably been turned into housing developments.

What else? In her *International Encyclopedia of Cooking*, Myra Waldo defines the dish as "rice and peas, often with ham." Typically, none of the recipes mentioned so far except Elizabeth David's agrees; most mention no meat at all, while Ada Boni calls for diced *pancetta*, which is closer to seasoned but unsmoked bacon. Waverley Root perversely insists that the taste of celery should predominate in the dish; none of the other of our cooks seems to think so, though recipes can be found that do.

Where they all do agree is that the seasonings should be simple: a little parsley and onion (whether yellow or spring), and that sautéed in melted butter (or, for Ada Boni, a mixture of butter and olive oil). The liquid in which the rice is cooked should be a broth made of chicken or meat, although Waverley Root suggests (and it's a nice touch, I think) using water in which the discarded pea pods were briefly boiled, then flavored with only a few spoonfuls of broth.

When we come to proportions, though, our cooks again agree to disagree, and in every possible way—from a tablespoon of butter to a stick, from a handful of Parmesan to a cupful, to the very ratio of rice and peas. However, I'm not going to go on any further about that, nor about the finer points of preparation. By now, I think, your thoughts on these points are as lucid as mine.

In other words, if I've interested you at all in this debate, I've already made my point: you find you have your opinions, you feel your recipe, your way with *risi e bisi* is already taking shape in your fingers. Thick or loose, wet or dry, rich or meager, pungent or subtle, more green or more white, laced with strips of prosciutto or bits of *pancetta*, showered with coarse pepper or dotted with fennel or celery, dusted or drenched with cheese, spooned or forked . . . and suddenly this simple, uncomplicated dish comes alive in a richness of possibility, enough to fire up any genuine culinary sensibility.

Juxtaposing all these good cooks provides us with an experience far more valuable than any one of them can offer, because we are suddenly liberated from this nonsensical notion of a seamless cookery. We experience that art as it is and should be: opinionated, argumentative, contradictory, with each cook making the exact same "traditional" dish in his or her own particular way, all the while swearing it is the only conceivable one.

This experience is not a substitute for being there, maybe, but it now begins to find something like integrity. Observing, listening, tasting, we feel inside ourselves a shifting of that complex balance of option, opinion, and taste—the living logic of the dish—as it settles itself into the shape that *we* will want to make. And then we find ourselves on the other side—the before side—of the recipe, which is just where, I think, a good cook wants to be.

Getting to that place—somehow—is what this book is all about. The ways are various but the goal is the same. Over the years, out of all the food I've tasted or read about, a certain group of familiars have clustered round, tagged by appetite as dishes I can never know too much about. They attract my eye on restaurant menus, suggest themselves as I push the cart past their components in the supermarket, flag me down when I leaf through a new or unfamiliar cookbook. And it is through such tiny increments of understanding—historical anecdotes, evocations of place, surprisingly different ways of making, sharp disagreement with other cooks—that I have learned to bring these foods to life, to move them off the page and into the fingers of the cook.

Risi e Bisi (risotto style)

8 tablespoons (1 stick) butter
2 cups freshly podded peas
3½ cups good chicken stock
1 small onion, minced
2 slices prosciutto, diced (optional)

1 cup Arborio (or long-grain) rice
Salt and freshly ground pepper
1 tablespoon finely minced parsley
1 cup freshly grated Parmesan cheese

Melt 2 tablespoons of the butter in a medium-size pot. When it has just melted, add the peas. Turn down the heat as low as possible and cook the peas, covered, until just tender, about 10 to 15 minutes. If the heat is kept gentle enough, the peas should not stick or burn, but if you fear this, add a little water or extra chicken stock. Do not overcook. Set aside.

Heat the chicken stock until it starts to steam. Lower the heat and have it ready. Melt the remaining butter in a large, heavy pot. When melted and starting to foam, add the minced onion and sauté over medium heat until translucent. Add the prosciutto if used and then the rice. Sauté for about 3 minutes, or until the grains take on a translucent cast. Then begin adding the hot stock, a generous splash (or ladleful) at a time, stirring constantly, until the stock is absorbed by the rice. Continue adding the stock until the rice is plump and not too soft, and the mixture moist but not soupy. Taste for seasoning, adding salt as needed (the amount will depend on whether prosciutto is used and if the stock was previously salted) and a generous grinding of pepper. Gently stir in the parsley and cooked peas, and cook for another 2 minutes. Turn into a serving dish and sprinkle with half the Parmesan, reserving the rest to be added separately at the table. Serve at once.

(Serves 4)

Risi e Bisi (soup style)

3 tablespoons butter
1 small onion, minced
2 slices prosciutto, diced (optional)
2 cups freshly podded peas
1½ quarts good chicken
  stock

1 cup Arborio (or long-grain)
  rice
1 tablespoon finely minced
  parsley
Salt and freshly ground pepper
1 cup freshly grated Parmesan
  cheese

Melt the butter in a large, heavy pot. When melted, add the minced onion and sauté over medium heat until translucent, about 3 minutes. Add the prosciutto if used and the peas. Sauté 2 minutes or so, until the fat on the prosciutto glistens and the peas are coated with butter.

Pour in the chicken stock and bring to a simmer. Sprinkle the rice into the stock, lower the heat so that the liquid steams but does not boil, and let cook for about 20 minutes, or until the rice is plump and soft and the peas are done. Stir in the parsley and taste for seasoning, adding salt as needed (the amount will depend on whether prosciutto is used and if the stock was previously salted) and a generous grinding of pepper. Turn into a serving dish and sprinkle with half the Parmesan, reserving the rest to be added separately at the table. Serve at once.

(Serves 4)

I

PERSONAL PASSIONS

A Cup of Cocoa

❀

Summer on a Maine island means a host of rainy mornings, even days, spent in front of the fireplace. The gray light in the window, the feathery murmur of rain on the roof, the banshee wail of the fog siren down past Doughty's Landing at the naval station, the resonant splash of rainwater tumbling into the rain barrels—the signs were there the moment I woke up, huddled in a bundle of flannel sheets and army blankets. Not a morning to stay in bed—the fog had seeped through the cottage and into the covers—but a morning for a fire. A quick dash to the outhouse, then logs wrestled from the cache under the stairs, kindling chopped—and a tongue of flame would flicker up, the tang of bubbling resin and salt rising from the driftwood to mingle with the aroma of eggs and bacon frying and coffee brewing.

I would select a mystery from the corner bookcase stuffed with vintage, dog-eared paperbacks, and—breakfast dishes pushed to one side of the fireplace and feet propped up against the other, well-wrapped in a blanket and the rocker tilted to catch some light from the nearest wall fixture—I would hold the book open with one hand while warming the other with a steaming mug of cocoa.

The mug itself—the captain's mug, I called it, for it rippled out at the base to assure firm footing on a suddenly slanting table (years later I learned it was, in fact, a barber's shaving mug)—possessed a rich clear glaze even then old enough to be as shot through with tiny veins as a good piece of Stilton cheese. Hence, it had character enough to be regarded as less an object than a boon companion . . . the cocoa was the communion between us.

I would get up periodically through the morning to fill it with a fresh cup, whisked up and poured in steaming hot over a tablespoon or two of Marshmallow Fluff, and return to the fire to enjoy its continued company and that of Gervase Fen, Lord Peter Wimsey, or Father Brown. The Fluff would soon melt and broach the surface of the cocoa, while still remaining maddeningly out of reach. Only when the cup was empty could it be seized: the last swallow was a chocolate-and-egg-white-tasting sweet and luscious mass, the treat's treat. I loved the vulgar stuff, not only the taste but its visual pleasure: that thick, vivid smear of white swirled into the dark brown sludge that floated at the bottom of the cup.

All this came to mind recently when I contracted a nasty virus that lodged in my chest, filled me with fever, cough, and lethargy, and dulled both mind and appetite. After a few disbelieving hours before the television set, I ransacked my shelves for light reading (current favorites, P. M. Hubbard and Anthony Price) and disinterred the cocoa pot. (The mug still lords it over the other crockery at the Maine cottage. As much as I've always wanted it, it belongs to there, not to me.) Sans mug, then, and—worse—sans fireplace, but there was still the same pleasuring comfort in the cocoa: soothingly warm, rich, subtle-flavored and sweet.

Ordinarily, I'm a coffee drinker: the cocoa pot, dusty and unused for months, was glad to see me. Cocoa-drinking represents a slower-paced pleasure than I usually allow myself. For it is a drink meant to be savored, just like good coffee or tea. But unlike those beverages, whose straightforward stimulation sets us up for a good talk or a day's work, cocoa offers only simple pleasure as its reward. And it's a pleasure that—unless we've just come in from an afternoon of cross-country skiing—seems too full of unjustifiable calories and subsequent guilt. A cup of something like Swiss Miss carries less onus because, though its calories can be equally real, its "instant" banner translates into "made by someone else." The soothing notes of the packaging speak to us as surrogate mother, saying "you look good and tired, dear— let *me* make you something nice and hot," thus providing comfort while relieving us of guilt. Too bad it tastes like cardboard impregnated with chalk.

Most of these instant mixes actually bill themselves as "hot chocolate"—so much so, I think, that this phrase now summons from most of us a wince and an image of the machines restaurants haul out of storage when the weather grows cold to replace the instant iced tea maker. Time was, however, when just as reliably as *cocoa* would conjure up Red Cross rescue workers, tugboat captains, and red-cheeked children, *hot chocolate* would bring to mind courtesans sipping from Limoges china as they soaked in their morning tub, and dandies, throated and cuffed in lace, gossiping over the morning papers and silver chocolate pots.

Hints, in short, of a suspect sensuality. Hot chocolate is the very drink of love: a cup in which a few ounces of Tobler or Suchard bittersweet have been melted in hot milk offers an intoxicating voluptuousness that easily explains chocolate's reputation as an aphrodisiac. And worse, it is an indulgence as sinfully expensive as it is rich. Since there is a lot more in a chocolate bar than chocolate, it takes about an ounce and a half or more to make a cup—or, say, half a $1.75 bar of Tobler Tradition bittersweet to make a cup. But what a cup. . . .

At this point, it's worth pausing to note that a roasted cocoa bean, before processing, is about 55 percent pure cocoa butter—a self-descriptive natural vegetable oil with a melting point of 90°F—or mouth temperature. In its natural form, chocolate is incredibly rich to eat, more like frosting than what we know in the familiar bar, too much for most digestive systems. In the last century, a Dutchman, C. J. van Houten, discovered a way to press out this fat, separating it from the chocolate solids, and later a way to treat the solids themselves to make them less acidic (making them not only more digestible but also more soluble). Cocoa has a cocoa butter content of about 22 percent, whereas a chocolate bar has more like 35 percent, the rest being the cocoa solids, sugar (40 percent in a bittersweet bar), and, in milk chocolate, a good proportion of powdered milk.

Hot chocolate, then, is characterized by a rich, sweet flavor and velvety texture, while cocoa is brisker and thinner, with a cleaner, sharper presence on the tongue. However, the puritan-leaning virtues of cocoa-making can be carried too far. Though a cocoa drinker by preference myself (Droste), I still don't hold with the traditional Yankee way of making it in hot water, tempering it with a splash of milk and a bit of sugar. This may have been more than Yankee thrift at play: older recipes often call for more cocoa and less sugar in the cup, hinting perhaps of a taste for a bitterer brew. *The Picayune Creole Cookbook,* for example, doesn't even mention sugar at all. In *Down and Out in Paris and London,* George Orwell describes a night spent in a doss house where the indigents were given a breakfast of butterless bread and sugarless (and milkless) cocoa—nasty stuff, but perhaps in the warden's eyes no worse than black, unsweetened coffee.

Apart from its caloric wallop, chocolate is not as soluble as cocoa: before modern processing techniques, it wasn't soluble at all. Hot chocolate recipes from countries where chocolate was first introduced often carry over into modern times strategies originally introduced to deal with chocolate as it first was—extremely rich and difficult to dissolve. A traditional Spanish method beats in an extraordinary amount of cornstarch, so much so that a spoon can be stood on end in a cup of what tastes like not-quite-set chocolate pudding. Originally, the cornstarch provided a thickener that kept the chocolate particles in suspension and some starch to balance off the fat. Today, neither is required, and that version is best avoided altogether. Not so, however, the recipes that use either egg yolks or whole eggs as a thickener. They give hot chocolate a glossy smoothness and thicken it only enough to heighten that velvety sensation on the tongue.

Even with the use of such thickeners, the chocolate particles could only be kept in suspension by constant beating (a task often assigned to servants), since the slightest pause would precipitate the chocolate to the bottom of the pot. To prevent this, hot chocolate drinkers carried their own special tool, a tiny beater, some very elaborately and expensively made, called a *molinillo* by Spanish-speaking peoples and a *moulinet* by the French. (In strictest accuracy, the term denotes both the beating tool itself and the pot it was used in, but today the reference is almost always to the tool.) The stem is held between the palms of the hands and rapidly rotated until the hot chocolate is topped with froth. The *molinillo* is most popularly associated with Mexican hot chocolate, a concoction made with flavorings such as cinnamon and crushed almonds, but the tool itself can be used to froth any hot chocolate, adding a dramatic and useful touch, though a regular kitchen whisk does just as well.

The dividing line between hot chocolate and cocoa drinkers seems to cut between the northern and southern European temperaments: you are more likely to be offered cocoa in Norway and Britain and hot chocolate in France, Italy, or Spain. We could draw conclusions from this that would probably prove unwarranted; most likely the taste for a rich hot chocolate was already firmly rooted in countries where chocolate was first introduced by the time cocoa came along. What chocolate has gained in digestibility by being made into cocoa, it has lost in pleasure. A tongue that has acquired a taste for the former may never be swayed into accepting the latter, no matter the interests of the stomach, as you may discover for yourself from one of the hot chocolate recipes shared on the following pages.

Whether we enroll in the party of hot chocolate or cocoa drinkers, the important thing is to squelch the nagging voice that presumes to scold when we take down the cocoa tin without some justifying stigmata such as frostbite or fever's ague. Try slipping cocoa back into your life. Nothing is nicer, coming in out of the cold and damp, than standing over the range with that rich, creamy smell of hot milk warming the nostrils, chilled fingers beating smooth that heaping, pleasuring spoonful.

Because it has only a hint of caffeine to tingle the nerves, cocoa is a morning drink for children—except on that rare morning when you yourself have time to linger, watching the steam patterns frozen on the windowpanes, as you sit, lazy, quilt-wrapped, in the easy chair, sifting through the paper for the crossword, brain purring on idle. This is where it comes into its own, our special cocoa recipe, with its grating of cinnamon or vanilla bean or twist of orange peel, the dab of whipped cream or shameless gob of Marshmallow Fluff.

Then, and in the evening, late, when we want to be warmed and filled and soothed before we slip off to bed, stimulated only just enough for sleep, or some other tumble into bliss. Since I began by evoking the solitary pleasures of a cup of cocoa, it is fitting to close by remembering its connubial ones. Cocoa, in more innocent times than ours, was considered a mild aphrodisiac, Cupid's nightcap, warming cold fingers and stimulating sweet thoughts on chilly nights.

A Cup of Cocoa

1 cup milk
1 heaping teaspoon Dutch process cocoa
1½ teaspoons sugar

Pour the milk into a small, thick-bottomed pot. Add the cocoa and sugar. Over low heat, whisk the mixture together, being sure to clean the side of the pan of any cocoa that sticks to it as it heats. When the mixture begins to steam (do not let it boil) remove it from the heat and whisk it vigorously until the mixture foams. The process of whisking not only helps keep a skin from forming over the top of the cocoa but also brings out more of the cocoa flavor. (Variations: A twist of orange peel—never use extract, which is too potent; a tiny drop of vanilla; a large dollop of whipped cream or Devonshire cream; a sprinkle of well-chopped toasted almonds or hazelnuts; a marshmallow or heaping tablespoon of Marshmallow Fluff.)

(Serves 1)

Hot Chocolate

Scant pint of milk
1 3-ounce bar imported chocolate (either milk chocolate or semisweet)

Pour ¼ cup of the milk into a small, thick-bottomed pot. Break the chocolate into small bits and add to the milk in the pot. Over very low heat, let the chocolate melt, then pour in the rest of milk, bit by bit, whisking well with each addition. When the chocolate is melted and the milk faintly steaming, remove from the heat, beat vigorously with a whisk until frothy, and serve. (Variations: A small amount of chocolate-based liqueur, such as Cheri-Suisse, Vandermint, or Droste Bittersweet is liked by some. Other options appear in the following recipes. Of course, unsweetened baking chocolate can be used instead. Use the same proportion: 1½ ounces of chocolate per cup of milk and sweeten to taste.)

(Serves 2)

French Hot Chocolate

2 cups milk
1 3-ounce bar imported semisweet chocolate, broken into bits
2 egg yolks

Prepare the hot chocolate as directed in the recipe above. Beat the egg yolks in a small bowl. When the hot chocolate is ready, remove from the heat. Take a teaspoon of the hot chocolate and beat into the eggs. Mix in a few more teaspoonfuls the same way, and then mix the egg and chocolate mixture into the hot chocolate in the pot. Whisk vigorously until frothy and serve at once. With a croissant for dunking, there is *no* better breakfast.

(Serves 2)

Belgian Cocoa

2 large egg whites at room
   temperature
2 cups heavy cream
¼ cup confectioners' sugar,
   sifted

¼ teaspoon vanilla
4 cups milk
2 tablespoons Dutch process
   cocoa

Beat the egg whites in a bowl until they hold stiff peaks. Beat the cream to soft peaks, then add the sugar and vanilla, and continue beating until the cream also holds stiff peaks. Gently fold the egg whites into the whipped cream and divide the mixture evenly among 6 large mugs. Heat the milk in a saucepan, whisking in the cocoa until the cocoa is dissolved and the milk hot (do not let it boil). Pour the cocoa into the mugs and serve at once.

(Serves 6)

Swiss Hot Chocolate

¶ This recipe cannot be given exactly, but it is simple enough to make if you have the required paraphernalia. Although the Swiss treat it more familiarly, you will probably want to reserve this for a very special breakfast treat.

Set 2 or 3 small heat-resistant pitchers on a rack in a pot and pour water around. Break a different 3-ounce chocolate bar into each of the pitchers, using one milk chocolate, one semisweet, and (if a third pitcher is used) some other solid, flavored bar, such as mocha, nut, or even white chocolate. Gently heat the water but do not let it boil, stirring the chocolate in each pitcher with a small spoon to help it melt. Heat milk in another pot and pour into a larger pitcher. Each person makes a personal cup of hot chocolate (in demitasse cups) by mixing the different chocolates together to taste and stirring in the hot milk.

Mexican Chocolate

4 cups milk
3 ounces unsweetened chocolate
½ cup *piloncillo* (dark brown
   sugar) or ⅔ cup honey

2 or 3 cloves or pinch of
   ground cloves
⅓ cup sliced almonds
½ teaspoon ground cinnamon
   or 1 cinnamon stick

Pour the milk into a thick-bottomed pot. Over low heat, melt the chocolate in milk. Stir in the sugar or honey. Crush the cloves and almond slices with the cinnamon in a mortar and mix with the hot chocolate. Whip the mixture with a *molinillo*, a whisk, or with an egg beater until the mixture is well blended and frothy.

(Serves 4)

Spanish Egg Chocolate

2 ounces unsweetened chocolate
2 cups milk
Tiny pinch salt
¼ cup sugar

1 teaspoon ground cinnamon
½ teaspoon vanilla
1 egg

In a double boiler gently cook the chocolate and milk together to a velvety consistency. Keep stirring as you add the salt and sugar, then finish up with the cinnamon and vanilla. Remove the chocolate from the heat. In a chocolate pot or other pitcher beat the egg until frothy. Slowly pour the hot chocolate into the pitcher, stirring. Froth it well with a whisk or *molinillo* and serve at once. (A piece of real vanilla bean, split open and heated with the milk and chocolate, makes this even better.)

(Serves 2)

A Bowl of Porridge

❀

Our supper was porridge. The porridge pot was set down in the
middle of the floor, and we all sat around with great bowls of
milk and ladled the porridge into the milk. . . . —EDWIN MUIR

There are several kinds of oatmeal—Scotch, Irish, Canadian, and
American. . . . It seems as if the Canadian and American should
be best because the freshest; but the fact is the others are considered choicest. —MARIA PARLOA (1880)

Breakfast cereal is terrible stuff. We eat it because for some strange
reason we think it's good for us, because it's cheap and goes down
easily, and, mostly, because it's what everybody else eats for breakfast. Not me, no more. Apart from a brief flirtation with granola in
the sixties, I haven't touched a bowl of it for almost twenty years.

I mean, of course, the cold stuff. I love hot cereal: Wheatena,
Maltex, Hot Ralston—they have aroma, taste, a sense of substance,
the presence of the actual grain they come from. But while I'll gladly
eat most any of them, the standby on my own larder shelf is a metal
canister of McCann's Irish oatmeal. Pop it open and you'll find something the hand can get hold of, real chunks and bits of grain, not the
processed silt that pours from all those other boxes.

People who say they don't like oatmeal have probably never tasted
it. Our own oat porridge is mostly made with rolled oats, at best, or
"instant" oats, mixed up right in the bowl, yielding a substance as
much like real oatmeal as instant coffee resembles the genuine brew—
not very much at all. An honest batch of oatmeal must simmer in a
pot for at least a half hour. That gentle cooking brings out its nutty
taste, its velvety aroma, a texture the mouth can linger over, and a
warmth that glows in the stomach until lunchtime. And, best of all,
like cornmeal mush or a bowl of grits, oatmeal is company. Sit down
to your Hot Ralston and there's nothing to do with it but eat it. But
oatmeal has depth. The spoon slips down and lifts up memories.

Some are our own, some not. Because breakfast is our most conservative meal, many favorite morning foods reach further back into

the past than anything else we set on the table. A child reading an old storybook feels suddenly at home with those strange folk of yesterday when they sit down to hot buttered toast or a plate of ham and eggs. And this sense of connection endures even when the story itself fades away.

Take *Oliver Twist.* If you remember anything at all about that novel, you remember "Please, sir, I want some more" . . . and the sudden silence in a roomful of starved boys, bowls polished clean, fingers licked for any bits of gruel (porridge-cum-water) that might have splashed on them. The empty porridge bowl is all the more powerful an image because oatmeal is at once so cheap and so comforting that grudging it becomes an act of genuine cruelty. If corn flakes had existed then, they would have had no analogous resonance to give the novelist: there is no comfort or warmth in *them*.

And I have my own private memories. For a spell of years I worked as a mailboy for a corporate headquarters near Wall Street on a shift that started at 7:00 A.M. I've never been a willing early riser, a reluctance then compounded by lack of a bed. I slept on a bamboo mat spread out on the floor and had that much further a climb from warmth to wakefulness. Even worse was winter, when my Lower East Side apartment got no heat in the morning until after I had left.

My solution to so unbearable a situation was this: when the clock radio snicked on at 6:00 A.M. sharp, I would scramble off the floor and hurry into the kitchen to turn on the hot water tap in the bathtub (it was next to the refrigerator—the toilet, happily, did have a room of its own) and set a cup of water to boil on the stove. In went a pinch of salt and two handfuls of oatmeal—and I fled back to bed. Exactly half an hour later, the oatmeal was done and the kitchen (blocked off from the rest of the apartment by a tacked-up army blanket) was warm from the tubful of hot water. (The oven would have done the job as well, but I paid for the gas; the landlord paid for the hot water.) My clothes were waiting on the kitchen chair. I pulled them on, gobbled down the oatmeal, and dashed down Ninth Street for the First Avenue bus. The radiators would start to bang as I went out the door.

One reason why old-fashioned oatmeal is still found on the grocer's shelf, despite quicker-cooking versions, is that some of us take as much pleasure in its company on the stove as in the bowl, putting our personal mark in its cooking as well as in its eating. Some, in fact, still swear by the hulled groats, bringing them to a boil and then steeping them overnight in the cooling water.

But most of us choose either oatmeal or rolled oats, the latter being groats flattened into flakes by huge steel rollers to a more uniform thickness. Oatmeal produces a coarser, more variegated porridge; the rolled oats, a smoother, more uniform one. The choice is up to you. Since each process calls for a different proportion of grain to water, I suggest following the directions on the container, though a reliable golden mean is two handfuls of oatmeal to each cup of water and a good pinch of salt.

Some suggest slowly dribbling those handfuls into the simmering water over the first ten minutes of cooking time so that the finished porridge contains oats in all stages of cooking. Others suggest adding no salt until the cooking is half done, to keep the grain tender. In any case, the oatmeal should be vigorously stirred while the grain is dribbled in to prevent lumps, and then, heat low, left strictly alone (like a pot of rice) until done. Continual stirring breaks down the oat particles and lessens the distinctive granular texture. Better to do as I do and set the pot into a double boiler and slip off to the tub (or back to bed) while it simmers itself to perfection. It needs a good half hour to reach full flavor and body. The finished product should be substantial enough to hold up the stirring spoon (or chopstick, my own version of the Scottish "spurtle"—or oatmeal stirring—stick).

The old Scottish way was to eat it straight from the pot with no decoration save that pinch of salt and a pat of butter; when milk was added, it was kept in a separate bowl. The spoon was dipped first into the oatmeal, then into the milk, giving the mouth the contrast of hot and cold at once, rather than a simple, lukewarm mouthful.

We, of course, eat it with milk and sugar (and butter, too); brown sugar makes an ideal flavor match. Some choose cream over milk, others buttermilk. Some, bolder still, stir in a raw egg or take it plain, with a glass of stout or ale on the side. And then there's the Scottish laird who claimed to start his day with a bowl of porridge generously sprinkled with brown sugar, then covered over with a wee dram of scotch. A breakfast, he said, to put hair on any chest.

My own secret? I make mine with milk instead of water, mixing in some sweet butter and a spoonful of clover honey, eating it thick and hot with a puddle of cream in the center—and make enough extra to cool, cut into squares, and serve cold with whipped cream as the next night's dessert.

Oatmeal is soothing when eaten as a bedtime meal. In hard times, I've made a regular dinner out of it by mincing some scallions and a carrot or two, and sautéing them in butter or some lamb or beef drippings before adding the same two handfuls of oatmeal. Into this I stir a cup of milk and two or three cups of meat broth, making a rich-tasting, delicious, and inexpensive soup.

In those parts of Britain (and elsewhere) where the oat once served as a principal food grain, there are a host of other oatmeal recipes for such as dumplings, stuffings, puddings, soups, and breads. Perhaps the most common of these is the oatcake, a flat, sometimes unleavened, pancakelike affair that can be made savory or sweet. Indeed, the Scots, Welsh, Irish, and northern English all have their own version of the oatcake, which differs partly by regional taste, but also by the available means for baking them: on a griddle, in the stove, or on the hearth itself.

If you are curious to try them, a generous sampling can be made by mixing a cup of fine oatmeal (I give my coarse Irish oats a few seconds in the food processor) with a half teaspoon each of baking powder and salt in a small bowl. Add to this two tablespoons of butter or bacon fat and about a half cup of boiling water, just enough to make a stiff but pliable dough. Knead this with floured hands until it forms a smooth ball.

This dough is treated like cookie dough, rolled out in a round circle as thin as possible on a flour-dusted board ("thin as a penny, wide as a plate" is the saying), pinching the split edges back together with your fingers. Cut this round into four quarters (farls) and set them on an ungreased griddle over medium heat. When they curl at the edges, turn them over, cooking both sides to a light biscuit color. (They can also be baked in a preheated 375°F oven, unturned, for twenty minutes). Eat hot with butter and cheese.

Our own oatmeal cookie may be their grandchild, or perhaps it's second cousin to Swedish oatmeal wafers, which it also almost resembles. The oatmeal cookie seems a relatively recent addition in our cookbooks, but it's surely an American creation; we are unique in our taste for the big, coarse, sweet thing that that cookie most often is. I like them fine when you forget the raisins, but most of all I love them the way Mrs. Appleyard makes them.

Mrs. Appleyard, you may remember, was a fictional creation of Louise Andrews Kent, whose sturdy but impish Down East manner spilled over from the best-selling (1940) novel *Mrs. Appleyard's Year* into one of the few good New England cookbooks published this century. Her oatmeal cookie recipe—adapted here to my own taste— is a gem.

Toasted Oatmeal Lace Cookies

¶ Because of the large amount of sugar and butter in the recipe, these cookies spread out in a large, irregular circle, crispy brown at the edges and with a smooth praline glaze underneath. Expect the dough to seem too wet, use your heaviest cookie sheets, and don't try making them on a humid summer afternoon.

2¼ cups rolled oats	½ pound sweet butter
2¼ cups light brown sugar	1 egg, slightly beaten
2 tablespoons flour	½ teaspoon vanilla
½ teaspoon salt	¼ teaspoon ginger

Preheat oven to 375°F. In a large, ungreased frying pan over medium heat, stir the uncooked rolled oats for about three or four minutes or until they release a sweet nutty aroma and crisp up a little around the edges. Turn into a large mixing bowl and let cool enough to handle. Then mix in the sugar, flour, and salt. In a small pan, melt the butter, letting it become completely liquid but not to foaming. Pour it into the bowl with the other ingredients, stirring until the sugar has melted. Then beat in the egg, vanilla, and ginger.

Drop the batter from a teaspoon in small balls set about 2 inches apart. Don't try to flatten them and don't crowd them; you'll get about 9 cookies to a sheet. Bake for about 6 to 8 minutes, or until they just turn golden brown. Let cool only until they are hard enough so that a spatula can be slid under them, then immediately transfer to a sheet of wax paper spread out on the counter, where they can cool without touching each other. Let them cool completely before putting them away. They will freeze successfully, or they can be put into an airtight tin between layers of wax paper. Kept dry like this, they will stay crisp as long as there are any left. Mrs. Appleyard says she kept some once for almost two days.

(Makes about 50)

Corn Cakes

❀

Johnny or hoe-cake, hot from the fire, is better than a Yorkshire
muffin.   —BENJAMIN FRANKLIN

Her corn-cake, in all its varieties of hoe-cake, dodgers, muffins,
and other species, . . . was a sublime mystery to all less practiced
compounders.—HARRIET BEECHER STOWE, *Uncle Tom's Cabin* (1852)

First, there is the griddle. I would love to own a soapstone one and
someday—when my ship comes in—I will. But I am happy enough
with this one, cast-iron, weighty, well seasoned. I fell in love with it
the first time I laid eyes on it, but it took decades of convincing before
my grandfather would give it up—and then only when I had moved
upstairs and would come down and make him hotcakes when he was
in the mood.

Myself, I use it mostly for griddle breads—scones and biscuits and
shortbreads—the sort of thing most people stick away into the oven
to mind its own business. But I am a fiddly sort of cook and am only
happy when there's something in front of me to stir, poke, shake,
sniff, lift, and peek under.

This is especially true in the morning, when I am sleepy and hungry
and looking for something to do with myself while the coffee beans
are roasted, ground, brewed—a space of twenty minutes. Plenty of
time to make some oatmeal or coddle an egg, and I do those things,
but usually I want something I can take with my mug of coffee into
the living room and then find with blind fingers, my nose buried in
a journal.

I'm a slow starter, my biorhythms inverse to the world's. They take
their slow and grudging time to climb up to operating level and then—
late in the evening—abruptly nose-dive me into sleep. So, I am
dilatory and sluggish at the start of my day and want nothing more
than to wrap myself in a blanket and flop in the wicker armchair by
the one sunny window, the buzz of some bright and gossipy voice in
the ear, coffee and idle eating ready at the side.

This is why my breakfast companions of late are often corn cakes . . . about six of them, spread out on the plate so they'll keep their crispness. Sometimes I fry them up with little bits of bacon or, in season, with tiny Maine blueberries. But they're fine made plain and eaten just the way they come off the griddle, crunchy-textured and with that wonderfully sweet and delicate taste of corn.

I eat them with my fingers, plain. It's curious that we don't consider pancakes finger food; they're sized right and we eat small breads that way, drenched with butter and honey no matter. What it is, I think, is their flabby feel. No matter how much your ordinary flapjack might pleasure the tongue, its touch has all the trusty firmness of an undertaker's handshake.

Each corn cake, on the other hand, has its own integrity: the coarse-textured meal gives it a crust a finger feels no immodesty in touching. In fact, there's tactile pleasure to the whole making of these cakes that makes them so attractive as morning fare, offering a little playfulness before we pull on the grim visage of the day.

You go grab your Aunt Jemima box—you'll still be blearily looking for the directions while I'm finishing mixing my batter. The basic proportions are so simple they can be set to memory: for every cup of cornmeal use a slightly greater amount of buttermilk, a scant teaspoon of baking soda and half that of salt, and a tablespoon of corn oil or melted butter; add an egg if you're feeling extravagant. Stir all that together with your finger until it is mixed more or less smooth, the thickness of loosely whipped cream (thinner for thin cakes).

Heat the griddle until a drop of water skates across and then lightly grease it with a pastry brush dipped in melted shortening or lard. Then dot the griddle with the batter. I use a coffee scoop (two tablespoons) for each, but you can just as easily tip it out of a pitcher. You will find they cook quicker and turn easier if made small, no more than three inches across. Also remember that they take longer to cook than other pancakes; make sure they've firmed on the top before turning them. I get about six corn cakes from every half-cup of cornmeal/flour used in the batter: judge your portions from that rule.

Corn cakes are delicate and ask for patience and a gentle hand, but if you are willing to bear with them, you will find them amazingly adaptive to inspiration and ingredients on hand. Some cooks blend in a little white or buckwheat flour to lighten and make them less fragile. A delicious corn cake is made from fresh corn kernels beaten into a pulp—a moister version of the way all corn breads once were made, when the meal was beaten from cobs plucked from the field.

Buttermilk is used in many of the traditional recipes collected below because it reacts with baking soda to make a "natural" leavening. (Of course, the earliest corn cakes were leavened with nothing at all.) But if you prefer to use fresh sweet milk, simply substitute one and a half teaspoons of baking powder for every teaspoon of baking soda in the recipe. Other leavenings can be used, too—eggs are often used and I have seen more complicated versions using yeast.

The sampling below will give you a sense of the wide range of corn cake cookery, along with some hints about traditional meals and toppings. If you find them to your taste—as I think you will—let them find a place at your dinner table, too. No soup was ever so good as when a little corn cake was broken into it, and nothing sits so fine beside a plate of barbecue.

A soapstone griddle greased with a ham rind makes the tastiest griddle cakes.
                                                    —A SHAKER COOK

Virginia Cornmeal Batter Cakes

1½ cups cornmeal, water-
    ground from Boone County
    white corn
2 tablespoons flour
½ teaspoon baking soda

¾ teaspoon salt
1½ cups buttermilk
2 tablespoons melted butter
2 eggs, separated

Sift together the cornmeal, flour, baking soda, and salt, and pour in
the buttermilk gradually, beating hard. Beat the egg yolks until foamy,
and then mix these and the butter into the batter. In a separate bowl,
beat the egg whites until stiff and fold these in gently but thoroughly.
Fry the cakes on a greased hot griddle.

(Makes about 18 cakes)

Cornmeal Griddle Cakes

¶ *From Good Living*, by Sarah van Buren Brugiere (1890).

2 eggs, lightly beaten
4 cups sour milk or butter-
    milk
2 tablespoons molasses
½ cup flour

3 cups (approx.) cornmeal
1 tablespoon lard, melted
1 teaspoon salt
1 teaspoon baking soda

Mix together the eggs, milk, and molasses, and add these to the flour.
Mix in enough cornmeal to make a batter the thickness of rich cream.
Add the lard, then the salt and the baking soda, dissolved in a few
drops of boiling water. Beat very hard. Have the griddle very hot and
greased with a piece of fat salt pork. Test a little of the batter; it
should run easily and make cakes so thin that you can only just turn
them with a cake turner. If too thick, add a little more buttermilk
and a pinch of soda as before; if too thin, add a bit more cornmeal.
"Delicious. Recommended."

Texas Sweet Corn Flapjacks

1½ cups sweet corn kernels
(cut from about 3 ears)
1 egg
1 tablespoon melted butter
2 tablespoons light cream

2 tablespoons fine cracker
crumbs or flour
½ teaspoon salt
¼ teaspoon freshly ground
pepper (optional)

Grate the corn kernels into a bowl, reserving all juices. (If corn is plentiful and bursting with juice, run a sharp blade down the ear through the center of each row of kernels and, using the back of the knife, squeeze out the tender pulp and milk until you have 1½ cups.) Beat the egg until foamy, then beat in the corn bit by bit, beating thoroughly and very hard. Add the butter and then the cream. Stir in the crumbs, a tablespoon at a time, until the mixture holds together. Drop onto a lightly greased griddle by the heaping tablespoon and cook until golden, turning when the tops seem solid. (*Note:* If you have a food processor, making these is a snap. Insert steel blade and process the batter following the procedure above, aiming for a slightly pulpy texture. Delicious at breakfast with syrup, and even more wonderful spiced with a bit of Tabasco sauce and served as a side dish at dinner.)

(Makes 8 to 12 pancakes)

Cornmeal and Rice Griddle Cakes

¶ From a Shaker recipe.

2 eggs, separated
2 tablespoons melted butter
1 cup cold boiled rice, white,
brown, or Indian
1 cup cornmeal (for lighter
cakes, half white flour and
half cornmeal)

1 cup half and half
1 teaspoon baking powder
1 teaspoon salt

Beat the egg yolks well and mix in the butter. Then stir in the rice and beat until the rice is pulped. Stir in the cornmeal, half and half, baking powder, and salt, and blend until smooth. In a separate bowl, beat the egg whites until stiff and then gently fold into the batter. Have the griddle hot and well greased and make the cakes large. Bake until nicely browned and serve with maple syrup.

(Makes 8)

Corn Bread Crumb-Cakes

1 cup crumbled stale corn bread	1 teaspoon sugar
	1 egg, well beaten
¾ cup milk	¼ cup heavy cream
½ teaspoon salt	3 tablespoons flour
2 teaspoons baking powder	

Soak the stale corn bread crumbs overnight in the milk. Next morning, add the salt, baking powder, sugar, egg, cream, and flour to make a pourable batter. Beat 1 minute, then ladle batter onto a hot, greased griddle. Serve hot.

(Makes 8 to 12)

Southern Lacy-Edge Corn Cakes

¶ There are various recipes for this corn cake, made famous by the once-annual "Batty Cake Brekfus" on the morning of the Kentucky Derby, where they were served along with "sawsidges, 'lasses, sputterin' coffee, and fried apples." (Sugar is added to this recipe not for sweetness but for a crisper texture.)

1 cup cornmeal	¼ cup flour
2 teaspoons sugar	1 egg, well beaten
½ teaspoon salt	1½ cups buttermilk
½ teaspoon baking powder	1 tablespoon melted butter

Sift the dry ingredients together in a mixing bowl. In another bowl, beat the egg into the buttermilk and the butter. Stir this into the dry mixture, beating until smooth. It should be very thin. Heat the griddle until it sends a drop of water skating. Grease well with lard or vegetable oil (and again after each batch) and drop the batter by the tablespoon. When the bubbles are set and the edges brown, turn and quickly brown the other side. The cakes should be edged with a crusty lace. Serve at once, stacked in threes with butter between, with molasses or cane or maple syrup. (*Note:* Keep batter thin by adding buttermilk as needed.)

(Makes 24 to 30)

Rhode Island Griddle Cakes

¶ Adapted from June Platt's *New England Cook Book*.

1 cup jonnycake cornmeal (see page 25)	Pinch ground ginger
½ cup flour	1 tablespoon molasses
1 scant teaspoon baking soda	1½ cups buttermilk
½ teaspoon salt	

Sift the dry ingredients together in a mixing bowl. Dissolve the molasses in a little hot water, and mix it in with the dry ingredients. Then stir in the buttermilk, splash by splash, until you have a stiff batter. Bake griddle cakes on a hot greased griddle and serve with a bowl of butter creamed with powdered sugar and dusted with cinnamon.

(Makes 12)

A NOTE ON JONNYCAKE

Rhode Island jonnycakes are NOT easy to make.

—IMOGENE WOLCOTT

Let's be honest: unless you come from Rhode Island, a true jonnycake isn't worth making for anyone but yourself. They're tricky to make and no one will thank you for the effort—at least until they've acquired the taste. Why make them? Well, they taste like that crisp crust that forms on the bottom of the mush pot, a mouthful of hot crunchy corn. If that and the pleasure of working a delicacy out of unpromising and reluctant material is the sort of thing to appeal to you, the effort pays for itself.

You'll need a well-seasoned griddle and a cup of genuine Rhode Island flint cornmeal. Heat them both: the cornmeal to just warm in a bowl in the oven, the griddle to very hot indeed. Set some water in the kettle to boil. When the cornmeal is warm, stir in a half-teaspoon of salt, and beat in the water, bit by bit, until you have a loose batter, just fluid enough to pour (not fall) off the spoon. Add one more tiny splash of water and beat the mixture for four minutes. This will help it hold together on the griddle.

Grease the griddle with bacon fat or shortening and dot it with the batter—a tablespoon per cake—setting each well apart from the others. The batter should spread out thin; if it doesn't, beat in more boiling water. The trick to a jonnycake is to have it thin enough so there is no wet mush in its center but thick enough to hold together when turned.

Despite its thinness, a jonnycake takes longer to cook than a regular pancake. Don't try to turn it until it seems completely solid on top. Then work a tentative spatula under: if it holds together, take a peek. If the bottom is a delicate fawn, it is time to turn it. Cook the other side to the same color.

Eat jonnycake plain with butter; even the best maple syrup overpowers it. In some parts of Rhode Island, a tablespoon of milk is stirred in before the batter is poured, to give the cakes a slightly smoother texture. Others mix the meal with cold milk to make a batter, but this is mere pancake-making, the result no true jonnycake at all.

SOME THOUGHTS ON INGREDIENTS

The Cornmeal

> There is a partiality in the North for yellow meal, which the Southerners regard as only fit for chicken and cattle-feed. The yellow may be sweeter, but I acknowledge I have never succeeded in making really nice bread from it.
> —MARION HARLAND (1883)

The simpler the corn cake, the more important the flavor of the meal, which is one reason why modern corn bread and corn cake recipes often call for the addition of sweeteners. Mass-produced cornmeal has a flat, dead flavor, the tongue tasting it as if through a layer of tissue paper. This is partly because of the type of corn and partly because of the way it is milled. Cornmeal that is meant to sit on the pantry shelf indefinitely is degerminated so it won't spoil . . . and tastes like it.

The South is willing to fight for decent cornmeal and gets it in their widely grown Boone County white, but in the North this is not so. Even the natural-food-store versions are only adequate: their cornmeals are moist and sweet but their flavor remains dim. The only exception is in Rhode Island, a state still passionate about its jonnycake and willing to support the few mills that grind superlative cornmeal from the low-producing but flavorful native White Cap flint, a corn almost unknown anywhere else. The simplicity of jonnycake means that the taste and texture of the meal is everything. The corn must be carefully and slowly stone-ground into a flat meal whose slightly coarser texture is a guarantee of flavor, since the grain is not overheated by the grinding.

The image that comes to most minds hearing "stone-ground" is a lazily creaking mill wheel, but not to mine: the cornmeal I use is ground by a stone turned by a 1946 Dodge truck motor. That is Gray's Grist Mill, where Timothy McTague produces what is simply the finest cornmeal I have ever eaten. It is made entirely from Rhode Island White Cap flint: clean, fresh, and delicate, with wonderful aroma and flavor. Although sold as Rhode Island Johnny Cake Corn

Meal, this designation is more a guarantee of quality than a statement of limitation. It has become my meal of choice for my corn bread baking, as well as for the testing of the recipes given here. (Gray's Grist Mill also grinds and puts up a traditional Boston brown bread mix of cornmeal, rye, and wheat flour. Write to: P.O. Box 422, Adamsville, RI 02801.)

THE TOPPING

Although I encourage you to try corn cakes as a side to pan-fried fish, roast duck, and country sausage patties, no one could question their appeal on the morning breakfast table with a jug of hot syrup in which a fat chunk of butter is melting. Maple syrup, of course, goes just fine with corn cakes—as does any fruit syrup—but my topping of choice is Louisiana cane syrup, the uptown cousin of ordinary molasses. It is bittersweet and suavely silky, famously compatible with a corn cake's simple sweetness. Easily found in the South, it is a rarity in the North (as is decent molasses). An exceptionally fine cane syrup is made in Vermillion Parish, Louisiana, by a mill in operation since Reconstruction and sold by Community Kitchens. (Write for their catalogue: P.O. Box 3778, Baton Rouge, LA 70821.)

Macaroni and Cheese

❀

Macrows: take and make a thin foil of dough, and carve it in pieces, and cast them on boiling water, and seeth it well. Take cheese and grate it and butter cast beneath and above . . . and serve forth.   —*The Forme of Cury* (circa 1390)

School cafeterias have so stigmatized macaroni and cheese that it's hard to convince anyone that it can be a good meal.
      —MIRIAM UNGERER, *Good Cheap Food*

More than men, I think, women share important memories as tokens of their love. One recollection so given me was of a small girl watching her father making macaroni and cheese. A man for taking great pains in the perfection of small things, his method was a loving ritual of sustenance. The ingredients were prepared and mixed in a large, heatproof mixing bowl, which was then set directly in the oven and periodically removed during cooking for further incorporation of a precisely gauged amount of additional cheese. By the time the dish was ready, the elbow macaroni sported in it like dolphins in a savory orange-yellow sea.

The strong fatherly arm stirring the bubbling ingredients with a sauce-coated wooden spoon . . . the fragrant heat wafting out the open oven door . . . the gold and glistening mound of freshly grated cheese waiting on the counter . . . the hungry little girl whose fascination and ardent appetite were to the cook a special seasoning . . . these are powerful images.

But their power is also of a special kind, and shows the difference between two very different kinds of culinary experience, that of the eater and that of the cook. Because if appetite is stirred by this account, it is at a level deeper than the simple desire to eat. The empathetic resonance of *this* memory makes us want to go into the kitchen and cook.

As it happens, I'm very fond of macaroni and cheese, and keep a special spot in my heart for cooks who genuinely love it: they are not that many. But I've been thinking of it lately as a kind of familiar food that seems especially vulnerable to commercial corruption—like homemade marinara sauce, vegetable soup, baked beans . . . dishes less out of style than no longer possessing any style at all. Simple foods made of simple, honest ingredients, they have been polished by the use of so many hands that their features have been rubbed entirely smooth.

And so we have turned away from them, thinking them too ordinary to interest us. But the truth is that we no longer know *how* to be interested in them, which is a very different thing. For while these things cannot command interest, like many good things whose character has been dimmed by time and use, they can richly reward us should we choose to give it anyway. They do this by becoming entirely our own, as the old chair, plucked from the rubbish, refinished, and set in some corner of the study or bedroom, shows its gratitude by melding into its new space as if it had been there forever. It is the homely that turns house into home.

If we don't see this, it may be because we have become more accustomed to think about food as eaters, rather than as cooks. Eaters think in terms of taste. Reaching for the jar of Progresso marinara sauce or Campbell's chunky vegetable soup, they regard it simply as something about as good as they could make themselves. And they may well be right: if most homemade chicken broth was as different from the canned version as some like to claim, College Inn would have been out of business long ago. The difference is there, but it is up to the eater to decide to notice it.

For the cook, however, the story is not quite the same. One important dimension of kitchen experience is what I have previously called —for lack of a better term—*resonance,* a palpable depth to the things out of which we make our meals. In their way, these things speak, and it is our ability to hear, to enter into a kind of conversation with them that marks our crossing over from kitchen worker, however skilled, to true cook.

In the modern kitchen, this resonance is often only barely perceptible; someone else in the kitchen might not be aware of it at all. But the cook, even if not consciously attentive to it, *is* aware, because to the extent we can coax it into being, we increase the reality, the meaningfulness of the cooking experience. And this resonance is strongest in those ordinary, familiar dishes with no aura of specialness to distract us from the actual experience of making.

Making macaroni and cheese, this resonance starts with the familiar heft of the cooking pot as I pull it from under the counter. Cast iron and coated with orange enamel, scoured and stained through years of use, it has been a companion through my entire life as a cook. As I fill it with water, the handle presses against my hand with the firm assurance of a friend.

From the refrigerator, a chunk of Wisconsin Cheddar, richly pale as clotted cream. Its lactic presence unfolds not only back to the farm and the cow but also to the cheese counter where it was chosen over the Argentine Parmesan that seemed a little too bitter and thin, the darkly orange Leicester, rich and crumbly and so expensive, the Vermont Cheddar that, for this dish, had too much character by far.

The grater set over my largest mixing bowl, the cheese slips into shreds, heaps into a generous pile, a whole pound of it—minus the bits that break away and tumble to the side, appetizers for the cook. The water boils. I take down the noodles, in this instance, half a box of rotini, one of the more playful shapes of the pasta tribe and not at all the best choice for this dish, since the thick sauce may refuse to adhere to their tight spirals. But it's all I've got, so in it goes anyway, handful after handful, into the roiling water.

Butter is cut to bits, the can of evaporated milk rooted out from its hiding place and spiced with a fat scarlet drop of Tabasco, two eggs taken from the fridge and beaten to a frothy mass. One of the rotini must be speared and tasted. The pasta must be caught at just the right moment, still with a tiny bit of "spine" or crunch, so it can finish its cooking absorbing the taste and savor of the sauce.

After a quick shake in the colander, they are tumbled into the mixing bowl, tossed with butter, mixed with everything else, the cheese stirred in bit by bit to keep it from clumping into lumps, some of it—and some of the evaporated milk—held back for later. The bowl is slid onto the oven shelf with a glance at the clock—and the rest you already know.

All of this is absolutely ordinary, and yet there is much here to take pleasure in. The dish is put together without recipe, memory tugged for ingredients, proportions, and timings that are obvious and simple and fall together easily. Each step puts a familiar kitchen tool through its paces; each step asks for small but necessary decisions. And, also, the work is framed in pleasant anticipation, begun when I chose the cheese at the store and not done until I scrape and eat the last tasty bits of baked cheese from the sides of the mixing bowl.

Around all this is a net woven of association. My recipe draws in large part from my mother's, but it is still my own, changed by my own taste and by the lives that have impinged on mine, such as that oven-going mixing bowl. It is also association that has me use evaporated milk, whose sweet/sour tang evokes for me the version made by the Irish lady who kept house for my grandmother, and who also added (as I also sometimes do) fresh tomato—peeled, seeded, cut in chunks, and drained on paper towels before being mixed in.

At the same time, the very simplicity of the dish means that it welcomes spontaneous gesture—the handful of chopped, cooked ham, the rotini substituting for elbow macaroni (or pasta replaced entirely by a chopped head of cauliflower). In the same way, one time it is seasoned with Tabasco, the next time with nutmeg, and on and on.

I don't want to pretend that ordinarily all or even part of all this is consciously articulate—just the opposite. Even specific decisions hardly ever flicker into word. As my hands do their work, I listen to music on the radio and think about other things. Even so, I know that it is there around me—like the sound of talk in the next room—a hum not quite audible to the ear but still companionable, useful, breaking into my thoughts now and then to remind me of something forgotten, like bidding me to make sure that the sauce does in fact cling to the rotini. And for the rest of it, it is simply there, enriching my kitchen time and giving—at least for me—some palpable patina to the dish itself.

If I had spent about the same amount of time making this meal from a box of Kraft macaroni and cheese dinner, the work would have been less, but the experience would evaporate into nothing. Directions are printed on the package; most of the ingredients are provided. No chain of association leads me from the garish orange "cheese" powder to cheese itself, let alone the cow. And while I could elect to add some other things, the dish would still unequivocally belong to Kraft (if only because, on my own accord, I would never purchase the individual components—whey, granular Cheddar, powdered buttermilk, etc.—to make this dish from scratch). There is nothing here with anything to give to the cook . . . only to the person who does not want to be a cook.

On the other hand, however, there is also nothing in the making of macaroni and cheese—or vegetable soup or baked beans or tomato sauce—to offer true challenge to the good cook. If kudos are wanted, they must be earned making something else. But mastery of the difficult is only one of the rewards of cooking, and it is worth remembering now and again that there is a humbler gift a dish can give the cook: the pleasure of its company.

A NOTE AND A RECIPE

A good dish of macaroni and cheese is hard to find these days. The recipes in most cookbooks are not to be trusted, in some instances because they refuse to leave well enough alone, vulgarizing the dish with canned cream of celery soup or a dollop of port wine cheese spread. But most usually it is their vexatious infatuation with white sauce, a noxious paste of flour-thickened milk, for this dish flavored with a tiny grating of cheese. It is the basis for a familiar crumb-topped casserole baked in a Pyrex lasagna pan, a casserole universally bland, dry, and rubbery. Contrary to popular belief, this is *not* macaroni and cheese but macaroni with cheese sauce. It is awful stuff and every cookbook in which it appears should be thrown out the window.

Instead, that recipe will remain the popular one: it is cheap to make and pretty to look at. *Real* macaroni and cheese is unkempt. It is also generous with cheese, using at least four times more than what is put in cheese sauce. The recipe below, the *real* recipe, lives a life of exile in its own country . . . biding its time in the few homes willing to grant it sanctuary, awaiting the counterrevolution. This version originally appeared in *The Home Comfort Cook Book*, published in 1937 by the Wrought Iron Range Co., makers of the Home Comfort wood-burning kitchen stove. I give it, however, as adapted first by my mother and then by me, with special thanks to a memory.

Macaroni and Cheese

½ pound elbow macaroni
4 tablespoons (½ stick) butter, cut into bits
Dash Tabasco sauce
1 12-ounce can evaporated milk (or use whole milk mixed with a little cream)

1 pound sharp Cheddar cheese, grated
2 eggs, beaten
1 teaspoon dry mustard, dissolved in a little water
Salt and freshly ground pepper

Preheat oven to 350°F. Boil the macaroni until just barely done in salted water. Drain and toss with the butter in a large, ovenproof mixing bowl. Mix the Tabasco into the evaporated milk. Reserving about ⅓ cup, stir the milk into the macaroni, then add three quarters of the cheese, the eggs, and the mustard. When well combined, season to taste with salt and pepper, and set the bowl directly in the oven. Every five minutes, remove it briefly to stir in some of the reserved cheese, adding more evaporated milk as necessary to keep the mixture moist and smooth. When all the cheese has been incorporated and the mixture is nicely hot and creamy (which should take 20 minutes, all told), serve it at once, with a plate of toasted common crackers to crumble over.

(Serves 4 to 6)

No matter how closely you follow my instructions, your macaroni and cheese will never taste exactly like mine, but we'll hope. I never made the dish exactly the same way twice, but each time it gets more divine. —PEARL BAILEY

Bread and Olives

❀

The last dinner of each month, when money simply was not there to be stretched, called for a favorite of my grandmother: hot lemon tea served with a variety of olives called *throumbes* . . . and brown bread.
— RENA SALAMAN

It is quite affecting to observe how much the olive tree is to the country people. Its fruit supplies them with food, medicine and light; its leaves, winter fodder for the goats and sheep; it is their shelter from the heat and its branches and roots supply them with firewood. The olive tree is the peasant's all in all.
—F. BREMER (1863)

Olives. If there is a single flavor whose presence gives shape to the eating of all the Mediterranean, it is theirs. Street markets reek of their acescent aroma, brine-soaked tubs proclaim their gaudy multitude: bruise-purple, glaucous, pure emerald green; some plump to bursting, others withered as any prune. In Provence alone, there are dozens of varieties and hundreds of cures, touching every note in a register of bitter, pungent complexity.

How can we understand this appetite? Olives, *their* olives, are so hard to like except one by one—the piquant touch on the hors d'oeuvres tray, some tiny slivers scattered over the salad, pasta, or pizza. And even then, we prefer them at their most suave—*niçoise*, Kalamata, Ponentine—sleek miniatures of what is in truth a coarse and gargantuan hunger.

The cookbooks reflect our taste, not theirs. It is rare to find any olive-flecked offering beyond the usual roast duck or beef or chicken stew. And rarer still is mention of a simple eager eating—of what is perhaps the most ordinary of any Mediterranean meal or snack—a glass of wine, a bit of bread, some salt and oil, and a whole plate of them, with an empty saucer for the pits.

All those olives; so few words. How can we hope to take the measure of a cooking when its most basic hunger eludes our palate, when we stand agape at curbside vendors offering paper cones of them, sold and eaten with the same happy abandon that you and I invest in an ice-cream cone? Our tongue resists the shape: the natural grain of our appetite runs the other way. American cooking, after all, is a cuisine designed to master abundance, not make the most of scarcity. Salt and sugar—the seasonings of satiety—are our favorite seasonings because they urge flagging appetite on past hunger. The habits of hard work and thrift that form our character abhor waste. From our industry and fertile soil comes an abundance that—however, somehow—has to be tucked in, the plate cleaned. (Thus we subsume so much edible food into "garbage," reducing the amount of "food" we feel responsible for eating.)

In much of the Mediterranean, appetite marches to a different drummer. The essential flavors of its cooking—sour, pungent, bitter—cause the mouth to pause. Garlic, anchovy, lemon, and all their familiars give the eater a pungent spurt of pleasure that balances against a bland and starchy bulk of pasta, rice, bread, mush—or simple hunger itself. The complex taste of a brine-cured olive halts appetite in its tracks, the tastebuds tracing the pattern of a sensory brocade.

Our mouths, unused to this sensation, meet it with difficulty, even distaste. Our favorite foods, based on meat and dairy, are bland and rich, meant to pass quickly over the tongue. We find our pleasure in the long and blissful slide to a familiar fullness.

Or so, at least, I explain all this to myself. From the moment I first tasted it, olive oil won over my appetite. I can drink it from the bottle. But for the longest time I hated all but the blandest, most buttery of olives. If I've persevered toward liking them, it was because my tongue knew that somewhere buried in that bitter flesh were a few drops of unguent gold—if I could only learn to discern and savor them. Happily, the rest of the equation had an instant, magnetic appeal. The glass of wine, the bread, the olive oil—all these drew my appetite. I had only to see how to this pleasure the olive itself was the essential pivot. And so we begin without the olives, just the rich and unctuous slice.

BRUSCHETTA

In the regions of Italy that have olive oil, it is a great treat for snack or appetizer to have large slices of country bread toasted, rubbed with garlic, and covered with green oil, especially in the season of the year when the olives are newly pressed. The oil, still warm from the olive press, is poured over the bread, creating a flavor never to be forgotten. —GIULIANO BUGIALLI

No further proof is needed of the deep love for olives and their oil that flows through all Mediterranean cooking than the warmth that fills the text when this simple food is mentioned—and in the litany of familiar tags by which it is known in Italy alone: *bruschetta, fetta unta, pancrocino, schiena d'asino*. At its purest, it is nothing more than a coarse-textured slice of peasant bread toasted over burning embers, rubbed with raw garlic, and dipped into the first fragrant pressings of the olive crop.

We know this, of course—distant cousin though it is—as garlic bread, made by mashing a bit of garlic (sometimes with some fresh oregano or basil) in butter, to be spread on bread slices then reassembled into a loaf and heated in the oven. Good as this is, it has already moved a great distance from the original: garlic bread is a small component, an appetite stimulant in what is usually a very large meal. *Bruschetta*, however, is a meal in itself or almost a meal, eaten as a midday snack or a country-style breakfast.

Because of this, the logic of its making is different, starting with the need for that slightly stale, coarse-textured bread. This isn't misplaced empathy for its peasant origins but the need for a crisp contrast against the oil's sweet lubricity: dip into it a soft-crumbed slice and the result is a greasy mush. The contrast is sharpened still further by slicing the loaf thickly (leaving each slice as much crust as possible) and toasting it until just speckled with brown. This was traditionally done over open coals—giving the bread a wonderfully smoke-grazed flavor—but the oven broiler does the job (the slices should be cut too thick to fit in any toaster).

The toasting having crisped the bread and brought out its flavor, the slice is rubbed with raw garlic and brushed and dribbled with an oil carrying the taste of the fruit. Eat. Full-flavored and succulent, it is no more greasy-seeming than well-buttered toast. This balance of taste and texture is fine tuned to personal taste, some eaters preferring to fry the bread in hot oil; others crush the garlic cloves directly into the oil to intensify its flavor. Most potent of all is the Provençal *roustido dou moulin*, where the bread slice is dunked in oil, topped with crushed garlic and anchovies, and then oven-baked until crusty!

Far more sociable is a milder version from Catalonia, *pa amb tomàquet*, where the bread is toasted and both sides rubbed with garlic and fresh tomato pulp before being dribbled with olive oil. (Nor is this the only Spanish version. In another, *pan de costra al ajo*, garlic cloves and dried hot red pepper are pounded together, seasoned with salt and pepper, and wetted with the juice of half a Seville orange and a little olive oil. This mixture is spread on bread that is then toasted before being eaten.)

But however you make it, bread and oil isn't to be eaten by the plateful, like hot buttered toast. It's that equilibrating pungency of the garlic that both adds a sense of substance and slows the tongue. And once educated that much, my appetite began to make sense of a meal of bread and olives, that fruit having both the richness and pungency the balance requires. I still thought of olives as culinary singletons—bits of seasoning, really, no different than a garlic clove. This was to change.

OLIVADA

> This is an excellent black olive "mash" preserved in virgin olive oil, wonderful as a spread or . . . in the preparation of sauces, or even as a pasta sauce.   —ALFREDO VIAZZI

Excellent, yes. The first time I ever saw it I knew exactly what it really was—olive jam—and my ecstatic appetite wanted into it so badly, I had the cap loose hardly out of the store and I hunkered down on a stoop just around the corner to devour the whole of it, a French loaf as knife, plate, and napkin. I went back and bought a second jar "for home."

The brine-cured olive transformed—pitted, pulped, put up in oil— it was no longer seasoning, but food. My tongue learned to wag a new way. It wasn't just the change in the olive; it was making the necessary connection with bread: the idea of olive jam. People do, of course, eat "real" jams straight from the jar—"spoon sweets," it's called—but usually a jam or jelly calls up an automatic image of toast and butter. Here, toast and olive oil (or—naturally—any starch: baked potato, pasta, polenta, pizza). Far from the prickly monad I had taken it for, the olive's pungency was really to foil a starch's subtler-tasting bulk. No wonder the moniker Italians fondly bestowed on fat, rebarbative Oliver Hardy: *Olio. Stanlio e Olio.*

Like *bruschetta*, *olivada* exists this side of recipes. You just make it the way you want, choosing your own type of olive and any flavorings your mind tastes with them. Only one bit of caution: Don't skimp on quality. Watery olives or flavorless oil will produce something worse than the sum of its parts. To give some sense of the range of the possible, here are several attractive options, the first—and simplest— closest to the store-bought import I first tasted, that of *Crespi e Figli* of San Remo.

OLIVADA I.   Pit firm black olives (such as *niçoise*, Ponentine, or Kalamata), and either force the flesh through a sieve or process in a blender or food processor into a coarse paste, adding just enough extra virgin olive oil to moisten thoroughly. Then mix in a pinch of dried oregano. This can be kept cold for up to a week, but it should always be served at room temperature.

OLIVADA II.   This version, from the Italian Riviera, is an obvious though muted relation to a Provençal *tapenade*, with its hint of garlic and anchovy. Prepare as directed above, but to every ½ cup of the olive mixture, blend in half a small garlic clove, crushed, and ⅛ teaspoon anchovy paste. (These amounts can be increased to taste. And whole anchovy fillets, well rinsed of salt, patted dry, and then finely minced, can be substituted for the paste.)

OLIVADA CON BASILICO.   This is a very pleasing variation with a crisp herbal aroma, especially fine on pasta and made much like *pesto alla genovese:* 1 cup black, firm brine-cured olives, pitted; 2 cups firmly packed fresh basil leaves; 1 small clove garlic, crushed; and ¼ cup extra-virgin olive oil. Put all the ingredients except the oil in a food processor or blender. Then, with blade turning, pour in the oil in a fine stream of droplets, making a smooth paste.

MASLINE FRECATE. This is not an *olivada* but a close cousin from Romania, an incredibly rich and unctuous spread, perfect slathered on a thick slice of black bread. One cup each black olives and sweet butter, plus a finely minced addition of chives or scallion, sweet pepper, fennel, and/or parsley to taste. Pit the olives, and either rub through a sieve or mix them with a little olive oil and blend into a coarse puree in a food processor or blender. Soften the butter with the flat of a knife and work in the olive pulp. Work until the mixture is well blended and smooth, then work in the flavorings.

It's impossible to write about *olivada* without sharing my friend Matt Lewis's spectacular inspiration—splitting hot-from-the-oven corn bread, spreading the bottom half with *olivada* and thin slices of choice mozzarella, and then putting back the top half, letting things stand just long enough for the cheese to melt and the olive aroma and flavor to permeate the corn bread. Really super stuff and a meal by itself—at least with a side of ripe, sliced tomatoes. Her own special recipe (cooked Arborio rice stirred into the corn bread batter) is part of an article on corn bread-making that appeared in *Petits Propos Culinaires* #19, and I'm not giving it away. Your own favorite corn bread (but not a sweet one) should work just fine. (To get Matt's recipe and take a look at *PPC*, a British-based journal of the higher sort of food thought, make out a check for $6.20 to Jennifer Davidson and send it to her c/o *PPC* North America, 5311 42nd St. NW, Washington, DC 20015.)

PAN BAGNAT

[P]an bagnat (bathed bread). What the bread is bathed in is olive oil. A round bun is sliced in half, soaked in the oil, and between the halves are placed various items of the Nice repertoire—always tomato, green pepper, and black olives, sometimes slices of onion, slices of hard-boiled egg, radishes, or anchovies—or all of them.
—WAVERLEY ROOT

Sadly, the definitive account of Mediterranean junk food has yet to be written, we addicts assembling what we can from the bits and pieces let slip by food writers on route from one three-star restaurant (or granny) to the next. Even so, it doesn't take much research to learn that the familiar "Italian sandwich"—or sub or hero or hoagie—is a love child born of Italian taste and American *abondanza*. Judge the authenticity of your local favorite by whether—discarding cheese and meat—you still have something worth eating. In Italy itself, at least where meat is still something worth noticing, your salami is served by itself on a plate. A sandwich is made with what we over here know as the "come withs"—black olives, sour pickle, hot pepper, onion, tomatoes, and greens—all dressed with a generous splash of oil.

Pan bagnat, the fabled sandwich of Nice, is a case in point—and also nicely draws to a close this course of gustatory logic. Here, bread, oil, and olive provide a solid basso continuo to improvisational flights of Mediterranean flavor: anchovy or tuna, tomato, sweet pepper, garlic, onion, cucumber, celery, hard-boiled egg. If this sounds familiar, it is very much a *salade niçoise* tucked between slices of bread or, in Nice itself, in a special round loaf baked especially for the purpose. Unfortunately, *salade niçoise* has become one of those set pieces that grow more elaborate every year. But for *pan bagnat*, authenticity means winging it.

PAN BAGNAT. Slice a good French or Italian loaf in half horizontally. Rub each cut half with a garlic clove and then brush generously with a fruity olive oil. Dot the bottom half with bits of black olive and layer to taste with slices of tomato, cucumber, sweet pepper, scallion, radish, greens, capers, hard-boiled egg, and anchovy (or oil-packed Italian tuna). Cover with the top half, wrap tightly in plastic wrap or foil, weigh down with a plate, and leave for an hour or two to firm. Serve cut in slices.

PATAFLA A *patafla* is an evolutionary half step between what *pan bagnat* was once (a sort of bread salad) and the sandwich it became—minus the anchovies. And it's delicious, especially if you have some truly juicy tomatoes; this is a sandwich that needs all the moisture it can get. (Amounts are approximate: judge them from the size of the loaf.) A handful each of brined green and black olives, pitted and pulled into bits; 1 clove garlic, minced; 2 large ripe tomatoes, coarsely chopped; 1 sweet red or green pepper, cored, seeded, and chopped; ½ small red onion, finely chopped; and 1 tablespoon capers with their liquid—plus a loaf of Italian or French bread, salt, pepper, and olive oil. Cut the bread in half horizontally. Carefully pull out the moist center from the bread, leaving the crust intact. Tear the removed bread into small bits, and toss in a bowl with all the other ingredients, seasoning to taste with salt and freshly ground pepper, and drizzling with enough olive oil to moisten well. Spread this mixture over the bottom crust, cover with the top one, and wrap in plastic or foil, pressing the halves gently but firmly together. Let this meld together for several hours—even a whole day—in the fridge. Then slice at an angle and serve.

PAN BOLOGNA.   1 loaf Italian bread, cut in half horizontally; 1 or 2 cloves garlic; 2 tomatoes, cut in half; 2 tablespoons finely chopped onion; 1 teaspoon capers, chopped; 1 teaspoon whole capers; ¼ teaspoon minced fresh hot pepper or dried red pepper flakes; ¼ cup olive oil; 1 teaspoon minced fresh basil or parsley; salt and freshly ground pepper. Toast the bread halves under the broiler until just tinged with brown. Rub with the garlic and then the tomatoes, leaving as much pulp as possible on the bread. Sprinkle on the onion, chopped capers, and hot pepper. Then drizzle with the olive oil, season with the salt and pepper, and decorate with the basil or parsley and the whole capers. Serve as is or cut at an angle into uniform slices.

The preface to Maggie Klein's *Feast of the Olive* quotes in part a reminiscence of Elizabeth David meeting Norman Douglas, in a restaurant terrace lined with orange trees and overlooking the cliffs at Capri, for a glass of the local white wine and

> . . . *a bowl of olives, a carafe of green oil, some peasant bread, salt. And, of course, some of the most scandalous conversation in Europe.*

May we all have the chance to dine so well.

The Tian

❁

A tian is a Provençal specialty, halfway between a gratin and a thick omelette, and there is hardly any vegetable, or combination of vegetables with meat or fish, which cannot be tian-ized.
—*The Mediterranean Cookbook*

A tian is a Provençal dish. Calling it a "specialty," however, may be going too far, suggesting that you might see it chalked up outside some local bistro as the day's special, the chef's treat. Possible, but not more likely than finding your local restaurant featuring macaroni and cheese. A tian, essentially, is a vegetable casserole, a modest penny-stretcher meant, whether served hot or cold, as the main course or a side dish, to provide the bulk of the meal at the least possible cost. Unlike most casserole dishes, however, its list of virtues doesn't start and end with economy. The defining characteristic of a tian—slow cooking in olive oil and seasonings—brings out the best of taste and texture in a host of vegetables. Furthermore, it is a dish especially amenable to improvisation, permitting an amazing range of combinations and adaptations without threat to its essential nature. And finally, a tian is an excellent vegetarian dish, since its nutritional content can be enhanced via several attractive options without recourse to meat.

Originally, the tian was a simple peasant dish of vegetables that took its name from the vast, heavy earthenware terrine it was cooked in—a *tian*—the classic shape of which, we have on good authority, was round (Elizabeth David) . . . square (Roy Andries de Groot) . . . rectangular (Julia Child) . . . oval (Mireille Johnston). It was packed full and carried to the village baker to be cooked in his oven once the bread was done (and seasoned by the tang of woodsmoke), its heavy weight necessary to absorb heat and continue the cooking process as the oven itself began to cool. Today, when even the poorest villagers have their own ovens and the village bakery is often only a memory, the *tian* is as likely made of Pyrex or Corningware as clay; the American cook can easily make do with a casserole.

The tian might only deserve a culinary footnote if it hadn't managed also to evolve with the times. Cooks who could no longer justify the cost and time of the long baking (which had once been unsupervised and cost-free) found a way to cut the oven time through precooking and to expand the role of the dish by adding starch and protein, making it more substantial and nutritious. And for the most part, these modern adaptations have been accomplished while still maintaining the dish's central logic—vegetables gently heated in olive oil until succulent and tender—while greatly expanding the scope of its possibilities.

The result of this evolutionary voyage is a dish almost unique in its accessibility to a cook's immediate needs and resources. A tian can be simple and quick or rich and complicated, and assembled from one, two, or several vegetables: spinach, Swiss chard, zucchini, pumpkin, squash, potatoes, broccoli, red peppers, eggplant, tomatoes, carrots, onion, mushrooms, green beans, cauliflower. Not only do all these vegetables (and many others) make an excellent tian, but they can be combined to make even more tempting combinations—eggplant and red peppers, say, or green beans, zucchini, and onion. And once the cook has chosen the vegetables, the range of options continues: the tian can be cooked as is; expanded with rice, chick-peas, or macaroni; enriched with eggs and cheese.

At this point, it's worth pausing to look at two examples of what is the simplest—and probably earliest—sort of tian: a single vegetable slowly cooked to perfection. From them, we can get an idea of the dish's immediate appeal and of the strong central logic that underlies the more elaborate presentations usually found in contemporary cookbooks. (These two recipes are adapted from Richard Olney's *Simple French Food* and René Jouveau's *La Cuisine Provençale*—possibly Olney's own source of inspiration.)

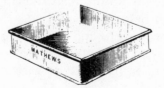

Spinach Tian

2 pounds fresh spinach
Salt and freshly ground pepper
¼ cup olive oil
¼ cup homemade bread crumbs

Preheat oven to 375°F. Stem the spinach, carefully rinse away any grit, shake the leaves dry, and chop fine with a sharp knife. Put the chopped spinach in a bowl and toss with salt and pepper to taste. Oil a casserole dish with 1 tablespoon of the olive oil. Pack the spinach tightly into the casserole and sprinkle evenly with the bread crumbs. Dribble the remaining olive oil over the spinach and bake for 50 minutes to 1 hour, or until the leaves have been reduced to a moist, savory mass and all the excess liquid is cooked off. (*Note:* This is excellent just the way it is, providing the olive oil is good, the spinach still young, tender, and sweet, and the bread crumbs crumbled from decent bread. However, you might like to flatten a garlic clove and let it flavor the oil for an hour before assembling the dish; or add a pinch of nutmeg with the salt and pepper; or mix a handful of pine nuts in with the chopped spinach before packing the casserole.)

(Serves 4)

Pumpkin Tian

One small pumpkin (3 to 4 pounds)
¼ cup flour
6 cloves garlic, finely minced
Generous pinch fresh thyme (approx. 1 teaspoon)
2 tablespoons freshly grated Parmesan cheese
Salt and freshly ground pepper
⅓ cup olive oil

Preheat oven to 325°F. Remove seeds, string, and rind from the pumpkin flesh, then cut flesh into ¾-inch cubes. Set the pumpkin cubes into a colander and toss with the flour until the cubes are coated and the excess flour has escaped. Toss again with the garlic, thyme,

Parmesan cheese, and season with salt and pepper to taste (pumpkin is sweet and bland and requires a fat pinch from the salt box). Rub the interior of a casserole with a generous amount of the olive oil, pack in the floured and seasoned pumpkin cubes, and dribble the remaining oil evenly over the top. Set in the preheated oven and bake for 2 to 2½ hours. The top of the dish will form a dark rich crust; the pumpkin within dissolves in the mouth into molten succulence. (*Note:* Although pumpkin is quite fine in this dish, the actual squash used for it in Provence is *courge rouge,* which is similar but more flavorful and less sweet. It is just now starting to appear in American markets, somewhat pumpkin-shaped but of a deeper, reddish hue. Home gardeners can find seeds for it in specialty catalogues [see page 157 for one of them].)

(Serves 4)

Both of these tians are excellent when prepared as directed; the pumpkin tian especially, so savory and redolent of garlic, will surprise and delight palates that have unjustly relegated that squash to Halloween duty and the pie pan. Even so, it's hard not to notice the extravagant cooking times—an hour for the spinach and over two hours for the pumpkin—an expensive use of oven heat, unless the tian is pushed in back of a turkey.

So, not surprisingly, more modern recipes drastically cut into that time by sautéing vegetables in olive oil before they go into the oven, thus wilting the spinach and cooking out much of its moisture and softening the pumpkin pieces. And since this range-top prep essentially cooks the vegetables, the integrity of the oven baking is retained by expanding the tian's identity to embrace a mélange of vegetables and play a more substantial role in the meal. The spinach now goes into the oven, perhaps, with a cupful of rice (just barely cooked so that it can absorb any remaining spinach liquor) and a mixture of egg and feta cheese. As for the pumpkin, precooking it permits the cook to add other ingredients that would have otherwise been overcooked.

Pumpkin Tian with Cheese and Rice

One small pumpkin (3 to 4 pounds)
¼ cup olive oil
¼ cup homemade bread crumbs
1 onion, minced
1 cup cooked rice

½ cup freshly grated Parmesan or Gruyère cheese
Handful chopped parsley
1 egg, beaten
Salt and freshly ground pepper

Preheat oven to 375°F. Remove seeds, string, and rind from the pumpkin flesh, then cut flesh into ¾-inch cubes. Heat 1 tablespoon of the olive oil in a large skillet and sprinkle in the bread crumbs. Stirring constantly, toast them to a rich gold and remove to a small bowl. Add another 2 tablespoons of the oil and sauté the onion until tender and translucent. Add the pumpkin cubes and sauté for 10 minutes over gentle heat, turning the cubes with a spatula. Remove from the heat and let cool. Blend together the rice, cheese, parsley, and egg, seasoning the mixture with salt and pepper to taste. Mix the onion and pumpkin into this mixture. Rub the inside of a shallow casserole with half the remaining olive oil and pour in the pumpkin mixture. Sprinkle the top evenly with the toasted bread crumbs, dribble over the last of the olive oil, and bake for 20 minutes or until the mixture is heated through.

(Serves 4 to 6)

Cooking time reduced from two and a half hours to thirty minutes, the pumpkin combining with cheese and rice to make a quick-cooking, substantial tian that will provide four with a meal or six with a side dish. In the above version, only a single egg is used to bind the mixture together; in other tian recipes more eggs are used so that the result is something like a Basque *pipérade* or an Italian *frittata*. Because so many cookbooks feature tians with the full panoply of options—rice *and* eggs *and* cheese—it's important to note that a sophisticatedly flavored and substantial tian can be composed without any of them. Take, for instance, the following recipe.

Tian with Roasted Red Peppers and Mushrooms

3 large red bell peppers
1 pound mushrooms
¼ cup olive oil plus 2 tablespoons
¼ cup homemade bread
  crumbs

6 shallots or 3 scallions,
  minced
6 cloves garlic, minced
Handful chopped parsley
½ cup dry white wine
Salt and freshly ground pepper

Preheat oven to 375°F. Roast the peppers directly over an open burner flame, turning frequently with a pair of tongs so that all sides are equally blistered and blackened (or, if your range is electric, bake on a baking sheet in a preheated 400°F oven for 30 minutes, also turning frequently). Remove peppers from the heat and seal in a paper bag, letting them steam loose the burned skin as they cool. When they can be handled, remove and discard all skin, stem, and seeds, slicing the remaining flesh into long, thin strips.

Slice the mushrooms thickly. Heat 1 tablespoon of the olive oil in a large skillet and sprinkle in the bread crumbs. Stirring constantly, toast these until they turn golden, and set aside in a small bowl. In the same pan, heat ¼ cup olive oil and add the mushrooms, sautéing them until they are soft and wilted and their juices have cooked off. Add the shallots or scallions and the garlic. Continue to sauté for 2 more minutes, then remove from the heat. Combine this mixture with the roasted strips of red pepper. Mix in the parsley and wine, and season to taste with salt and pepper. Oil a shallow casserole with the remaining tablespoon of olive oil. Add the vegetable mixture and sprinkle evenly with the bread crumbs. Bake for 30 minutes. Serve either hot or cold.

(Serves 4)

Not only do many cookbooks present the tian just in its Sunday best, but they imply as well that it owns but a single suit. Moving, say, from Anne Willan's *French Regional Cooking* to Roy Andries de Groot's *Auberge of the Flowering Hearth* to Child and Beck's *Mastering the Art of French Cooking*, volume 2, we find an almost identical tian recipe—

zucchini, rice, cheese, and eggs. This is the sort of bland, rich vegetable dish that used to be served in expensive restaurants as an accompaniment to the meat when high caloric intake was still chic, but it doesn't work as a solo dinner dish.

However, if we add a good portion of some astringent green, Belgian endive, a head of romaine, or Swiss chard, that hint of bitterness serves as an appetite-enhancing foil to the unctuous richness of the rest, as can be tested in the following recipe.

Tian with Zucchini and Swiss Chard

2 pounds zucchini
½ cup raw rice
1 pound Swiss chard
¼ cup olive oil plus 2 tablespoons
1 medium onion, finely chopped
¼ cup homemade bread crumbs

2 cloves garlic, minced
4 eggs
Pinch minced parsley
½ cup freshly grated Parmesan or Gruyère cheese
Salt and freshly ground pepper

Coarsely grate the zucchini, spread it out on a clean towel, sprinkle with salt, and set in a colander to drain for an hour. At the hour's end, wrap up the towel and wring out as much moisture as possible.

Preheat oven to 375°F. Cook the rice in a generous cup of salted water until done and set aside. Clean the Swiss chard of any grit, cut away any tough stems, and finely chop the rest. Heat 1 tablespoon of the olive oil in a large skillet and sprinkle in the bread crumbs. Stirring constantly, toast these to a rich gold, then remove them to a small bowl. In the same skillet, heat ¼ cup of olive oil and add the onion. When it is soft and translucent, add the garlic, zucchini shreds, and Swiss chard. Stirring constantly, cook over moderate heat for about 5 minutes, or until the Swiss chard has completely wilted. Allow to cool a little. Beat the eggs in a large bowl. Stir in the parsley, half the grated cheese, the cooked rice, and the vegetable mixture. Taste and season with salt and pepper. Oil a shallow casserole dish with the remaining tablespoon of olive oil. Pour in the combined ingredients, then sprinkle the top evenly with the remaining cheese and the bread crumbs. Bake for 35 to 40 minutes, or until the eggs have set and the bread crumbs are golden. (*Variations:* If Swiss chard is unavailable or not liked, spinach may be substituted. An equal amount of fresh basil can be used instead of the parsley. Also, if available, zucchini flowers can be added to the recipe with the zucchini, sautéing them in the olive oil with the zucchini itself and the Swiss chard.)

(Serves 6)

By now, I hope, you are getting a sense of how a tian is put together. The improvising cook will find that many options naturally suggest themselves as a particular tian is composed. With vegetables that tend to give up moisture while cooking, undercooked rice or noodles can be used to absorb it. On the other hand, if the dish needs a bit of additional moisture to keep it from drying out, a liquid ingredient can be chosen to add to the flavor balance. In the roasted pepper and mushroom tian above, for example, a little dry white wine was added to offset those vegetables' sweetness; a generous dash of a good wine vinegar could be used to serve the same purpose. Vegetables that might tend toward bitterness, however, might be balanced instead with some milk or cream.

These, of course, are final adjustments. The basic balance of texture and taste should be struck out of the combination of vegetables itself. Thus, in the following tian, the acidic presence of the tomato offsets the blander, richer-tasting eggplant, while the chick peas, used instead of rice, give the dish a contrasting firmness of texture. As a strictly vegetable composition, this tian works deliciously well, but for a formidable presentation, it can be expanded to include cheese as well. For the final touch, the cook might decide to include a handful of diced raisins or, moving in a different direction entirely, bits of pitted, brine-cured olives. If the tomatoes prove on the sweet, bland side, the dish might also call for a squeeze of fresh lemon or a bit of balsamic vinegar. And finally, while the version including cheese is prepared to give the dish a layered effect (something that can be used to add visual appeal whenever contrastingly colored vegetables are used), the ingredients can also be simply mixed together.

Tian with Eggplant, Tomatoes, and Chick-Peas

½ cup dried chick-peas
1 medium eggplant (about 1½ pounds)
3 medium tomatoes (about 1 pound)
¾ cup (approx.) olive oil
1 medium onion, minced

½ teaspoon ground allspice
1 teaspoon dried red pepper flakes
3 or 4 fresh basil leaves, shredded
Salt and freshly ground pepper

The night before preparing the dish, rinse the chick-peas, picking them over for any pebbles, put them into a small saucepan, and pour over 2 cups cold water. The next day, add enough additional water to cover the chickpeas by 1 inch, cover, and simmer gently for 2 hours or until just tender. Drain and reserve. (Or, if time presses, you can of course substitute about 1¼ cups drained canned chick-peas instead.)

Preheat oven to 375°F. Peel the eggplant if you wish and cut it into 1-inch cubes. Set the cubes in a colander and sprinkle them evenly with a generous pinch of salt (about 2 teaspoons). Leave them to drain for an hour, tossing them once halfway through. Quickly rinse the salt off the eggplant under cold water and pat the cubes dry. Remove the eggplant cubes from the colander. Put the tomatoes in the colander and pour boiling water over them to loosen skins. Then peel, seed, and coarsely chop the tomatoes, setting the pieces to drain on paper towels. Heat ½ cup of the olive oil in a large skillet and sauté the eggplant over moderately high heat, turning the cubes with a spatula, until they are lightly browned on all sides, adding more oil if necessary. Remove the eggplant from the skillet to a large bowl and add 2 more tablespoons of the olive oil. When this is hot, sauté the onion until it is tender and translucent. Add the chopped tomato and cook over medium heat until the mixture is slightly thickened. Season with the allspice, red pepper flakes, and basil, seasoning to taste with salt and pepper. (If adding the egg and cheese mixture, turn now to the instructions below.)

Oil a large casserole with 1 tablespoon of the olive oil, and layer the ingredients, starting with half the eggplant, then half the chick-peas, then the entire amount of tomato-onion mixture, then the rest of the chick-peas, ending with the remaining eggplant. Dribble the remaining tablespoon of olive oil over the top and bake for 40 minutes.

(Serves 4)

Variation with Egg and Cheese: To the ingredients above, add the following:

½ cup ricotta cheese
1 egg
¼ cup freshly grated Parmesan cheese
½ cup heavy cream

Prepare the recipe to the point where the mixture is to be added to the casserole. Preheat oven to 375°F. Put the ricotta in a large bowl and beat in the egg until the mixture is glossy and smooth. Add the Parmesan, bit by bit, to form a thick, pastelike mixture, reserving about a tablespoon. Then stir in the cream, also bit by bit, adding enough to make the mixture moist but not runny.

Oil the casserole with 1 tablespoon of the olive oil. Set down about half the eggplant across the bottom of the casserole and sprinkle with half the chick-peas. Now pour in the tomato-onion mixture, topping that with the cheese mixture. Now, in reverse order, add the remaining chick-peas and the remaining eggplant. Sprinkle with the reserved Parmesan and the remaining tablespoon of olive oil. Bake for 40 minutes.

Needless to say, I have only scratched the surface of possible tian combinations, not even mentioning several traditional versions made with ingredients not easily come by nor any calling for meat or fish (salt cod tian is another Provençal favorite). Readers wanting other examples of this delightful dish should turn to the volumes marked with an asterisk(*) in the following list of consulted sources, and especially those by Richard Olney and Mireille Johnston: James Beard, *The New James Beard;* Elizabeth David, *Summer Cooking;* Roy Andries de Groot, *Auberge of the Flowering Hearth;* Jane Grigson, *Vegetable Book;**

René Jouveau, *La Cuisine Provençale;* * Mireille Johnston, *The Cuisine of the Sun;* * Marian Morash, *The Victory Garden Cookbook;* * Anna Mac-miadhacháin, et al., *The Mediterranean Cookbook;* Richard Olney, *Simple French Food;* * Fay Sharman, *The Taste of France;* and Anne Willan, *French Regional Cooking.*

Pasta and Beans

❀

This dish, very common and popular in Italy, is almost unknown abroad. Served far more often in homes and in simple trattorias than in restaurants frequented by tourists, it is warming, nourishing, and inexpensive. —ANCEL AND MARGARET KEYS

Pasta e fagioli—or pasta fazool as it comes out in some neighborhoods—is a simple, hearty dish so characteristic of Italian cooking that it's hard to find a cookbook that doesn't have a recipe for it—or two cookbooks that have the same recipe. This is because, really, the dish exists this side of recipes: it's an impromptu, put-up meal easily and cheaply assembled from foods on hand. In fact, the broken pasta often called for is, in Italy (where pasta is sold loose), truly bottom-of-the-barrel stuff, sold at a pittance the pound and often mixed and bagged indiscriminately, giving a delightfully haphazard texture to the finished dish.

Just as with rice and peas, pasta and beans are nutritious complementaries (one reason they taste so good together) that allow the creation of a variety of strictly vegetarian dishes or, more commonly, dishes where the meat is only a flavoring. But pasta and beans also work together in other ways, the beans giving body to pasta dishes and the pasta giving lightness to bean dishes that, while full of flavor, tend otherwise to take a long, slow, noisy time to digest.

Finally, for those of us addicted to a relaxed, impromptu style of cooking, this notion of combining pasta and beans provides one of those sudden flicks of perspective that alters our whole bag of tricks. Here is a dish that can gracefully slide from soup to salad to entree with very much the same ingredients. And no dish is happier to help us segue from end of summer into fall, offering, at our pleasure, lighter dishes full of fresh-picked harvest vegetables to more substantial plates, warming the body while the finger still hesitates to wake the still-snoozing thermostat for its new stint of duty.

I also hope that the recipes below will stimulate your appetite for ventures all your own. Working on these pages, visions of dishes tempting but untried kept floating through my mind—lamb meatballs baked in a casserole with white beans, orzo, and pine nuts . . . spinach with black-eyed peas and broken macaroni, dotted with bits of sun-dried tomato . . . lentils, vermicelli, and sweet corn. . . . *Buon appetito!*

BASIC BEAN PREPARATION.   After being rinsed off and picked over for pebbles, dried beans (except such as lentils, split or black-eyed peas) need long soaking in ample water: either overnight or 2 hours after being brought to a boil for a few minutes. Use this as an opportunity to give the dish more flavor. Into the soaking water add such flavorings as carrot ends and peelings, celery tops and leaves, chunks of garlic and onion, and a big pinch of the same herbs that will season the dish as it cooks. When the draining water is discarded— as it should be—remove these flavor agents, adding fresh ones for the cooking. But never salt the soaking water, and do not salt the cooking liquid until the beans are half done. Italian cooks add a tablespoon of flour to the soaking water, saying it produces yeasts that tenderize the beans. Finally, to use fresh or canned beans instead of dried ones, double the amount, using 2 cups fresh or canned for every cup dried (1 pound dried beans equals about 2½ cups).

SOUP

Pasta and beans are so obviously a natural for a soup that it's no surprise that the combination is well represented all over the Mediterranean, from the basil-sauced *soupe au pistou* of Provence to the richly sustaining Moroccan lamb soup, *harira souiria*. Even in the Italian repertoire, there are enough different recipes to fill a book of their own. Fortunately, while each differs from the other in the hand-honing of personal experience, they are linked together by the underlying logic of their making:

— A *sofrito*—a flavor base of sautéed aromatics—is made from onion, garlic, celery leaves, and such, finely minced and sautéed in olive oil or leaf lard, into which is poured

— a broth (usually water, but sometimes beef or chicken stock),

— the beans themselves, which can be almost any variety, but most usually red or white *(cannellini)* kidney beans, chick-peas, lentils, or small white beans,

— a choice of vegetables—usually tomatoes, but also cabbage, carrots, potatoes, celery, sweet peppers, and so on—plus a few fresh potherbs—including sage, rosemary, and basil—and a tablespoon of tomato paste, and

— a flavoring presence of olive oil and/or fatty meat, sometimes a meaty ham or beef bone or lamb shank—or some meat scraps such as pork rind, pig's feet, or sausage chunks—or (sometimes) anchovies. Prosciutto rind, which is usually cut away and discarded at the deli counter, is superb in these dishes (as is the bone itself) and can sometimes be begged for nothing. All this is then slowly simmered together until the beans are almost ready, at which point is added

— the pasta, usually either spaghetti broken small or the smaller pasta shapes, cooked until half done, then added to finish cooking in (and help thicken) the soup. When brought to table, the dish is then sprinkled—or not, as appropriate—with a fresh grating of Parmesan.

This grasped, the limited conjugation that follows need only suggest in its singular the savory wealth in the plenitude of its plural.

Pasta e Fagioli I

1 pound dried white beans, presoaked as directed above

Salt and freshly ground pepper

¼ cup olive oil

1 large sprig fresh rosemary or ¼ teaspoon dried

3 cloves garlic, minced

2 tablespoons minced Italian parsley

½ pound small macaroni or broken pasta

Put the beans in a heavy pot with 3 quarts water, bring to a simmer, and cook for 1 hour. Then season liquid to taste with salt and pepper. In a small sauté pan, heat the olive oil and the rosemary together over gentle heat. When the oil is suffused with the aroma of the rosemary, if using the fresh herb remove and discard it. Add the garlic and parsley to the flavored oil and cook an additional minute. Add this to the soup and continue to simmer it until the beans are soft or about two hours. In a separate pot, cook the macaroni in salted water until half done. Drain, stir into the soup, and cook until the pasta is just done.

(Serves 8)

Pasta e Fagioli II

2 to 3 pounds soup bones

1 pound dried white beans, presoaked as directed above

2 tablespoons olive oil

3 cloves garlic, minced

1 tablespoon chopped fresh basil

5 medium tomatoes, peeled and coarsely chopped

1 tablespoon tomato paste

Salt and freshly ground pepper

½ pound small macaroni or broken pasta

2 tablespoons chopped parsley

Freshly grated Parmesan cheese

Place bones and beans in a large pot and cover with water. Bring to a simmer. Check occasionally to skim off any scum, adding more water as necessary. Cook 1½ to 2 hours, or until the beans are soft and tender but not mushy. Then remove from the heat, discard the bones, and pour off all but about a cup of the remaining liquid (if any).

In a skillet, heat the olive oil, and sauté the garlic until it turns translucent. Add the basil, tomatoes, and tomato paste, then taste and season with salt and pepper. Cook gently for 5 minutes. Cook macaroni in salted water until just done, and quickly drain. Mix together the sauce and the macaroni in the pot with the beans. Simmer an additional 4 minutes to heat through, and then serve, topped with parsley and Parmesan cheese.

(Serves 8)

Pasta e Fagioli III

2 tablespoons olive oil
2 medium onions, coarsely chopped
1 clove garlic, minced
2 stalks celery, coarsely chopped
1 20-ounce can chick-peas, drained
1 cup shredded cabbage

4 large tomatoes, peeled and coarsely chopped
2 quarts beef stock
Salt and freshly ground pepper
½ cup orzo (a rice-shaped pasta)
½ cup freshly grated Parmesan cheese

Heat the olive oil in a large, heavy pot and sauté the onions until translucent. Add the garlic and celery, and when they release their aroma, add the chick-peas, cabbage, and tomatoes. Pour in the beef stock, taste and season with salt and pepper, and cook for 30 minutes. Meanwhile, in boiling salted water, cook the orzo until almost done. Drain and add to the soup pot. Continue simmering until the orzo is just done. Serve with the Parmesan cheese on the side.

(Serves 6)

SALAD

The secret to a good pasta salad is to make and eat it with the pasta just cooled to room temperature. Only the tiniest pasta doesn't get heavy and soggy when cold, which is why so many take-out pasta creations look so good and turn out so deadly.

Pasta and Bean Salad

1 pound dried Great Northern or *cannellini* beans, presoaked as directed above
2 medium onions, quartered
2 stalks celery, with leaves
juice of 1 lemon
1 teaspoon salt
½ teaspoon freshly ground pepper

3 tablespoons chopped parsley
2 teaspoons chopped capers
1 teaspoon fresh rosemary or ½ teaspoon dried
¾ cup olive oil
½ pound penne, cooked in salted water until just done and drained thoroughly

Cover the presoaked beans with water in a large pot, add the onions and celery, and bring to a simmer. Cover and cook about 2 hours, or until tender. Drain well. Mix together the lemon juice, salt, pepper, parsley, capers, rosemary, and olive oil. Gently stir this dressing, the pasta, and the beans together in a large bowl. Let cool to room temperature and serve.

(Serves 8)

Pasta and Bean Salad with Tuna

1 cup dried Great Northern
  or *cannellini* beans, presoaked as directed above
1 small onion, finely chopped
3 tablespoons good olive oil
2 teaspoons fresh lemon juice
Salt and freshly ground pepper

¼ cup chopped fresh basil or
  parsley
1 7-ounce can tuna packed in
  olive oil
½ pound ziti, cooked in
  salted water until just done
  and drained thoroughly

Cook the beans in unsalted water for 45 minutes. Drain. Mix with
the onion, olive oil, and lemon juice while still warm. Season to taste
with salt and pepper, and let reach room temperature. Then mix in
the basil or parsley. Drain the tuna (saving the oil) and break into
small chunks. Add the tuna and the ziti to the beans and mix gently.
Dribble the olive oil from the tuna over the salad and serve. (*Note:*
If you prefer to use water-packed tuna, discard the liquid and dress
with a little olive oil.)

(Serves 4 to 6)

MAIN DISHES

Pasta and Beans with Pancetta, Celery, and Carrots

¼ pound *pancetta* or 2 ounces
  prosciutto and 2 ounces salt
  pork
2 stalks celery, with leaves
2 carrots
¼ cup olive oil

1 pound dried Great Northern or *cannellini* beans, presoaked as directed above
Salt and freshly ground pepper
½ pound fettuccine
1 red onion

Cut the *pancetta* (or the prosciutto and salt pork) into large dice. Finely
mince the celery leaves. Cut the celery and carrots into bite-size pieces.

Heat the olive oil in a Dutch oven or heavy pot with a cover. Sauté the *pancetta* or salt pork until translucent. Add the celery leaves, the celery and carrot pieces, and continue to cook until vegetables soften. Add the beans (and the prosciutto if using) and enough water to cover. Cover and simmer for 1 hour. Add salt and pepper to taste and continue cooking until beans are tender. Cook the fettuccine in salted water until just tender, then drain well and divide among six bowls. Serve the beans over, with or without the liquid, as you prefer. Slice the red onion as thinly as possible and serve separately as a garnish.

(Serves 6)

Bacon, Beans, and Noodles

¶ This dish from northern Italy is also excellent made with lamb or veal breast instead of the slab bacon.

1 cup dried Great Northern beans, presoaked as directed above	3 cloves garlic, crushed
	½ pound flat egg noodles
	1 tablespoon chopped parsley
¼ pound slab bacon, cut into large chunks	Salt and freshly ground pepper
1 cup chicken stock	Freshly grated Parmesan cheese
1 medium onion, chopped	

Cook the beans and the bacon in the stock for 1 hour. Remove the bacon and slice thinly. Add the onion and garlic to the beans, bring to a boil, and add the noodles. Cook briskly for 12 minutes, then stir in the parsley and the bacon slices, adding salt and pepper to taste. Serve in deep bowls, with the Parmesan cheese and warm bread.

(Serves 6)

Lamb Shanks, Orzo, and Beans

1¼ cups (about ½ pound) dried Great Northern or *cannellini* beans, presoaked as directed above
2½ pounds lamb shanks
¼ cup olive oil plus 1 tablespoon
1 cup orzo (a rice-shaped pasta)
1 medium onion, minced
2 cloves garlic, minced
1 tablespoon tomato paste
Pinch ground cinnamon
1 cup dry red wine
Salt and freshly ground pepper

Set the presoaked beans in a large, heavy pot and cover with water. Simmer 1 hour, checking occasionally and adding more water if necessary. Brown the lamb shanks in 1 tablespoon olive oil and add to the beans, seasoning liquid to taste with salt and pepper. Simmer gently another hour. Drain the beans, reserving cooking liquid, and remove lamb shanks to cool.

Cook the orzo in boiling, salted water until almost done (there should still be a crunchy "spine" in their center). In the same pan used to brown the lamb shanks, heat the remaining ¼ cup olive oil and sauté the onion until translucent. Add the garlic, and when that begins to darken, the tomato paste, cinnamon, and wine. Bring mixture to a boil, then lower heat and let simmer a few minutes, stirring. Remove the meat from the lamb shanks and cut into bite-size pieces. Give bones to dog and combine the beans, lamb meat, and orzo together and spread evenly into an ovenproof casserole. Pour the flavoring mixture over this, adding enough bean liquid, if necessary, so that the beans, orzo, and lamb are completely covered. Taste for seasoning, cover—or cap with foil—and set in a preheated 325°F oven for about 1 hour. By then, the liquid should have been absorbed by beans and orzo. If not, uncover, raise temperature to 375°F, and bake until the excess moisture evaporates.

(Serves 6 to 8)

Stuffed Grape Leaves

❀

In springtime in the islands [of Greece] when the young wheat
comes up, the fields are green, and all around the hills are like
velvet; then the people celebrate the many beautiful customs of
the season.   —THEONIE MARK

Like poetry, cooking suffers in translation. It doesn't even matter
if the ingredients are the same; the mouth still stumbles over the
flavors, as if tasting with a stranger's tongue. So it was with my first
encounter with a stuffed grape leaf, a small, dense, enigmatic bundle
pried from a can, holding tight to its secret burden of savory rice,
lemon, and mint. Chewy, herby, cool—they have come to fill a niche
in my summer eating so uniquely their own that they have an almost
shy and tentative quality, little culinary orphans whose corner of the
table is held at sufferance of the palate's whim. It takes a large step
of imagination to grasp Rena Salaman's assertion in *Greek Food* that
"stuffed vine leaves are the crown of Greek cuisine." What are these
little things when we are the strangers at table and they the ones at
home?

Walking in early summer in our own fields and woods, we would
not hesitate, finding a berry patch—strawberries, raspberries, blueberries—to pick a bunch and bring them home to make a pie, a pot
of jam, or just for eating out of hand. But where we surrender to the
sweet, we veer away from the aromatic, the pungent. Not so the
Greeks. There the herbs we shake from bottles or coddle in our
gardens grow wild on the flinty hills: thyme, rosemary, mint, oregano,
sage, fennel, chamomile—these are the smells of landscape, not merely
of the kitchen shelf. The spring rains come to spur their growth, the
summer sun to draw and dissipate their aromatic oils. Then their
scent floats down into the villages, to mingle with the smell of charcoal, the aroma of roasting lamb.

And, to most Greeks grapevines themselves aren't plants associated
with distant vineyards: they're familiar and everywhere. Wine, after
all, until quite recently was the safest way to purify water after boiling

it—and the next best way to get it, after a well. Wine was as necessary to the table as bread, and while it might be as good or as bad as that loaf, it was no more a luxury. Even today, in Greece, many people still make their own.

Grapevines also mean shade—no mere luxury in so sunny a country. Everywhere you go, there are grapevines overhead, straddling cobbled alleys and waving over courtyards. They are the first thing planted when some tiny space is found for a garden, and so poignant a symbol of spring that an armful of cuttings is the first choice of a gift of season for some city cousin without a vine.

In Greece, as in all countries of the Middle East, stuffed grape leaves are made fresh with whatever herbs and greens are new and sweet. For these people, each grape leaf is a green fist that clasps in its pungent fingers those same fresh herbs whose odors season the air itself, mellowed by fruity oil and set off by the tart tang of lemon in a chewy bite of rice.

I don't mean, of course, to slight the other peoples with a claim to this dish, for it is a taste that circles the Levant and climbs high into the Caucasus: the grape leaf is the Armenian national emblem. But whatever the version—Bulgarian, Turkish, Yemenite, Lebanese— the resonances are the same in their subtle differences, the variations the flavor and texture of a landscape.

This is a dish, then, if we want to know it on its own terms, to be made fresh—the grape leaves, if possible, but certainly all the rest; nothing does it in so quickly as dried herbs or dull greens. Feel free to improvise with what is choice and at hand. (The best Rena Salaman ever had were made by a farm woman using fresh spinach just picked from her garden.) One need only adjust quantity to pungency. It is a mouthful of summer you are setting on the table, nothing else.

FRESH LEAVES.   Any growth of unsprayed grapevine, wild or domestic, can provide you with fresh grape leaves, and with wild vines especially, the leaves are sometimes better than the grapes. In Greece, the season for collecting them is early summer, but in milder climes, where the leaves stay tender, they can be taken almost all season. Wear a long-sleeved shirt and stuff a pocket with rubber bands. Pick those free of insect damage and neither too big nor too small. Traditionally, only the second and third leaves of each vine were taken (this was to protect the vine and the grapes from sunburn). The leaves chosen should be thin, flexible, and smooth, the dull (reverse) side not yet turned coarse and white. Each should snap off easily from the stem. Shaded leaves will be more tender than those that get full sun. Stack them up all the same way, rolling up each handful into a bundle and securing it with a rubber band.

Once home, rubber bands removed, use kitchen tongs to hold each stack of leaves for 30 seconds in boiling brine, 2 teaspoons pure (pickling) salt per quart of water. Then lift them out and drain them briefly by squeezing them gently in a colander (set over the cooking pot if you plan to preserve the leaves). The leaves are now ready to be used in cooking, to be wrapped up in bundles in aluminum foil for freezing, or preserved in brine. To preserve them, roll them into tight bundles and pack these vertically in pint preserving jars. Mix a pickling liquid of 1 cup fresh lemon juice to each quart of the cooking brine, and bring this mixture back to a boil. Pour the boiling liquid over the leaves, close the jars, and process for 15 minutes in a boiling water bath (see any up-to-date preserving manual).

BASIC RECIPE.   Fresh leaves should be boiled briefly in salt water before using (see above), preserved leaves rinsed well in icy water. (Some foreign-packed grape leaves are preserved in an excessively salty brine and require several rinses—even a short parboiling—before use, but domestic leaves should not.) Any thick, tough stem (not only the nub but also the part that runs up into the leaf) must be trimmed out with scissors or a sharp paring knife. Only finicky cooks trim off every nub.

Whether fresh or preserved, the leaves should be picked over, with torn leaves and tough-looking customers set to one side. Use these to line the cooking pot—a heavy cast-iron Dutch oven is best—covering the bottom and overlapping on up the sides. This keeps the stuffed bundles from sticking or getting scorched should the pot momentarily boil dry.

The leaves to be filled should be turned dull side up. The filling—usually about a teaspoonful if uncooked rice is used (it expands when cooked) or scant tablespoon with bulgur (which doesn't)—is set in the center. The bottom is wrapped up over the filling and the two sides, one after the other, are folded to embrace it. Then the bundle is rolled right up to the tip of the leaf and set, seam side down, in the pot. When the bottom of the pot is full, start a second layer, and so on until the filling is used up.

It's hard to predict how many leaves you can expect to find in a jar; the range is wide. A 1-pound jar can hold up to 100 and should have 80, but some of those may be tattered and useless. The estimates given in the recipes below are, hence, conservative. So, don't be surprised, let alone upset, if you end up with a surplus of leaves. These can be tucked back into their brine and refrigerated for another week or two without penalty. And if there are too few for another batch, they can be put to good use in a dill crock, or in your cooking as a potherb or grill wrap (see page 183). You may also find yourself with fewer (or more) stuffed grape leaves than a recipe promises; one cook's teaspoonful can be another cook's fistful. Traditionally, the tinier the bundles, the greater the compliment to the eater. But if your stuffed leaves burst open while cooking, you can be sure your measure was too generous.

Now, the filling used up, the cooking liquid is poured over and tradition then sets a plate over the bundles to keep them intact while cooking and make sure they are submerged in the broth. The pot should be brought to a gentle simmer, the flame lowered, and an eye kept on the contents to make sure they never boil dry.

Cooking times vary widely from cookbook to cookbook. Bulgur, especially, requires a very short cooking time and raw rice hardly more than an hour. If the rolls are overcooked, the freshness is lost. Forty-five minutes seems to me a good median point for a sampling—for which the wise cook will add a few extra stuffed leaves to the pot. They are done when the rice is just cooked to a firm softness and the leaves tender.

Custom has it that meatless fillings are to be served at cool room temperature (not, please, cold) and those with meat, hot. The case for the latter is strongest when the meat is lamb, congealed mutton fat pleasing few palates. But otherwise, let personal taste rule over fiat. One final word of advice: They are always even better the next day. Make them ahead of time, and make many.

A Greek Filling of Fresh Herbs

¶ This is the best of all stuffed grape leaves, but its simple perfection depends on respect: use your best olive oil and don't substitute dried herbs for the fresh ones called for: it's better to find an appropriate substitute.

30 to 40 grape leaves, fresh or preserved
½ cup fruity olive oil
1 bunch (6 to 8) scallions, finely chopped
½ cup finely minced fresh dill or fennel
¼ cup chopped parsley
2 tablespoons minced fresh mint
⅔ cup long-grain rice
Juice of 1 lemon
⅔ cup boiling water

Prepare the grape leaves as directed in the basic method. Heat the olive oil gently over low heat. Add the scallions, dill or fennel, parsley, and mint, and heat until they wilt and release their scent. Stir in the rice, add the lemon juice and the boiling water, and cook until the water is absorbed. The rice will be only partly cooked. Let this mixture cool, then use it to fill the grape leaves, a generous teaspoon per leaf, and roll as directed in the basic method. Put each seam side down in a pot lined with spare grape leaves. Pour in 2 cups of water, and set a heavy plate on top to weigh down the stuffed leaves. Bring the liquid to a simmer, and cook about 45 minutes, tasting them for doneness. When ready, let cool and serve, if you wish, with plain yogurt on the side.

A Greek Filling of Lamb, with Egg-Lemon Sauce

50 to 60 grape leaves, fresh or
  preserved
2 tablespoons olive oil
1½ pounds lean ground lamb
1 medium onion, minced
4 or 5 scallions, minced
½ cup minced fresh dill or
  fennel

¼ cup chopped parsley
2 tablespoons minced fresh
  mint
¼ cup long-grain rice
¾ cup boiling water
Salt and freshly ground pepper

For the sauce:
  2 egg yolks
  Juice of 2 lemons, strained
  The cooking liquid left in the pot after cooking the stuffed
  grape leaves

Prepare the grape leaves as directed in the basic method. Heat the olive oil gently over low heat. Cook the lamb and onion for 5 minutes, or until the lamb is no longer pink and the onion soft. If the lamb is fatty, drain off the excess fat. Stir in the scallions, dill or fennel, the parsley and mint, plus salt and pepper to taste, and continue cooking until these wilt and release their aroma. Then add the rice and pour in the boiling water, stirring until the liquid is absorbed. The rice will be only partly cooked. Let this mixture cool, then use it to fill the grape leaves, a generous teaspoon per leaf, and roll as directed in the basic method. Put each seam side down in a pot lined with spare grape leaves. Pour in 2 cups of water, and set a heavy plate on top to weigh down the stuffed leaves. Bring the liquid to a simmer, and cook about 45 minutes, tasting then for doneness.

When the stuffed leaves are cooked, pour off the cooking liquid into a bowl. There should be a generous cup's worth; add water if necessary. In another bowl, beat the egg yolks vigorously until they are light and creamy. Gradually work in the lemon juice and then, finally, the hot liquid, adding it in a thin, steady stream. Serve the stuffed grape leaves hot, the sauce separate.

A Greek Filling of Summer Squash

¶ This version, like the Caucasian prune and bulgur recipe to follow, is meant to be served as a meat substitute during Lent.

30 to 40 grape leaves, fresh or preserved
½ cup olive oil
2 medium onions, minced
1 pound small yellow squash or zucchini, finely chopped
2 tablespoons minced fresh mint

Juice of 1 lemon
¾ cup cooked, pureed plum tomatoes
Salt and freshly ground pepper
½ cup long-grain rice
½ cup boiling water

Prepare the grape leaves as directed in the basic method. Heat the olive oil gently over low heat. Add the onions and, when they turn translucent, add the squash, mint, lemon juice, and tomato puree, adding salt and pepper to taste. When the vegetables are just heated, add the rice and pour in the boiling water. Cook until the mixture absorbs most of the liquid. Remove from the heat and let cool. Then roll each leaf with a teaspoon of this filling, setting each seam side down in a leaf-lined pot. Pour in any liquid left from the filling plus 1 cup of water. Set a heavy plate on top to weigh down the stuffed leaves and simmer for 45 minutes. Serve hot.

A Turkish Filling of Pine Nuts and Currants

40 to 50 grape leaves, fresh or preserved
2 large onions, minced
1 cup long-grain rice
3 tablespoons chopped black currants
2 tablespoons chopped pine nuts
¼ cup minced fresh mint

¾ cup chopped parsley (stems reserved)
¼ cup minced fresh dill (stems reserved)
2 teaspoons ground allspice
2 tablespoons lemon juice
½ cup olive oil
Salt
2 lemons, cut into wedges

Prepare the grape leaves as directed in the basic method. Mix together the onions, rice, currants, pine nuts, mint, parsley, dill, allspice, lemon juice, and olive oil, adding salt to taste. Fill each leaf with a teaspoon of the mixture and roll into a bundle as directed in the basic method. Set seam side down in a pot lined with the parsley and dill stems. Cover with water (about 3 cups). Weigh the bundles down with a heavy plate and simmer until the rice is tender and the water absorbed, about 45 minutes. Add more liquid if necessary. Remove from the heat and let cool. Serve cold with the lemon wedges as a garnish.

An Armenian Filling of Lamb and Bulgur

40 to 50 grape leaves, fresh or preserved
1 cup coarse bulgur
1 pound lean ground lamb
1 onion, finely chopped

1 teaspoon salt
Freshly ground black pepper
½ cup tomato puree
Juice of ½ lemon

For the sauce:
1 cup plain yogurt
½ clove garlic, crushed
Pinch salt
1 tablespoon chopped fresh mint or 1 teaspoon dried

Prepare the grape leaves as directed in the basic method. In a bowl, soak the bulgur in 2 cups of water for 30 minutes. Then pour off the liquid, pressing the grain to squeeze out as much as possible. Combine the lamb, bulgur, onion, salt, a good grinding of pepper, and half the tomato puree in a mixing bowl. Mix the ingredients by hand until well blended. Fill the leaves with a tablespoon of this mixture, rolling them as directed in the basic method. Put each seam side down in a pot lined with spare grape leaves. Mix the lemon juice with the remaining tomato puree and 1¼ cups of water and pour over the stuffed grape leaves, weighing them down with a heavy plate. Bring the liquid to a simmer, lower the heat, and cook for 30 minutes. Make the sauce by mixing the ingredients well and letting this mixture stand while the stuffed leaves cook. Serve hot, with the sauce separate.

A Caucasian Filling of Lentils, Bulgur, and Dried Apricots

¶ In the Caucasus, this dish is made with fresh plums and plum syrup and is served as a Lenten dish instead of a meat course.

40 to 50 grape leaves, fresh or preserved
¼ cup brown lentils, picked over and rinsed
⅓ cup coarse bulgur
3 tablespoons olive oil
1 small onion, finely chopped
1 tablespoon chopped pine nuts
4 dried apricots, finely chopped

2 tablespoons minced fresh mint
2 tablespoons finely chopped currants
1 teaspoon salt
½ teaspoon freshly ground pepper
1 teaspoon ground cinnamon
2 tablespoons lemon juice
¼ cup apricot nectar or pomegranate juice

Prepare the grape leaves as directed in the basic method. Simmer the lentils in lightly salted water for 15 minutes. Drain thoroughly and let cool. In a bowl, soak the bulgur in a cup of water for 30 minutes, then pour off the liquid, pressing the grain to squeeze out as much as possible. Heat the olive oil in a saucepan over low heat, then add the onion and pine nuts and sauté until the pine nuts take on color and the onion becomes translucent. Remove the pan from the heat and mix in the lentils, bulgur, apricots, mint, currants, salt, pepper, and cinnamon. Stir well. Mix the lemon juice and apricot nectar and pour over. Use this mixture to fill the grape leaves, a tablespoon per leaf, and roll as directed in the basic method. Put each seam side down in a pot lined with spare grape leaves. Cover with 1½ cups of water and set a heavy plate on top to weigh down the stuffed leaves. Bring the liquid to a simmer, and cook about 45 minutes, tasting then for doneness. Serve cool.

A Russian Version with Dill and a Buttermilk Sauce

40 to 50 grape leaves, fresh or preserved
1 tablespoon butter
1 pound lean ground lamb
1 onion, finely chopped
1½ cups cooked rice

1 tablespoon minced fresh dill
Salt and freshly ground pepper
1 cup hot lamb stock or chicken stock

For the sauce:
1¼ cups buttermilk
1 clove garlic, crushed

Prepare the grape leaves as directed in the basic method. Melt the butter, and gently sauté the lamb and the onion until the onion softens and the lamb is no longer pink. Remove from the heat and stir in the cooked rice and the dill, and season with salt and pepper to taste. Use this mixture to fill the grape leaves, a generous teaspoon per leaf, and roll as directed in the basic method. Put each seam side down in a pot lined with spare grape leaves. Pour in the hot stock and set a heavy plate on top to weigh down the stuffed leaves. Bring the liquid to a simmer, and cook about 45 minutes, tasting then for doneness. Meanwhile, make a sauce by mixing the buttermilk and the garlic, seasoning this with a little salt if you wish. Serve hot, with the sauce separate. (*Note:* 1 cup sour cream diluted with ¼ cup milk can be substituted for the buttermilk.)

A Jewish (Sephardic) Version with Beef and Honey

¶ Adapted from Suzy David's *The Sephardic Kosher Kitchen* (see page 259).

25 to 30 grape leaves, fresh or preserved
1 pound extra-lean ground beef
¼ cup rice
1 medium onion, finely chopped

currants
1 tablespoon minced fresh dill (stems reserved)
2 tablespoons minced parsley
1 teaspoon salt
Generous pinch freshly ground pepper

For the sauce:
2 tablespoons olive oil
¼ cup tomato paste
2 tablespoons minced fresh dill
1 tablespoon honey

1 teaspoon red wine vinegar
Juice of ½ lemon
Salt and freshly ground pepper

Prepare the grape leaves as directed in the basic method. Moisten the beef with ¼ cup water and then mix in a bowl with the rice, onion, currants, dill, parsley, salt, and pepper. Fill and roll each leaf as directed in the basic method, a generous teaspoon for each. Set them seam side down in a pot lined with dill stems and spare grape leaves.

Make the sauce by heating the olive oil in a small pan. When hot, stir in the tomato paste and heat, stirring, for 2 minutes. Then add 1 cup cold water, the dill, honey, vinegar, and lemon juice, and cook for another few minutes, or until the mixture is hot. Season to taste with salt and pepper and pour over the grape leaves. Weigh them down with a heavy plate and simmer gently for 1 hour over low heat. Serve hot.

Readers interested in further investigating this dish might want to consult the following: Vilma Liacouras Chantiles, *The Food of Greece;*

Suzy David, *The Sephardic Kosher Kitchen;* Arto der Haroutunian, *Middle Eastern Cookery;* Venice Lamb, *The Home Book of Turkish Cooking;* Viviane Alchech Miner, *From My Grandmother's Kitchen, A Sephardic Cookbook;* Rena Salaman, *Greek Food;* and Sonia Uvezian, *The Cuisine of Armenia.*

Strawberries and Cream

❁

Raw crayme undecocted, eaten with strawberys or hurtes [whor-
tleberries] is a rurall mannes banket. I have knowne such ban-
kettes hath put men in jeopardy of they lyves.
—ANDREW BOORDE (1542)

Put them on the table in glass dishes, piling them high and lightly,
send around powdered sugar with them and cream, that the guests
may help themselves. It is not economical perhaps, but it is a
healthful and pleasant style of serving them—I had almost said
the only decent one.   —MARION HARLAND (1883)

Some twelve years ago, when my aged dog was a pup, I taught at a
small, independent school in the Berkshires. It was tucked right against
the side of a mountain, and fields spread out from it on either side.
Just the place for long, quiet walks—sometimes up to the mountain
through a dense, dank wood, other times off across a rambling stretch
of fields. Those fields, then abandoned and fallow, some boxed in a
fence of trees, were territory claimed only by red-winged blackbirds
and gardened by rabbits and woodchucks.

Crossing one of them on a bright blue June morning, the sunlight
hot around me, I was coaxed from self-absorption by a tantalizingly
sweet, familiar, yet strangely elusive aroma. Even when I had stopped
and stared around my feet, I saw nothing at first, the fruit so small,
the plants so green and brilliant. But then—as in a dream—I saw
them, all at once, tiny and scarlet, here and everywhere, a field full
to brimming.

As in a dream. I write that remembering not only the wash of sheer
delight I felt when they revealed themselves, but also their intensely
vital, utterly fragile perfection. Even in such surfeit they carried a
sense of rarity, not at all the jumbled tangle of the raspberry patch.
Parkinson wrote in 1629 of a variety "fit for a Gentlewoman to weare
upon her arm, as a raritie instead of a flower." These wild plants had
that same concise, even emblematic beauty—the crisp, ordered leaves,
the tiny white-petaled flower, the fine, arched stem, the bloodred

berry at its end, faceted like a jewel. Before such as this, reality loosens its fingers: the field under my feet became a highly ornamented border of a medieval book of days.

Sun-warmed, each left a hot smudge of perfumed flavor on the tongue. With all the willpower in the world, I could never save enough in a picking to make a pot of jam—just a full cup's worth—to eat that Sunday morning with cream and friends.

"Wee can not sett downe foote but tred on strawberries." This little berry patch was a remnant of that heritage, great-great-grandchildren of the berries the colonists first discovered in this country and sent back to Europe, the bright, fragrant, intensely flavored *fragaria virginiana*—Little Scarlet. The snobby *fraises des bois* that exclusive gardening catalogues carry can't hold a candle to them. Strawberries being far and away our most popular fruit, why our own wild berries aren't "semicultivated" like Maine blueberries and marketed locally is totally beyond me. The Indians grew them in such abundance that Roger Williams wrote, "I have many times seen as many as would fill a good ship, within few miles compass."

Except, perhaps, because they are so popular. To meet a huge and indiscriminate demand, hybrids have been developed for size and prolificacy—and which seem well matched to the taste of the American market. In her *Summer Cooking,* Elizabeth David warns us to cover any strawberries we put in the refrigerator, or their intense flavor will contaminate everything else. Little danger of that with most cultivated strawberries; we only pray they will end up tasting of themselves. Still, no one complains. The audience for things tiny, subtle, and fragrant has gone somewhere else.

So, unless you can grow or find your own—and then beat the birds to them—you must do the best you can. One particular trick is to buy twice the needed amount and ruthlessly discard the hard, the dull, and the whitish green. In midseason, even double the price is reasonable, and the pleasure of the dish increases out of all proportion to the cost. Your berries fresh and ripe and at hand, turn these pages for a few words on the choicest accompaniments: the cream pitcher, of course, the sugar bowl, and—maybe—a well-buttered, griddle-hot wedge of shortcake.

CLOTTED CREAM

He took a yellow cake of a bun formation. "Try this pleasure, Lomas. My design, executed by Elise. Sort o' saffron cake, with interior clotted cream and wild strawberry jam." —H.C. BAILEY

Clotted cream is to cream what the Missouri is to rivers—too thick to pour but too soft to slice. At its most fluid, it doesn't pour exactly, but oozes. At its thickest, it is next kin to butter. Unlike *crème fraîche*, its French cousin, British clot has only the faintest sour tang; it is sweet and rich. Unlike butter, however, it tastes like cream, not fat—just like very, very rich cream. At perfection, it is not unlike a very soft whipped cream without the air—smooth and light and dairy sweet in the mouth.

The two areas in Britain famous for clotted cream are Devonshire and Cornwall, where it is put in pies and pudding, and eaten with junket and fruit, both fresh or preserved. But, best of all, at tea with hot scones and jam. Even today, travelers in Cornwall will find "cream teas" served throughout the region. At its simplest—and only the greedy could want more—a cream tea consists of the pot of tea, a plate of fresh-baked Cornish spits (a small yeast roll) or scones, a dish of a local preserve, and another of clotted cream. The scone or split is broken open, spread with preserve, and heaped with clotted cream. That oozing morsel is then happily if messily propelled into the mouth.

The single complaint about these teas—or any meal where clotted cream is served—is that there never seems to be quite enough. However generous the wedge of pie, the dollop of clotted cream seems measured with the same scant teaspoon that scooped it onto the much smaller dish of canned peaches. This parsimony might be generously written off as a concern over the eater's weight problem, but is more likely product of an ironclad law: even in the best of circumstances, a pint of cream makes less than half a cup of clot. It costs.

Clotted creams differ—as all natural products do—by the nature of the silage and the breed of milk cow. Cornish cream, some aver, is a little coarser in texture than Devonshire's; others argue that the special flavor of Devonshire clot came from the tang of the peat over which it was once—but probably is no longer—heated. Neither will be exactly duplicated, even in the best of circumstances, in an American kitchen.

But the process is a simple one and requires only patience for its success. As I understand it, pans of raw milk were set out (about twelve hours in summer and twenty-four in winter) in a cool place to let the natural (and friendly) bacteria start developing. This was too short a time for their action to actually sour the milk but made it more susceptible to clotting over heat, while the heat then stopped any further bacterial action. The milk was set in wide pans over gentle heat (never enough to boil it) for a period of time, then allowed to gently cool for another day in the dairy. The resulting clotted cream was then carefully rolled or skimmed off into a jug and the remaining whey put to some good purpose (like feeding the pig).

This method was far from unknown in America. Mary Randolph gives the method (wisely heating the milk in a water bath, which keeps it from boiling). She called it "Edinburg cream." The Shakers also made it and called it "Shaker cream." However, so far as I know, indigenously made clotted cream is a lost dairy art; the only kind I have seen for sale is imported from England and can be found in some gourmet and imported cheese stores.

In the beginning, I was dubious about making my own. For one thing, the scanty bits of information I found contradicted each other, some asserting that the stuff was impossible to make with pasteurized milk. I searched for and did not find raw milk; finding unhomogenized milk was difficult enough. But if you can find that—and non-ultra-pasteurized cream—you're in business. Local natural food stores were a source of both of these for me.

Following the steps that I set out below, I produced a thick clot that closely resembles the written descriptions and photos I found of the real thing—a wrinkled texture lightly tinted yellow, with a sweet nutty taste and pleasantly grainy texture, which rasps the tongue just as it dissolves into a sweet softness. It comes away from the whey in a firm clot, but it can be softened with a little regular cream. (Heavy cream produces a richer-tasting clot, but not an appreciably larger amount of it.) However, it was not like the bottled, imported version. That is nearest duplicated by what I call "thickened cream," the recipe for which also appears below.

CLOTTED CREAM.   (*Note:* This is a 3-day process.) 1 quart raw or pasteurized (but *not* homogenized) milk and 1 cup light or heavy (*not* ultrapasteurized) cream. (Heavy cream makes the clot richer but not much more of it.) Pour these without mixing into the heaviest, widest frying pan you have (*not* cast-iron) and set it, covered, in the refrigerator overnight, so that all the cream will rise to the top.

The next day, carefully set the frying pan over the lowest possible heat (you may have to use a heat diffuser) and bring the milk slowly to about 140°F and keep it there for about 2 or 3 hours, until a faintly yellow crust forms on top of the milk/cream mixture. (If the milk gets much hotter, the butterfat will melt, giving the clot a waxy taste.) This is the clot.

Remove from the heat, being careful not to disturb the clot. When cool, set it—still in the pan—into the refrigerator to rest overnight. In the morning, you should be able to lift off the clotted cream with a spatula or palette knife and put it in a separate dish. If you like, thin it to a smooth consistency by stirring in a tablespoon or so of heavy cream. It should keep well for up to 5 days. It is, of course, wonderful with fresh strawberries, but you should reserve a few spoonfuls to have on toasted English muffins with raspberry jam. If there's a better thing on earth to eat, I don't know what it is.

BROWNED CORNISH CLOT. This is extremely simple to do, but the result is a little more granular in texture and has a nuttier taste. Put a well-scrubbed cookie pan on the middle shelf of the oven and pour into it a pint of light (not ultrapasteurized) cream. Turn the oven to its lowest temperature and leave the oven door ajar enough to keep the oven at about 160°F until a brown, wrinkled skin forms over the surface of the cream. Cool and let refrigerate overnight. Gently pour away any liquid. This produces a soft, custardy cream under a brown crust. Very tasty.

THICKENED CREAM. This method, which I came across by accident, comes closest to producing a clotted cream like the imported version, which is pure white and very soft. It is also the easiest to make—and furthest from the traditional method. One of the more authentic ways of reproducing a close approximation of *crème fraîche* is to sour it with a lactic culture and then set it in a Melitta-type coffee filter to let some of the whey drip out. However, I discovered—without using any added culture—that the whey would drip out of fresh (i.e., not ultrapasteurized) heavy cream, thickening *it* to the point where it became as dense as a soft cream cheese but still without a sour tang. (I suspect the air contact through the filter hastens the start of the souring process, which releases the whey, but not to the point where the cream tastes sour.)

To give it a try, pour non-ultrapasteurized heavy cream into a Melitta (or similar) filter set in the holder and perched over a dish large enough to catch the whey. Cover it with foil or plastic wrap and set it in the refrigerator. In a few hours, the cream on the sides of the filter should have thickened. Gently scrape this away with a soft rubber spatula. Keep doing this every hour or so until it has thickened to your liking. Pour and scrape it into a small bowl and stir it all to the same consistency. This will keep a day or two more in the refrigerator. At a density just thick enough to hold up a pencil, this was the closest simulation I got to commercial Devonshire clot.

SHORTCAKE

> Send [strawberry shortcake] at once to the table. Serve with it, if possible, a pitcher of cream. Milk cannot be substituted; better eat it plain, than to mix milk with berries.
> —SARAH TYSON RORER (1902)

Very possibly, we get our passion for strawberries and cream from our British heritage, but strawberry shortcake is a strictly American passion. As the name says, a true shortcake is a dense, rich concoction made from flour, butter, and sugar—and old cookbooks still give recipes for just such a thing. But when industrial genius introduced a commercial baking powder just before the Civil War, America—and especially rural America—went biscuit mad. At last, fresh, hot-from-the-oven bread could be set on the breakfast or dinner table without the delicate, time-consuming processes required by salt- and yeast-raised breads. And at some point late last century, "shortcake" just came to mean the richest-tasting biscuit possible.

Echoes of old-time biscuit-making ring loudest in Southern cooking, which has proven most resistant to change. Beaten biscuits, buttermilk biscuits, soda biscuits . . . mention these to a Southerner raised in time for World War II and you will stimulate memories of a whole cuisine—biscuits for breakfast with butter and cane molasses, with pork drippings or red-eye gravy, or just tucked cold in the pocket for a between-meal snack. But, for the rest of us, there's still the memory of strawberry shortcake.

I say memory and mean it: strawberry shortcake is on a downhill slide. It was most popular around the turn of the century, and cookbooks then gave a page or two of shortcake recipes. Now there's one recipe—for what amounts to just another biscuit. Nowadays, most people who eat fresh strawberries serve them on sponge cake.

Unpleasant stuff, sponge cake. It tastes like its namesake without the redeeming scrubbing power. Apart from the fact that you buy it ready to eat, its single virtue is that it easily absorbs strawberry juice and cream, collapsing into sweet mush. The flavors all combine into one single confectionary bite that identically repeats itself until the eater pushes away the plate. Kid stuff.

A bite of real strawberry shortcake, on the other hand, is a mouthful of contrast. The rich, sweet cream, the tart juicy berries, and the sour, crumbly texture of hot biscuit all refuse to amalgam into a single flavor tone, but produce mouth-stimulating contrasts of flavor—hot and cold, soft and hard, sweet and tart, smooth and crumbly. The mouth is alert and enchanted at once, just the way the ear responds when Oscar Peterson slides Billie Holiday into "These Foolish Things."

This kind of culinary counterpoint is one reason why, while most shortcake recipes call for an oven-baked product, my own preference is to make it on a griddle. This gives a further dimension to the final product: a nice, crisp, golden-brown crust. Especially with company present, the shortcake can be turned out after the meal proper, accentuating its "from scratch" nature and heightening anticipation of the coming pleasures.

My recipe is right out of Mary Lincoln's *Boston Cook Book*. I love it for many reasons, not least of which is that it uses no commercial baking powder, the modern stuff too often leaving a bitter aftertaste. The good old Royal brand was a mixture of cream of tartar and baking soda—just as Mrs. Lincoln calls for here.)

Mary Lincoln's Griddle Shortcake (1883)

½ teaspoon salt, scant
½ teaspoon baking soda
½ teaspoon cream of tartar
2 cups flour, measured, then
  sifted

4 tablespoons (½ stick) sweet
  butter
1 cup sour cream

Stir the salt, baking soda, and cream of tartar together and sift with the flour. Combine the flour and butter together into the consistency of oatmeal by rubbing them together quickly and gently with your fingers. Add the sour cream, cutting it into the dough with a knife, until it is just blended. Scrape the dough out onto a well-floured board, pat it into a flat cake, turn it over onto a floured surface, and roll it out gently until it is ½ inch thick. Cut it into rounds or wedges and set each on a preheated and lightly greased griddle, put over low heat. "Watch them and turn them, that all may be browned alike." When well puffed up, set a sliver of butter on the top of each and gently turn over. When browned on the other side and done (judge by cutting one partly open), serve immediately.

To serve properly, set sliced, sweetened strawberries on the table in one bowl and cream (clotted or whipped or plain) in another. Each eater should split a shortcake with his fingers (not cut it) and lavish the halves with strawberries and cream. The traditional method still works just fine: top the bottom half with strawberries and moisten well with their juice, top with the other half and heap on more strawberries and a generous dollop of cream.

STRAWBERY RYPE

The Strawberry is not everyone's fruit. To some it brings a sudden rash, and to others twinges of rheumatism. This fact must be admitted and faced.   —EDWARD BUNYARD

Indeed it must. Still, I know from personal experience that even those allergic to strawberries will suffer the rash for the pleasure of eating a dish of them—at least one dish—a summer. But let it be a dish worth the suffering. With strawberries as with tomatoes, all is not ripe that reddens. If you can't beg a taste of one, hold the carton up close and sniff. The more complex and deep the fragrance, the better the flavor: no aroma, no taste at all; they might as well be carved of balsa wood.

One dish of strawberries. . . . If we had to choose, what would it be? They are very good by themselves—otherwise we could pick them faster than we can eat them. They can simply be dipped in sugar. However, centuries of enjoyment have led cooks to two not mutually exclusive discoveries: the pleasure of their fragrant flavor is heightened in the mouth by folding them in a luscious wrap of cream or by stimulating the tongue with a hint of citric tartness. Almost all fresh strawberry dishes utilize either—or both—of those courses. And if strawberries aren't entirely your cup of tea, take heart: many of these recipes adapt nicely to fresh peaches. Peaches, raspberries, and cream—there's a dish to tease up an appetite, even in strawberry season. (*Note:* I have not given approximate servings for most of the desserts listed below. My rule of thumb is this: a quart of strawberries will serve six adequately, four amply, and two to surfeit.)

FRESHENED STRAWBERRIES

The simplest strawberry recipes simply "freshen" their flavor by soaking them for a while in some tart-flavored medium whose sharpness points up the strawberries' taste. This method is different from a maceration in that the juices of the strawberry aren't mingled with the freshening medium. Because of the simplicity of the flavors involved, it is important that only fresh ingredients be used.

Strawberries with Lemon and Mint

1 quart strawberries, washed and hulled
Juice of ½ lemon, strained
1 tablespoon superfine sugar
5 fresh mint leaves, torn into tiny bits

Toss the berries in the lemon juice, sugar, and mint in a large bowl. Let stand for a few hours, covered, in the refrigerator, to allow the flavors to mingle.

Strawberries with Lemon and Black Pepper

1 quart strawberries, washed and hulled
Juice of ½ lemon, strained
1 tablespoon superfine sugar
Freshly ground black pepper

Toss the berries in the lemon juice and sugar in a large bowl. Let stand for a few hours, covered, in the refrigerator, to allow the flavors to mingle. Season each serving with a twist or two of the pepper mill.

Strawberries in Orange Juice

1 quart strawberries, washed and hulled
Superfine sugar
Juice of 3 oranges

Combine the strawberries and orange juice and add just enough sugar for a pleasing taste of sweetness. Let stand as directed above.

MACERATED STRAWBERRIES

Strawberries can be sliced and macerated in a host of different agents, including fresh fruit juices and fruit-flavored liqueurs. They are then either served as they are, or on sponge cake, lady fingers, or meringues (and, if you like, topped with whipped cream sweetened with sugar and vanilla). Among the more popular macerating mediums are fortified wines like marsala or port, cognac or brandy, and various liqueurs, especially orange-flavored ones like Cointreau or raspberry-flavored ones such as Chambord. However, in Europe, the single favorite macerating liquid is a good local wine.

Strawberries in Wine

1 quart strawberries, washed and hulled
Juice of ½ lemon, strained
¼ cup superfine sugar
1 cup dry red wine

"Good red wine is made for strawberries," says Giuliano Bugialli rightly—and it need not be an overly refined one. "The strawberry," as Mr. Bunyard points out, "likes a little roughness in its wooing, so a young wine may be used; the delicate fruit is quite capable of holding its own." The French might use a Bordeaux or Beaujolais, the Italians a good Chianti. Recipes vary as to the amount of wine; some call for as much as a bottle to a quart of berries. Do as you like, but balance the sugar accordingly. Cut the strawberries in half; larger ones should be quartered. Mix the ingredients together and let the flavors marry for a few hours in a cool place—but no cooler than a temperature at which you would serve the wine by itself (and thus, not—except on the hottest days—in the refrigerator).

WITH PEACHES.   If you chance on ripe strawberries and ripe peaches together, the two make an excellent combination in red wine. A pint of strawberries, washed and hulled, and 4 ripe peaches, peeled and cut into chunks, combine well with the rest of the ingredients in the recipe above.

WITH WOODRUFF.   In Germany, May wine—a mixture of dry Moselle, sugar, and sweet woodruff—is often garnished with straw-berries, and conversely, this mixture makes a refreshing and unusual berry bowl. The problem, of course, is finding the woodruff. I used to have a jar around for making "mad dog chili"—and it gets used in Cajun cooking. Some grow it in their herb garden for its freshening scent. You can sometimes find "May wine" in the local liquor store—a mixture of inexpensive Moselle and woodruff. It will do well enough.

You'll need a bottle of May wine (or add a handful of fresh woodruff or 2 tablespoons of dried to a bottle of Moselle), a quart of strawberries, washed and hulled, and superfine sugar. Slice the strawberries and macerate in the woodruff-flavored wine for 2 or 3 hours in the refrig-erator. Taste and add sugar to taste after the first hour.

STRAWBERRIES AND CREAM

So long as strawberries can be eaten fresh with cream, it is van-
dalism to cook them. . . .   —MRS. C. F. LEYEL

There are many strategies for bringing out the best of this combination. My own favorite is that of Dorothy Hartley, as set forth in
that wonderful book, *Food in England*. Pour a cup of heavy cream
into a deep, cold bowl. Whip it until it is soft and thick but not stiff.
Gently stir in a quart of ripe berries, leaving the small ones whole
but slicing the larger ones, and mashing some slightly against the side
of the bowl. Let it stand, covered, for an hour or so in the refrigerator.
Then, "crust it over with dredged white sugar and serve forth, in
June, on a green lawn, under shady trees by the river." Some, by
the way, would call this a strawberry fool. Dorothy Hartley doesn't.

It seems unlikely that this can be improved upon, but many have
tried. One of the more attractive changes is to fold a quarter cup of
honey, bit by bit, into the whipped cream once it has started to hold
shape (and of course, to omit any sugar). This gives the cream a
tongue-coating richness and, with orange blossom honey, a hauntingly
delightful aftertaste that melds deliciously with the flavor of strawberry.

WITH CLOTTED, SOURED, OR THICKENED CREAM. The
method here is to set three bowls on the table, one of the cream, one
of superfine sugar, and the other full of strawberries (washed but not
hulled). Each eater first dips a berry into the sugar, then swirls it into
the thick cream, then slips it into the mouth. The hulls provide
handles and, left on the plate, a way of counting up and seeing which
greedy one has had more than a fair share.

Strawberry Cream

1 quart strawberries, washed and hulled
1 cup heavy cream
1/4 cup superfine sugar
1 egg white

Pick through the strawberries and set aside about a quarter of them, and those the smallest and ripest berries. Then press the remaining strawberries through a sieve or briefly puree them in a food processor. Whip the cream until it is stiff, beating in the sugar bit by bit once it starts to set. In a separate bowl, beat the egg white until it holds stiff peaks. Gently fold the beaten egg white into the whipped cream, and then combine with the strawberries. Taste for sweetness, then gently turn out into a shallow serving dish and decorate with the reserved whole strawberries. Keep chilled until ready to serve. Elizabeth David, whose recipe this is, calls it "a most exquisite cream," and notes that raspberries can be substituted—or, best of all, wild strawberries.

Frullato de Fragole

¶ This is one version of a drink served at refreshment stands all over Italy. If you like it, you'll find that the strawberries can be replaced with peaches, melon, or raspberries, with equally tasty results.

⅔ cup milk
⅔ cup strawberries, washed and hulled
1 teaspoon superfine sugar
¼ cup crushed ice

Combine these ingredients in a blender or food processor fitted with the steel blade and whirl just until the ice has melted and everything is cold and frothy.

(Serves 1 or 2)

Zemlyanika Po Romanovski/Fraises Romanoff

¶ Created by Antoine Carême for Czar Alexander I, this dish probably is more French than Russian, but it appears in the cookbooks of both countries. If possible, choose medium-size strawberries for this dish instead of the huge ones. If they are very big, you might consider cutting them into pieces.

1 quart strawberries, washed and hulled
Juice of 2 oranges (¾ cup)
¼ cup Cointreau or other orange-based liqueur

1½ cups heavy cream, chilled
¼ cup sugar
Vanilla

Put the strawberries in a bowl and add the orange juice and the Cointreau. Let them macerate for about an hour. Beat the cream in a cold bowl, gradually folding in the sugar and a few drops of vanilla. Spoon the whipped cream over the strawberries and serve at once. (*Note:* You may have first experienced this dish as I did—with the berries stirred into a mixture of whipped cream and soft vanilla ice cream. So far as I can determine, this is strictly an American version. But I don't think the Russians, with their passion for ice cream, would wholly disapprove. Prepare the same amount of strawberries exactly as directed above. Let 1 pint vanilla or sweet cream ice cream soften just enough to be stirable. Whip 1 cup of chilled heavy cream in an ice-cold bowl until stiff, and fold it into the ice cream. Gently blend in the macerated strawberries and serve at once.)

COMPOSITE RECIPES

There are many classic strawberry dishes that call for a combination of fruits, either as full partners or backfield support. Strawberry rhubarb pie comes to mind immediately and, with more prodding, strawberry and pineapple, but this berry lover's pulse quickens most at the mention of raspberry or peach. I've already mentioned combining strawberries and peaches in red wine; it's a combination that works well, too, in champagne. Raspberries are used in several famous French dishes, the simplest of which is:

FRAISES ET FRAMBOISES CHANTILLY. Chantilly cream is sweetened whipped cream, usually—but not here—flavored with vanilla. Robert Courtine's version of this dish goes as follows: wild strawberries and raspberries; brandy; black pepper; heavy cream; and superfine sugar. Pick an equal quantity of wild strawberries and raspberries. Pick them over, but don't wash. Put them in a bowl with a few spoonfuls of brandy and a grinding of black pepper. Let them steep. Whip the cream in a chilled bowl, sweetening it to taste (keeping in mind that no sugar has been added to the berries). Stir the berries well just before serving and heap the Chantilly cream over.

A variation of this approach is to crush the raspberries into a puree instead of leaving them whole, perhaps enriching their flavor with raspberry liqueur or crème de cassis. In *Fraises Ritz*, this dish finds its consummation in a puree of wild strawberries and raspberries, poured over cultivated strawberries and then topped with Chantilly cream.

Fraises et Framboises Cassis

1 quart strawberries, washed and hulled
Superfine sugar
1 cup raspberries (this amount can be increased with impunity
    to equal the amount of strawberries, depending on your purse
    or patch)
Crème de cassis or a raspberry liqueur

Sprinkle the strawberries with sugar to taste. Puree the raspberries through a fine sieve, discarding seeds, and, for every cup of puree, stir in 2 tablespoons crème de cassis or raspberry liqueur. Pour over the strawberries and serve with whipped cream if you wish.

Fraises Ritz

1 cup heavy cream
Sugar
Vanilla

½ cup wild strawberries
½ cup raspberries
1 quart strawberries, washed
and hulled

Whip the cream, sweetening it with a little sugar and flavoring it with a drop or two of vanilla. Either through a sieve or in a food processor, crush together the wild strawberries and the raspberries (if wild strawberries are unavailable, substitute a few of the ripest cultivated ones). Fold the crushed berries into the whipped cream and serve over the strawberries.

Toujours strawberries and cream.
—SAMUEL JOHNSON (1709–1784), complaining to Mrs. Thrale

Annotated Apple Pie

Of late the cook has had the surprising sagacity to learn from the
French that apples will make pyes; and it's a question, if, in the
violence of his efforts, we do not get one of apples, instead of
having both of beef-steak which I prefer.
—GEORGE WASHINGTON (1779)

Foliage season. Driving through the Berkshires in the western part
of Massachusetts, you see hill after hill of oak and maple stoked into
an autumnal glow, vistas broken only by an occasional straggling farm
or some houses crouched at a crossroads. It is easy to imagine—
deleting the macadam and electric wires—that what we see is now
much as it always was, empty, rustic, the bracken still broken by the
foot of the last Indian. But that is to see this landscape with a naïve
and sentimental eye. There is not a square mile in lower New England
unaltered by the white man's presence. Even but a hundred and fifty
years ago, this was an entirely different place.

Pull the car over onto the verge and climb up into the woods.
Inevitably there will be a stone wall and then another. This land was
once all cleared for farming, and pity the poor farmer who hoped to
raise some more profitable crop from its sullen soil. And, also almost
always, there is an apple tree—beaten by storm and savaged by pest,
but still clutching on to life. The fruit will tell you it didn't spring
from a random pip. Trees from seed revert to produce the tiny, sour
fruit of the true wild original, acidic for protection from worm, small
and many to up the odds that one, at least, will become another tree.

This one has been stripped by deer, their eager greed crushing
fruit underfoot to rot; the air reeks of its cidery ferment. But up higher
there are still a few, worm-riddled, of course, but with space at least
for one tentative, exploratory bite: the aroma bright, the taste still
fresh and sweet. Maybe a Roxbury Russet or Newtown Pippin, Northern Spy or Sheep's Nose, Winesap or Rome Beauty . . . the apple
too old, the tree too neglected now to tell, even if we had the mouth
to know.

It would be also naïve and sentimental to imagine the farmwife here, those hundred fifty years ago, filling what was a tiny home with the aroma of fresh-baked apple pie: she would be lucky to have an oven for baking, or the flour or sugar either. Most likely, they were pressed for cider and drunk; water was unsafe and ale cost money. Those eaten were most likely boiled in mush or made into pudding with cornmeal and lard.

But she wouldn't be surprised by our love of apples. Durable, adaptable, and fine-flavored, it has succored pilgrim and pioneer alike, providing food and drink, and mash for the pigs, and that through a large proportion of the year. Thomas DeVoe, writing in 1867, speaks of apples appearing in the South as early as May, and Winter, or keeping apples, are in the market through June. Their uses, he said, were as numerous as the varieties: ". . . for drying, apple-sauce, apple-butter, cider, tarts, jellies, fritters, dumplings, stewing, baking, dessert. . . ."

And, of course, apple pie. Earlier in that century, the recipe, not just for apple pie (which had a venerable history long before then), but *our* apple pie, had already appeared, made with brown sugar— white not being so familiar—but otherwise as simple-tasting and familiar as today. And as the nineteenth century progressed, each later cookbook had more recipes for it and more enthusiasm. And not only because pastry flour and sugar were more widely available and cast-iron cookstoves more affordable. Ironically, even as these modern amenities became widespread, so too did the pests that prey on apples. One unspoken but compelling reason for the sudden proliferation of those homey-sounding apple dishes—grunts, slumps, pandowdies, brown Bettys, and their like—was to put to good use the chunks and pieces frugal housewives salvaged, cutting out the worm holes and soft spots from otherwise useful apples. The flawless specimens were set away in the cold room, dried, or sent to market.

Our nation's apple passion crested at the turn of the century. At that time, according to John and Karen Hess in *The Taste of America*, there were over eight thousand varieties being grown. But more and more water became potable, grain was cheap (and, with it, beer), and cold storage and fast transportation offered a wider range of choices for the fruit bowl. The apple remained popular, even most popular, but it was no longer king.

Until recently, it seemed that competition and casual availability has condensed the apple into almost one bland taste, the few remaining varieties vying more to not offend than to please. But this may be changing. In the last few years local markets have welcomed apple season with a widening assortment: Rome Beauties, Idareds, Northern Spies, Macouns, Granny Smiths, Jonathans, and Winesaps. This year I tasted my first Pink Pearl, Melrose, Matsu, Gala, Holiday, and Grimes Golden.

Time, then, to reinvigorate enthusiasm for a really good apple pie. Still America's favorite, its lackluster performance of late is hardly due to benign neglect—no pie is more often made. Instead, it is due to shrinking expectations. We no longer expect from it anything but a mouthful vaguely sweet and vaguely nutritious; we forget the aroma, the flavor that could be ours. We forget that good apple pie needs more than a good recipe: it wants attention.

THE APPLE

> Apple pie depends, strangely enough, on the apples of which it is made. They should be tart and juicy. —MRS. APPLEYARD

The best rule, here, I guess, is to pick your apple tree and stick with it. My mother makes a great pie from the Wolf River apples that grow (and grew long before they ever got there) in the pasture of their old Maine farm. Hardly any source mentions the Wolf River; it is not so much rare as deliberately obscure, being not an immediately attractive apple. But it's there, fresh and free, so my mother has taken its measure, upping sugar and baking time when it's fresh and tart, and lowering both later, when it is neither. She knows that apple; this, not the apple, makes the difference.

Apples go on living after they're picked. After all, *they* want to be a tree. Their cells keep transforming the starch into sugar until there's no more starch; they then eat the sugar and collapse. This gradual shift in chemistry affects varieties differently. Taste a freshly picked Idared and it's nothing much, but it ages into a fine apple. The opposite is true of the Gravenstein, which is excellent fresh but soon deteriorates. Apples also have their years. This time your Macouns may be firm and juicy; next year they may be mealy and dry.

Not having a tree, the next best policy is to pay careful attention when buying them: apples should be unblemished and feel heavy for their size, resisting a gentle push with the thumb. Buy a few extra so you can discard the proverbial bad one. After that, find a favorite and stick with it. Famous for pies are Granny Smiths, Gravensteins (fresh!), Jonathans, Northern Spies, and Baldwins. All have juice and flavor and hold their shape when baked. Personally, I think McIntosh is better for sauce than pies. Golden Delicious has fans; not me. The important thing is to find *your* apple. If you love even Red Delicious enough, you can learn to make a pie from it.

The Crust

Just as there are dog lovers and cat lovers, there are bread and pastry makers. These things respond so differently to even loving hands that they pull at opposite temperaments entirely. Doggy bread dough exults in pummeling, contact, and warmth, and does its tricks almost unbidden, so eager to share affection. Pie dough, conversely, catlike, wants love, too, but from a coolly respectful hand and in short, sweet doses; only if you get it to its liking will it deign respond. Pie makers think bread work too easy; bread makers just hate pie dough. I'm a dog person, myself, and my only advice on pastry-making is to approach it cautiously and give it time to itself. Otherwise, please turn to a pastry person for your fine tuning.

Here's my recipe. Apple pie fanciers argue about lard versus butter crusts. Apple is a pie where a pure lard crust is easy to justify: flaky-light and with a flavor that easily marries with the filling, but the lard taste is definitely there. Yankee cooks compromise, tempering it with butter.

2 cups pastry flour, chilled an hour in the refrigerator
½ teaspoon salt
⅓ cup sweet butter
⅓ cup lard
⅓ cup (approx.) icy soda water

Mix the flour and salt. With icy fingertips or two table knives, work butter and lard into flour until no bits are larger than peas. Sprinkle with just enough cold water so that dough pulls together and holds its shape when rolled into a ball. It should not be sticky. Wrap in wax paper or plastic wrap and let rest in refrigerator for 1 or 2 hours before proceeding.

Divide the dough into two portions, one slightly larger than the other. The larger portion, remember, is for the *top* crust (the thicker crust goes on top to be flaky and delicious; the thinner crust underneath the filling just holds it in place). Put the larger piece back in the refrigerator until the bottom crust is rolled and fitted in an ungreased ("Never grease pie plate; good pastry greases its own tin"—Fannie Farmer) 9-inch pie plate. Roll out the crusts as directed in any competent cookbook, going easy with the flour.

(And, speaking of the devil, let's say it once and forever: flour belongs in the crust, not the pie. Sometime in this century, professional food writers started slipping flour into their pie fillings, first in the berry ones, then in the apple ones, convincing us that there was something terribly vulgar about a runny pie. But flour makes it gummy and clouds the flavor. Classic apple pie recipes never call for flour; almost every new baking cookbook does.)

The Filling

¶ This recipe, from an old (but not oldest) Fannie Farmer, is more or less the family recipe.

6 to 8 tart apples	¼ teaspoon salt
½ to ¾ cup sugar, white or brown	½ tablespoon butter
	2 teaspoons lemon juice
¼ teaspoon grated nutmeg or ground cinnamon	A few gratings lemon rind

This is about 3 pounds of apples. Long ago, most cooks used brown sugar in their pies; now most use white sugar, but I think brown gives a nice taste. Originally, Fannie Farmer used ⅓ cup of sugar. This amount has crept up over the years, even though apples get sweeter and sweeter: ½ cup should be plenty. Fannie Farmer used ⅛ teaspoon salt and later Wilma Lord Perkins upped it to the amount given. It is best dispensed with. Both sugar and lemon juice should vary (in opposite directions) in relation to the tartness of the apples (the sweeter the apple, the more lemon juice—up to 1 tablespoon).

While nutmeg seems the preferred old Yankee choice, cinnamon is more usual: there's already a hint of it in the apple itself. Some cooks resolve the dilemma by using both, halving the amount of nutmeg. You might also consider a tiny amount of ground or finely minced fresh ginger. Thomas Edison, says George Herter, the Bull Cook, liked a sprinkle of cocoa. Finally, I up the butter to 2 tablespoons. The original Fannie Farmer and some other cooks (such as Mrs. Appleyard) drop it down to a single teaspoon. The grated lemon peel is a nice touch—⅛ teaspoon will do, if we're measuring here—and it makes sure your lemon juice is fresh.

Preheat oven to 450°F. Pare, core, and cut the apples into eighths, ignoring modern cooks who tell you to slice them thin or drop them through your food processor slicing blade ("If you do, the juice will boil out before the apples are cooked, and the result will be tough and tasteless"—Florence White). They cook down just fine.

Mix the sugar and seasonings together and toss the apple chunks in it. Then sprinkle around the lemon juice (you've tasted and decided how much) and toss them in that. Working from the outside toward the center, but leaving a small space at the rim edge, neatly fill the pie, then mound the rest of the chunks on top. Sprinkle on any remaining sugar and spice left in the work bowl, then dot with the butter. Wet the edges of the bottom crust, cover with the top crust, and press the edges together neatly with the tines of a fork. Prick the top in several places.

Set pie on middle rack in oven and bake for 15 minutes; then reduce heat to 350°F and bake another 30 to 40 minutes, depending on the density of the apples and your intuitive sense of rightness. On this process, almost all cooks agree: the initial hot temperature firms the crust and steams the fruit in its own juices before they leach away.

Let cool at room temperature. As the pie cools, the apple slices will reabsorb their juices and plump up, so it's important to give them time. Serve the pie just warm. I agree with those who say apple pie should never be chilled: there never seems time to get it warm again. A pie should keep at room temperature for a day or two without any problem. The problem with a good pie is keeping it for the day or two.

VARIATIONS

SALT PORK AND APPLE.   Pork and apple complement each other nicely and this version is still favored in less trendy parts of New England. It is made exactly as directed above except with the addition of pea-sized bits of salt pork. To the Yankee taste, they're just tossed right in, but I think they should be blanched first to get rid of some salt. Cut 1 or 2 slices from a chunk, chop that small, simmer in boiling water, strain, and—if you like—brown before adding to the pie filling.

APPLE PIE AND CREAM.   Cut a circular vent the size of a dime in the center of the pie. When the pie is all but 5 minutes done, insert a funnel into the vent and pour in ½ cup of heavy cream. This is sometimes called "Dutch apple pie."

SHAKER APPLE PIE WITH CHEESE.   Take a slice of day-old apple pie, grate Cheddar generously over the top, and heat in a 350°F oven just long enough to make the pie hot and melt the cheese. World's best breakfast.

APPLE BRANDY PIE.   Mince 1 or 2 dried apple slices into small bits, cover generously with applejack or Calvados, and soak overnight. They will swell and absorb the brandy. Add the apple bits to the pie. They will have a chewier texture than the other apples (like raisins, only better), and will spread rumor of the brandy throughout.

> But, when I undress me
>   Each night, upon my knees
> Will ask the Lord to bless me
>   With apple pie and cheese.
>   —EUGENE FIELD (1850–1895)

II

PERFECT
PLEASURES

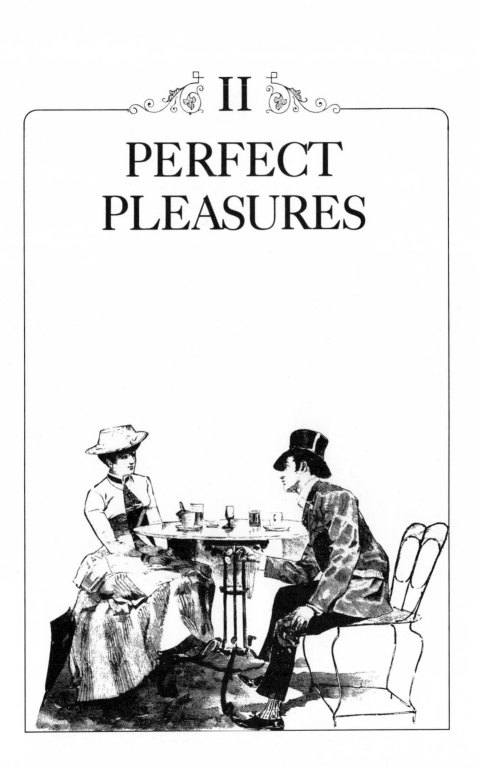

Beef on a String

✶

And since reading a restaurant menu is the customer's first course, as it were, allowing the eye to satisfy itself before the stomach, I particularly love to read—on the slate at the end of a slightly murky room, clear in the light from the hatch out of which floats the fragrant breath of the kitchen—these chalked up words: TODAY: *boeuf à la ficelle*.   —ROBERT COURTINE

Old cooking fads don't, like old soldiers, fade away. Instead, they linger on to fuel garage sales and book remainder piles. This is most obviously so with the meretricious gadgets we bought on impulse or that were presented to us by well-meaning relatives: the mini-fryer, for example, that never got hot enough to actually fry, and the crock pot, which turned out to do a good many things but none of them really well.

It is also true of other kitchen tools that were in themselves worthy but somehow didn't work out anyway, like the hand-cranked Italian spaghetti-maker now gathering dust up on top of the cabinet or the three-foot-long, polished-maple pastry roller, hefty as a baseball bat, that proved unmaneuverable on the counter and too long to fit in any of the kitchen drawers.

But there is also a third category of neglected kitchen equipment, well designed and once often used, but now abandoned because the dish it made has fallen out of style. Too good to throw away, it is tucked away in the closet with the mini-skirt wardrobe and the Brooks Brothers sport coats with the still-too-narrow lapels, in the hope of better days.

I think, for instance, of the rosette irons of a few years ago, the crêpe pan, the raclette melter, and especially the ubiquitous fondue pot. It's hard to remember back when it was actually a genuine novelty, fresh and fun and a break from the usual formal get-together. First came cheese fondue, then meat fondue, then chocolate fondue, then fondue cookbooks and "instant" Swiss fondue in the dairy case . . . then silence.

There's nothing at all wrong with real cheese fondue—delicious stuff, really, when you think back on it—but who has the courage to serve it, except to the family—and for the family, it's too much bother. Even quiche has fared better, variations still being proffered without embarrassment at brunch, the meal where it seems to have found its permanent home.

Anyway, all this came to mind the other day when, browsing through the remainder piles at the local bookstore, I came upon a book—a whole stack of the same title—devoted to the Mongolian firepot. This is a device used to make a sort of Chinese fondue. In it, a savory broth is set simmering, in which diced vegetables and shrimp or slivers of lamb or beef or chicken are dunked on chopsticks to be cooked, then eaten. The pot is a little like, but more elaborate (and more expensive) than, the fondue pot. I'm sure the two are getting along famously, though, now that the one has joined the other in the closet.

It is a juxtaposition of all these thoughts that brings us to the dish at hand, *boeuf à la ficelle*, prosaically translated as "beef on a string." It is (or, more truthfully, once was) a laborer's breakfast, served in the sort of tough, grubby Parisian bistro where you could well believe the fond rumor that the piece of string in question has been in use since the place first opened its doors. Like the firepot, *boeuf à la ficelle* is cooked in a simmering pot of rich broth, but the meat is fastened to a piece of string and dropped in all of a piece, since no Parisian laborer hungry for his breakfast would have either the time or the patience to dunk the meat in bite by bite.

To make it, a rich vegetable broth is essential, worked up from whatever pot vegetables suit your taste or happen to be on sale that day at the grocer's—leeks or onions, carrots, celery, turnips, and so on, but with lots and lots of small whole or quartered large (peeled) potatoes. These are mandatory, and so is plenty of freshly minced garlic and sprigs of herb—thyme, parsley, winter savory, bay—whatever and in what proportion seems good to you. All this should simmer together at least long enough to thoroughly cook the root vegetables, but preferably longer. Don't stint on contents or time; to flavor the beef during that meat's short poaching, the broth must have some real presence.

Then, cut a flavorful chunk of beef into steaks about three quarters of an inch thick—not choice cuts, but a tender chuck roast or London broil or perhaps some sirloin tip. Fasten a short, equal length of string to each steak, tying a loop at the other end. When ready to cook the meat, insert through the loops the handle of a wooden spoon long enough to rest across the top of the pot. Lift up the spoon, holding it by both ends, and lower the steaks into the simmering (but not boiling) broth. The meat should cook for five to eight minutes—the pieces still a little rare in the center when removed. The steaks are traditionally eaten with mustard and coarse salt, serving the pot vegetables (especially the potatoes) on the side. (In the bistro, more vegetables are added to the same broth to make the next round, and so the whole meal gets richer and better as the day goes on.)

Although I suppose it could be done, I'm not suggesting you try this at the dinner table, each guest holding onto his or her own string. No, this is a kitchen meal, to be eaten among friends with lots of beer or a fresh young wine, each guest hauling out his or her steak when deeming it ready, and given a free hand at the mustard pot. The broth can be eaten with the meal or put to good use later; the strings, if you like, can be saved for the next time, wrapped around the fondue forks.

Vegetable Love

❁

Ratatouille is a Provençal ragout of vegetables, usually pimentos, onions, tomatoes, and aubergines, stewed very slowly in oil. This dish has the authentic aromatic flavor of Provençal food.

—ELIZABETH DAVID

The zucchini hasn't been popular in this country long enough to have acquired a sufficient hate literature, though you'd think more people would be suspicious of a vegetable whose only virtue is that any fool can grow one. One? The whole problem with zucchini is that you *can't* grow just one; the amateur's first blush of pride in the vulgar fecundity of this squash soon enough turns to terror. Its much-touted versatility is just a polite way of saying that it constantly intrudes where it isn't wanted, a vegetable form of that blandly grating familiarity, "Have a nice day."

I would hardly bother concerning myself with a vegetable with the nutritional value, flavor, and texture of rained-on newspaper, if it hadn't insinuated itself into one of my favorite summer dishes, rendering it totally unappetizing: the ratatouille of Provence. This dish once was and still should be made of only onions, peppers, and eggplant (in a puree of tomato, redolent of herb and garlic). Now, even on its home turf, most *niçoises*, tendentious as they otherwise are about the preparation of that dish, give the nod to *la courgette* (or, more accurately still, *li courgourdéta*), zucchini's *nom d'un nom* in those parts. The battle, alas, is all but lost.

The goal of the good ratatouille, in Richard Olney's wonderfully evocative phrase, is to end up with vegetables that are "intact but puree-tender, cloaked in a syrupy reduction of their own abundant juices." And the problem with zucchini is strictly that its juices are *over*abundant: by the time they cook away, the dish has simmered into mush.

Even with the zucchini omitted, the dish is not all that easy to make ("ratatouille, contrary to popular belief, is a particularly long and tricky dish to prepare," boasts Jacques Médecin, mayor of Nice, in his *Cuisine Niçoise*), difficult not because of what it asks you to do, but what it asks you *not* to do, which is stir. This seems an easy-enough-to-follow injunction, but stirring turns out to be a tremendous temptation during that dish's long cooking. Logic constantly insists, all during the cooking process, that stirring is exactly what you should be doing to vegetables cooking in so little liquid.

Resist, resist . . . stirring will quickly break them up. The trick is to ever-so-gently *shake* them, especially at first, so that they do not stick. This soft but persistant shaking, which should send barely a tremor through the pan, is an art and requires practice, but you will be well rewarded, for it is truly the secret to this dish.

Ratatouille

8 tiny eggplants, ends trimmed away
4 red or yellow sweet peppers (or 2 of each)
4 perfectly ripe tomatoes
½ cup (approx.) good fruity olive oil
6 cloves garlic, minced
12 fresh basil leaves, minced
Pinch (½ teaspoon) thyme
Salt and freshly ground pepper
3 medium onions, sliced
½ cup dry white wine or a flinty Provençal rosé
Additional fresh basil and lemon wedges for garnish

Cut the eggplants in half and then cut the halves into slices. Sprinkle these with salt and let them sweat out their liquid in a colander in the sink for 30 minutes. Then spread them on paper towels and press firmly to squeeze out as much additional liquid as possible. Meanwhile, stem and seed the peppers and cut the flesh into strips.

When the eggplant is removed from the colander, put in the very ripe tomatoes (this is, remember, a summer dish), and pour a kettle of boiling water over them. When they are cool enough to touch, slip off their skins, quarter them, and squeeze out their seeds. Place the tomato pieces on paper towels, also to drain away any excess liquid.

Heat 1 tablespoon of the olive oil in a large heavy skillet . Add the garlic and sauté it until it just turns soft and translucent. Don't let it brown. Then stir in the tomatoes, the basil, and the thyme, seasoning with salt and pepper to taste. Cook, stirring gently (here it is permitted), until the tomatoes start to break down into sauce, about 5 to 10 minutes. Pour this mixture into a bowl and reserve.

Wipe out the pan and heat in it ¼ cup of olive oil. Add the eggplant slices and cook these for 5 minutes, turning them over once gently during the middle of the cooking. Add these carefully to the tomato mixture.

Again wipe out the pan, and again heat more olive oil in it, this time 2 tablespoons. Add the onion slices and pepper strips and sauté these for 5 minutes, or until the pepper is soft and the onion translucent. (Strict purists sauté these two vegetables separately, but I don't see the problem in combining them here, instead of moments later.) At this point, return the reserved vegetable mixture to the pot.

Over this mixture, pour the wine and stir just once with a wooden spoon to mix it in. Bring the mixture to a simmer, then lower the heat down to a mere flicker—the contents should gently steam but never bubble—and cook uncovered for about an hour, shaking the pan gently as necessary, until the liquid has thickened into a sauce and the vegetables are meltingly soft but still intact.

Ratatouille can be eaten hot, but I think it is best served at room temperature, strewn with bits of fresh basil leaf and with lemon wedges set at the side. With it, offer the rest of the wine and a good loaf of bread.

(Serves 4)

Afterword. Since writing these words in 1981 (and suffering the abuse of zucchini-growing readers who were afraid the antizucchini movement might spread to their neighbors), I've become a little more reconciled toward that vegetable, which is why you'll find it occasionally mentioned elsewhere in this book. As it turns out, there are varieties far more flavorful and tender than the one commonly found in most markets (see page 157) and—more importantly—I discovered that it can be salted and set in a colander (exactly like eggplant) to exude much of its noxious liquid. That treatment also tightens its texture and heightens what there is of its flavor. But my favorite recipe for it is still an adaptation of Dr. Johnson's instructions for cucumber—"slice it, dress it with salt, pepper, and vinegar, and throw it out as good for nothing."

Lost Bread Found

❁

Payn Purdeuz: Take creme or mylke, and brede of paynemayn
or ellys of tendyr brede. —Fifteenth-century recipe

It is called French, Spanish, German, and Nun's Toast; but egg
toast seems to best indicate the character of the dish.
—MARY LINCOLN (1883)

Do the French eat French toast for breakfast? The only French
cookbook I have found that mentions it suggests it as a fast and
economical dessert (as the British treat pancakes). Naturally, they
don't call it French toast (they don't have a single word for toast and
the designation "French" would be assumed as a matter of course).
They call it *pain perdu*, literally "lost bread," meaning bread that
would be tossed out if it weren't for this pleasurable form of resus-
citation.

Pain perdu is what they call French toast in New Orleans, too,
which is not surprising at all. What *is* surprising is that in *Louisiana
Cookery*, Mary Land gives a recipe for it from Madame Bègué, saying
that that lady "named her lost bread 'Poor Knight.' "

Surprising, because "Poor Knights"—or, more specifically, "Poor
Knights of Windsor"—is what the *British* call French toast. The British have been eating it for centuries; it was a passion in the court of
Henry V (1387–1422). Henry V beat the French at Agincourt, but
called French toast "payn purdeuz," which shows he wasn't one to
hold a grudge. (The Poor Knights, an order of military pensioners
established at Windsor Castle, was founded before Henry V but gave
its name to the dish at some point after him. Why, no one knows for
sure.)

I mention all this because, despite so rich and popular a history,
the dish did not, it seems, pass over the water with the rest of the
culinary baggage we inherited from Mother England. This much we
could even guess from Mary Lincoln's wild stabs at nomenclature, as
late as 1883. Perhaps there just wasn't enough bakery bread available

to ordinary home cooks for the dish to become widely known; until late in the last century we were more a country of quick bread and cornpone than yeast breads, which could be why we have no real tradition of a truly superlative loaf.

In any case, despite Mrs. Lincoln's vote for "egg toast," the French have clearly beaten out the Germans, Spanish, Russians ("Russian toast" was another name used at the time), and nuns. Perhaps this is because French toast appeared on the American scene at approximately the same time that we were taking our first cautious steps toward food snobbery, a market the French had already cornered and have zealously held on to ever since.

French toast, then, it is. But this simple, delicious breakfast fare needs no special gourmet luster to commend it—just some vociferous protection from the way it is usually made, out of ordinary store bread and drenched in syrup. Nor do most recipes help things by demanding such spurious ingredients as vanilla and outrageous amounts of sugar.

Perfect French toast requires that we restrict ourselves to a few choice ingredients and curb our sweet tooth. Most importantly, it demands forethought: the bread must be purchased a day or two beforehand, to give it time to stale, so that it can both hold its shape and absorb the cream-egg mixture it is dunked in. The loaf can be a good French or Italian loaf (by which I mean one with a firm and crusty exterior and an open, chewy interior) or, better yet, challah (an egg-rich, Jewish braided loaf). Leave it a day or two loosely wrapped in its wax paper bag (not plastic!) to reach the proper stage of stale. It should be dry, but not so much as to crumble into pieces when cut.

Now, as you linger under the glowing warmth of the comforter this next chilly Sunday morn, you can turn your mind toward a breakfast that not only provides the shortest distance from the first touch of cold floor underfoot to the first mouthful of hot food, but richly repays the effort.

French Toast

8 thick slices bread
8 tablespoons (1 stick) sweet
   butter
2 eggs
1 cup light cream or half and
   half

¼ teaspoon ground cinnamon
   or grated nutmeg
2 tablespoons confectioners'
   sugar

You have three simple tasks to perform before the bread is in the frying pan. First, slice the bread thickly, about three quarters of an inch, or twice the thickness of the standard slice. Second, melt the whole stick of sweet butter (salted butter is one reason so much sugar is dumped into French toast) in a large, heavy frying pan until it is hot enough to fry in, but not so hot as to turn brown. (Perfectionists clarify the butter before heating it to prevent burning, but care in adjusting the flame will take care of this just as well.) Third and last, in a wide, shallow bowl, beat the eggs into the cup of light cream or half and half (regular milk can be substituted, but not, please, skim). If at all available, use a non-ultrapasteurized product.

Dunk the bread slices in the mixture, letting them drink their fill. Let any excess drip back into the bowl. (If the bread falls apart, you have the wrong kind of bread. Fish it out and fry it anyway.) Lay out each slice gently into the bubbling butter, frying each side to a golden brown. As they crisp, mix together the cinnamon or nutmeg and confectioners' sugar. Sift this thickly over the finished toast (I use a tea strainer) and serve with extra butter.

(Serves 4)

You don't like cinnamon? The result isn't sweet enough for you? Well, all right, but don't reach for the syrup bottle. Maple syrup is delicious stuff, but it is no good on French toast, overpowering the subtle taste of egg, cream, and bread, and blotting out all the buttery crispness. Instead, consider spreading it with some good fruit preserve, raspberry or strawberry or peach, or mixing a tablespoon or two of brandy and a sprinkling of orange water in with the eggs and cream. Or try one of these choice variations:

YANKEE TOAST.   Core and slice lengthwise, but do not peel, 5 McIntosh apples. Fry these slices in butter with 3 tablespoons water and ¼ cup brown sugar. Serve on the French toast. *(Serves 4)*

FRENCH TOAST WITH SUGAR AND LIME.   Cut 2 fresh limes into wedges. Serve the French toast with butter, the lime wedges, and (preferably) a richly flavored, coarsely ground sugar such as Barbados or Muscovado, brown sugars made by simple evaporation and that thus contain flavors and nutrients lost in the more refined American "brown" sugars. *(Serves 4)*

HAITIAN TOAST.   A version discovered by Bert Greene during a stay on that island (he gives the recipe in his *Kitchen Bouquets*) and here simplified to my own taste. To the basic recipe, add 1 cup absolutely fresh-squeezed orange juice, while reducing the light cream to ¼ cup. Mix this together with the 2 eggs and a pinch of grated nutmeg, and make the toast in the melted butter as directed. Serve with lime wedges and brown sugar to sprinkle on top, preferably the Barbados or Muscovado sugar mentioned above. *(Serves 4)*

Potato Soup

❀

In reality—as Amanda told us later while peeling potatoes—Ole
Fritz merely wanted the recipe for her potato soup, which was
wholesome, he said, and soothed his gouty bones. . . . Amanda
seasoned [it] with mustard seed and caraway seed, and with herbs
such as marjoram and parsley. (Of course sausage can be boiled
with the soup or bits of fried bacon stirred in. Sometimes Amanda
cooked carrots in the soup, or leeks or celery for seasoning. In
the winter she put in dried mushrooms, or a few handfuls of
greenies [potherbs] and morels.) —GÜNTER GRASS, *The Flounder*

Potato soup. What wonderful stuff, and how likely it is you've never
had it—not vichyssoise, which isn't potato soup at all, just a buttery-
bland mouthful of weightless-seeming luxury for rich folk to start
their gorging on—but *real* potato soup, with no surfeit of cream or
leeks or anything else to crowd out that subtle earthy potato taste or
strangely ethereal aroma, the smell of a forest as it waits for the first
of the autumnal rains.

The problem is not that the potato is unknown to soup-making,
but too well known: that delicate flavor makes a wonderfully com-
plementary wrap for almost any other taste you can name. Hence,
for most cooks, "potato" comes up as "soup base" in every conceivable shuffle of their culinary deck. "The queen of soups," writes Dr.
Besançon, speaking for all, "is leek and potato. Next comes watercress
and potato, lettuce and potato. . . ." You'd think the good doctor
would note the constant in his litany and extrapolate the obvious, but
he hurries on oblivious.

Even in *The Great Potato Cookbook*, written, supposedly, as a paean
to "the incredible potato," Maria and Jack Denton Scott manage to
write a twenty-seven-page chapter on soup without once thinking to
try their subject vegetable by itself. It's potato this or potato that—
carrot, clam, cheese, cucumber, cabbage, pumpkin, etc. Really, it
staggers the imagination.

And it's not as if I'm a purist on this matter. Salt pork or bacon rind, caraway seeds, winter savory, marjoram, parsley, dill, butter or chicken fat, pot vegetables, a grating of cheese—there's no shortage of seasonings to bring a welcome spritz of savor to a good potato soup. But a good potato soup needs *only* a spritz of flavor. Add more and the potato retreats to play backup for someone else's show.

For just that reason it's worth starting with as minimal a set of ingredients imaginable, just to show what a few potatoes can do, given the spotlight and a little help from their friends. Here is a soup that André Simon in his *Concise Encyclopedia of Gastronomy* calls "the simplest—and best":

POTATO SOUP.   Simmer 4 or 5 medium-size peeled Maine potatoes in a quart of milk, mixed with a little water, for at least an hour. Season well with pepper and salt. Mash the potatoes, add a tablespoon or two of butter and pour into the soup tureen over some little snippets of stale bread, toasted in butter or some rendered sweet beef suet.

(Serves 6)

Deceptively simple, this soup—as admirable for what it leaves out as what it puts in. The stale bread is a nice touch—especially as opposed to the expected snippets of chive—little mouthfuls of crunch and fat that set off the potato's own flavor and richness. Most fiddling cooks would use cream instead of the milk and chicken or beef broth instead of the water. But milk adds a classic smoothness to the potato's delicate creaminess, which would only be smothered by real cream. And while broth would make this a fine-tasting soup, it would make it less of a potato one.

Plain water, in fact, works just fine in potato soup ("Beware the bouillon cube, my son!") when a grainier-style peasant soup is craved, such as this variant on Amanda's *ur-Suppe:*

Kartoffelsuppe

Small square salt pork, cut into tiny cubes, rind discarded, or 3 tablespoons butter
Pot vegetables such as a carrot, parsnip, onion, and/or celery top (as available), finely diced

1½ pounds Maine potatoes, preferably old ones, peeled and cut into ½-inch cubes, a little peel reserved and minced
2 teaspoons minced fresh marjoram or scant teaspoon dried
Salt
Minced fresh parsley and dill

Over medium heat, gently render the salt pork until it releases some fat (or melt the butter) in a heavy pot. Add the reserved minced potato peel and diced pot vegetables and sauté until they take on color. Then add the potatoes and, tossing occasionally, let cook until they turn translucent. Pour in 2 quarts of water, add the marjoram, and taste for salt. Cook 45 minutes, or until potatoes are soft and crumbly. Pour the soup through a sieve, pushing the vegetables through after it. Gently reheat to a simmer, and serve with the minced parsley and dill sprinkled over the top.

(Serves 6)

This is good soup. If you're not partial to marjoram, consider some of the other options suggested by Günter Grass; he knows whereof he speaks. Old potatoes are favored for two reasons: age has concentrated their flavor and they tend to crumble apart, producing a pleasing rough texture, which could be heightened still further by judicious use of a potato masher instead of a sieve. It's also worth noting that the best soup potato is a Maine potato: baking potatoes tend to disintegrate too much, waxy potatoes not enough to get the texture exactly right.

However, my own vote for the very best potato soup is a South American one, from the Andes, to be exact—home to the potato and a potato-based cuisine. Fittingly long-cooked and deep-flavored, it is only one version of a dish—*locro*—familiar all over that continent, made from whatever native starch is abundant and cheap. Like any peasant dish, there are many versions, but all start with an onion fried in butter or fat and end by mixing in some milk and a handful of crumbled white cheese. Some cooks add tomato (or some tomato paste) to the onion. I like it better with garlic.

Locro

4 tablespoons (½ stick) butter or fat
1 teaspoon sweet paprika
2 medium onions, chopped
2 cloves garlic, minced
4 pounds potatoes, peeled and quartered
1 pint half and half

¼ pound cheese, grated (a mild Cheddar, Monterey Jack, or by preference, queso blanco)
Salt
Pinch cayenne pepper (optional)
Two avocados, peeled, seeded, and cut into slivers (optional)

In a large, deep pot, melt the butter or fat. Stir in the paprika until dissolved, then add the onions and garlic. When they are translucent, add the potatoes and add enough water to cover (about 1½ quarts). Bring the water to a boil, reduce the heat until the soup surface barely quivers, and simmer for at least 2—better 3—hours. The potatoes should fall apart when prodded with a spoon. Mix in the half and half and cheese, stirring well. Taste for salt, and add a pinch of cayenne if you desire. Serve at once, alone or with a huge platter of avocado slices.

(Serves 6 to 8)

Crostini di Fegatini

❀

Crostini probably appear on every antipasto menu in every Tuscan trattoria, but all too often they arrive as gritty grey paste on soggy bread. At Ganino's, the bread is first grilled over an open wood fire, then brushed with good green olive oil and at the last moment anointed with capers and anchovy.

—LESLIE FORBES, *A Taste of Tuscany*

Funny how you can be vaguely aware of a dish for years without feeling a tremor of interest until a chance phrase, a moment's exposure to someone else's enthusiasm ignites a latent fire—and suddenly it composes itself into something palpably desirable. This kind of serendipitous surprise justifies, I think, the publishing of what are essentially the same recipes over and over again in different cookbooks. You never know what perspective will ignite that spark—as the above quotation did for me.

In menu Italian, *crostini* almost universally means delicate bits of crustless bread first toasted and then spread with some simple savory mixture such as anchovy butter, thinly sliced Parmesan and a drizzle of olive oil, or coarsely chopped and flavored olives, and almost always served as a first course or an hors d'oeuvre. When put to such duty, the bread usually specified is a fine-textured one, since the impression is to be elegant and the dish serve as no more than a whet.

However, *crostini* translates from the Italian as "little crusts"—and bread crust has a venerable place in that country's peasant cooking, which is full of clever ways of getting the last mile from the stale husk-end of yesterday's loaf. It was toasted into rusks, topped with cheese and anchovy, and baked crusty in the oven, or fried crisp in olive oil to be eaten as is or floated or dunked in broth.

Considering this last use, Leslie Forbes's dismissal of run-of-the-mill *crostini* as "soggy" is perhaps unfairly pejorative; our taste for crunchy toast is not everybody's. Pellegrino Artusi's recipe for *crostini* with chicken livers specifically prompts us to "remember that these *crostini* must be soft. . . . The bread may be soaked in soup after toasting it, so that the desired softness will be acquired."

Indeed, toasted crusts dipped quickly into a good chicken broth and then topped with chicken liver are very tasty and should be considered by those who would like to render the dish less fattening. (It also makes it more amenable to being eaten with a fork—if you require that to transform it into a meal.)

In any case, it's time to liberate *crostini*—and not just those with chicken livers—from automatic association with the canapé crowd. Let's see them not as the effete little tidbits that tide, time, and Miss Manners have made them, but as the hearty, substantial things they once were—an actual meal: thick toasted crusts of bread brought hot to table and lightly buttered or brushed with sweet-flavored olive oil, then thickly spread with a savory, coarse-textured mixture of seasoned chicken livers, all served with a simple salad of greens. Good . . . simple . . . easy to make.

Most cookbooks present this dish in its rather more complicated versions, but it is—by origins and temperament both—open to a more casual approach. The livers can be briefly poached whole in broth or wine, or sautéed in olive oil or butter (or a mixture of both). The seasonings can range from simple to complex, from salt and pepper to a flavorful mélange of herbs, capers, and juniper berries. One Tuscan version calls for minced spleen (*milza*), which must provide an unusual piquancy. (Chicken gizzards have been suggested as a substitute, but that seems progress in the wrong direction; anchovies would be better.)

Consider a quarter pound of chicken livers enough for one person if the dish is to be a meal, half that if for appetizers. The bread, sliced as thin or thick as you please, should be slightly stale—and should have the character to stand up to the other ingredients. Toast it all at once under the broiler (watching carefully), so that everyone gets his hot. (*Note:* Where I recommend a specific amount of seasoning, it is for a half pound of chicken livers; add or subtract accordingly.)

Pick over the chicken livers, cutting away any greenish bits. Heat a little sweet butter or olive oil in a sauté pan. When hot, add the livers and cook over moderately high heat until they are crusty without but still a little pinkish within, about four minutes. Remove them immediately to a cutting board and, with a sharp knife, chop them into a coarse mass, making sure to sever all connective tissue. Transfer this to a small bowl. In the pan, splash a tiny amount of wine (whatever you like from dry red to sweet Marsala) and, using a spatula or wooden spoon, scrape away any flavorful bits clinging to the sides and bottom and mix all this into a sauce. Pour it over the chopped livers, season to taste with coarse sea salt and a generous grinding of pepper, and beat to a spreadable but still rough consistency with a fork, moistening if necessary with a little more of the wine. Serve at once with butter or olive oil—and, of course, the toast.

This basic approach can be variously adapted: a half clove of garlic, minced, or a tablespoon or so of minced onion can be softened in the hot oil before adding the chicken livers; three or four crushed capers can be added at the same time as the wine, as can a teaspoon or so of tomato paste or rich broth.

Fresh sage is an herb that Italians are far fonder of than I, but it does do good things to chicken livers (as can fresh rosemary). Some mince the sage and mix it in with the livers, but I prefer to vigorously bruise one or two whole leaves with the back of a knife. Add with the livers and discard when making the sauce. Prepare as directed above, but this time season not only with the salt and pepper, but with a squeeze of lemon juice.

The dish can be heightened still further by adding about a tablespoon or so of finely minced, very fatty ham, letting this fry up a bit with the oil before adding the livers; the little bits of crispy ham fat give the liver mixture a delicious salty succulence. Or, again, a few pieces of dried *porcini* can be soaked for a few hours until soft, then minced and added with the livers to provide their own special flavor note.

Finally, if you find this dish to your taste, by all means sample the more sophisticated versions in Leslie Forbes's *Taste of Tuscany*, Giuliano Bugialli's *Fine Art of Italian Cooking*, Carol Field's *The Italian Baker*, Elizabeth Romer's *Tuscan Year*, and Alfredo Viazzi's *Cucina e Nostalgia*.

Carpaccio

Filetto Carpaccio is a dish of simply but artfully seasoned raw beef. It is claimed by the legendary Harry's Bar of Venice, the inspired improvisation of Giuseppe Cipriani to beguile the palate of an ailing contessa. It is made there—according to Richard Condon (in *Gourmet*, February 1982)—by searing the outside of an entrecôte of baby beef. This is allowed to cool, the seared portion trimmed away, and the meat then sliced as thinly as possible. The meat is presented decorated with a cold sauce of mustard and mayonnaise, the exact composition of which, alas, is *segreto di capo*.

Even so, the good news is that you already know enough, if not to replicate the dish, at least to turn out a truly voluptuous mouthful: there is no other raw beef preparation whose accompaniments play so well off its velvet succulency. It is so good, however, that one longs to know—however ultimately futile such knowledge might prove—the Cipriani secret.

But either because *Carpaccio* is a "restaurant dish" or because Harry's Bar is notoriously an American hangout, the recipe rarely appears in Italian cookbooks, especially the important ones. This is unfortunate. While Italian cooking is notoriously uncodable and its authorities rarely in accord even about what is, here they need only convince the Ciprianis to set the record straight.

And this they should do—if for no other reason than that less reliable cookbook writers, Italian and otherwise, have been treating us to "Carpaccios" that are neither authentic nor—usually—nearly so good. And while any chef has the right to meddle with an established dish to make it his or her own, there is no excuse for the food writer who, having failed—or not even tried—to wheedle out the real recipe, foists on the reader some horror concocted out of his or her perfervid imaginings instead.

For instance, a few years ago in a glowing article about Harry's Bar, a popular food magazine offered as an authentic *Carpaccio* a recipe that included Tabasco, Worcestershire sauce, dried mustard, and beef broth, all beaten into mayonnaise until the mixture had the consistency of "a very thick soup." If this is the true version, Mimi Sheraton needs her palate checked; she recently tasted the dish on its home ground and pronounced it "decent but bland." More likely, it's *not* at all authentic. No Italian chef would serve a concoction like that to a contessa, even a healthy one. And this version isn't the worst of the genre.

The problem is that the name of the dish is just too catchy for its own good. *Carpaccio* (named for a quattrocento Venetian artist) has become synonymous with any raw beef dish with Italian pretensions, and this only worsens the muddle. While the sauce itself may be original with Giuseppe Cipriani, his is neither the first nor the only Italian collation of raw beef.

For example, Francesco Ghedini's admirable *Northern Italian Cooking* offers three recipes, two very much of the *Carpaccio* genre. He calls these simply *insalada di carne cruda*, "salad of raw beef." Each is a variation of paper-thin slices of raw beef or veal fillet dressed with olive oil, fresh lemon juice, salt and pepper, and a generous amount of Parmesan cheese—simple, delicious, and not *Carpaccio*.

Even so, it is called that by the Romagnolis in their own version, which omits the Parmesan in favor of capers, parsley, and sliced mushrooms. Joe Famularo and Louise Imperiale similarly misname their own raw beef dish dressed in a vinaigrette seasoned with capers, chopped onion, mustard, anchovies, and sour gherkins, which is nothing like *Carpaccio* but not unlike an overfussy *carne crude alla genovese*, a Genoese dish where thinly sliced beef is brushed with olive oil, sprinkled with fresh lemon juice, and then scattered over with chopped *fresh* anchovy fillets, parsley, scallion, and tiny flecks of garlic. Again, excellent . . . again, not *Carpaccio*.

I've never been to Venice and have never tasted the genuine article. But I think the simplicity of the dish is its signature, not some arcane gustatory fiddling. Let the few known ingredients be chosen with respect and freshly prepared, and each mouthful will have the force and grace of its namesake, and will be a primitive yet cultured stimulant to appetite, a chef's *beau geste*.

Carpaccio should be made from a tender, succulent cut such as a piece of tenderloin, from, preferably, organically raised beef, trimmed of all fat. Some slightly freeze the meat to firm it for the requisite thin slicing. The original searing technique tightens the flesh to the same purpose. (Consider quickly searing it on all sides over natural mesquite or hickory coals and then not trimming it. The meat is framed in a blackened fringe with a delicious trace of smoke.) Anyway, if seared, the meat must be allowed to cool before slicing, and then refrigerated until just before serving.

The knife should be razor sharp and the slices as thin as possible, cut across the grain. Unless you are especially skilled at this, the slices will not be uniform, and no matter. (Some recipes call for pounding the slices between pieces of wax paper to make them huge and paper thin—a damnable restaurant trick, as abusive to good beef as it would be to smoked salmon or prosciutto.)

For this dish, the mayonnaise should be made in the genuine Italian manner, concocted simply of two egg yolks, two tablespoons of fresh lemon juice, a pinch of salt, and a cup of delicate extra-virgin olive oil, unmixed with any seed oil. The resultant voluptuousness is a perfect complement to the raw beef. To make it, let the yolks warm to room temperature and then beat with a good pinch of salt until they are creamy and light. Then, whipping briskly, dribble the oil into the yolks in a stream of droplets. When the mixture becomes stiff, thin it with a little of the lemon juice and continue until oil and lemon juice are both used up. (If all this is an unfamiliar task, turn to a good Italian cookbook for further advice.)

Most *Carpaccio* recipes add the mustard (of the Dijon type) when making the mayonnaise. This is a mistake, not only because Italians scoff at the idea, but, more importantly, because blending it in later allows this to be done to taste—a good idea, since recipes vary hugely here, from teaspoons to tablespoons. I suggest the smaller amount: it should serve only to stimulate the palate, not mask the rich but fragile taste of the beef.

That's it. You can, if you wish, mix in a little chopped parsley or basil or chives, for their visual tease, spreading the sauce decoratively on each slice. Serve cool but not icy cold, calculating two ounces per person for an appetizer, four ounces for a light main course, with a simple salad and a good Italian red wine. What better supper to greet a summer night, whether sitting down to table in Venice or on your own back porch. . . .

Boudin Blanc

❀

Breakfast was beer and boudin (a muscular local sausage of rice, pork and pork liver that can quickly become an addiction).
—*Time* (March 4, 1985)

Yes, indeed. And just how much an addiction, I'll be glad to tell. On my last visit to Louisiana, I bought a few pounds of boudin blanc in a little grocery in Lacombe to stuff in my suitcase for the trip back. The plane was held on the runway for an hour and the cabin temperature quickly shot up into the humid nineties. I could feel the heat seeping through my suitcase and setting off a wild orgy of bacterial action in the boudin blanc—to continue for the seven more hours before I could fling them into the fridge.

Of course, they should have been tipped straight into the garbage. My only concession to the imminent possibility of food poisoning was to eat the whole batch at once, before they had a chance to "spoil." And eat I did, the moisture pouring from my forehead only partly caused by the liberal seasoning of Tabasco peppers. I swore with each bite that from then on, at least in Massachusetts, I'd make my own.

Cajun boudin blanc (boudin noir is blood sausage) is really not much more than meatloaf stuffed in sausage skin, cooked rice replacing bread crumbs. Because of the proportion of meat to rice (and a substantial amount of greens), it is delicate in texture and, as sausages go, light on the calories. Cajuns often eat it as a side dish, but with salad and corn bread, it's a meal in itself. Bursting with flavor and vitamins, easy on the pocketbook, not all that difficult to make, it's all the invitation you need to break out the fiddle, invite the family over, and call in the pig.

But first things first. When you say "boudin blanc" to the folks down there, they won't know what you're talking about. That's because they say it a way no outsider—at least this one—can wrap mouth around. I pointed. "Oh," said the friendly counterlady, "yawl mean boo-dahhhnng." Yes, ma'am, I do.

The next thing is that it's *Cajun* boudin blanc we're talking about. That's only kissing cousin to the Creole version, which is made with breast of chicken, veal stock, and heavy cream, and nearly identical to the French original, which Jane Grigson describes as "of delicate flavor . . . the most expensive of sausages." With the Cajun version, none of these things is true.

Cajun boudin blanc was traditionally made at hog slaughtering time, or *boucherie,* a festive occasion when fiddlers played while family and friends worked in tandem to utilize every edible bit of the pig: the larger chunks of meat set to cure, the perishable entrails, offal, and bits and scraps transformed into a feast of sausage, headcheese, backbone stew, and *grattons,* bits of skin fried up crispy in their own fat. Obviously, at such an occasion, there is no place for cream or veal stock. Cajun boudin blanc is earthy stuff, used to being made by the dishpanful.

And, also because of its impromptu origins, recipes vary by family and ingredients on hand. Some make it with just pork, others add pork liver, still others the heart and kidney, too. Some are mostly rice and thus truly *blanc;* most have more meat and are really gray. They can be wildly hot or gently peppery or plain mild. In the same spirit, you should feel free to double the garlic, halve the cayenne, or toss out the sage. What follows is just to get you your fix on the thing.

To start with, if you don't have a meat grinder with a sausage tube, the task isn't worth the trouble by yourself. But with a food processor, a friend, and large funnel (about a half inch at the tip), you'll find it quickly done. Sausage casings can sometimes be found at butcher shops and ethnic markets. A reliable mail order source is The Sausage Maker (177 Military Road, Buffalo, NY 14207); their catalogue is free.

To prepare the casing, unravel a nine-foot length and soak it for about three hours in tepid water. Then cut into three equal lengths. Rinse the outside free of salt in cold water, then insert the tip of the sausage stuffing tube or funnel into one end of each of the lengths and gently, slowly, rinse out the inside. When the last length is rinsed, don't remove it: knot the far end and slip the whole length up over the tip until the knot presses against the opening. You are now ready to stuff your first sausage.

Boudin Blanc

3½ pounds lean boneless pork, trimmed and cut into large cubes
4 medium onions, chopped (about 2 cups)
1 bay leaf
12 peppercorns
Salt
2 tablespoons olive oil or vegetable oil
½ pound pork or lamb liver
6 scallions, minced

1 large green pepper, cored, seeded, and chopped
2 cloves garlic, minced
1 cup Italian parsley, chopped
2½ cups cooked rice, cooled
1 tablespoon dried sage
½ tablespoon cayenne pepper
½ teaspoon freshly ground pepper
3 3-foot lengths sausage casing, prepared as directed above

Put the pork in a large casserole and pour in enough water to cover by 1 inch. Bring to a boil over high heat and skim away any foam and scum that rise to the surface. Then add 1 cup of chopped onion, the bay leaf, the peppercorns, and a good pinch of salt. Reduce the heat to a bare simmer, and cook, partially covered, for 1½ hours. Then remove the pork and discard the flavorings and liquid.

Heat the olive oil in a large frying pan. When hot, add 1 cup of chopped onion. When these turn translucent, add the liver, season with salt, and cook over medium heat, turning once, for about five minutes or until just done. Remove at once from the heat and let cool in pan.

When the pork is cool enough to handle, combine it with the liver and its onions, the scallions, green pepper, garlic, and parsley, and crank this mixture through a meat grinder set for a coarse grind (or process to a coarse texture in a food processor fitted with the metal blade).

Put this ground mixture in a large bowl and combine with the rice, sage, cayenne and black pepper, and 1 tablespoon salt. Mix thoroughly with your hands and then beat with a wooden spoon until the mixture is smooth, moist, and light. Taste for seasoning.

Attach the sausage stuffing tube to the meat grinder (or get friend ready with funnel). Push the mixture through it into the casing, letting it feed slowly off the tube as it fills. Pack the sausage just firmly enough to prevent air bubbles, letting it form a coil on the table. Stop a good inch before the end of the casing and knot it tightly. Prepare the other two the same way. The boudin blanc may be cooked immediately or refrigerated for five or six days.

(Makes about 5 pounds)

To cook: Prick with a fork in 5 or 6 places. Heat 2 tablespoons of olive oil or butter in a heavy frying pan over medium heat. Cook the boudin in a coil until it is hot through and browned on both sides. One 3-foot length feeds two very well. (*Note:* Cajun cooks also poach boudin blanc in simmering water until good and hot, but I find it easier to handle in a frying pan.) "Eat them by holding the casing in your hands and sucking the insides from the casing" (Raymond Sokolov).

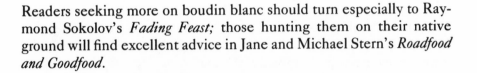

Readers seeking more on boudin blanc should turn especially to Raymond Sokolov's *Fading Feast;* those hunting them on their native ground will find excellent advice in Jane and Michael Stern's *Roadfood and Goodfood.*

Stifádo

❀

Riley was her name; his name was Nikos. She was a friend of a friend, which was how I knew girls then, and I ran into her one late winter's day out shopping on First Avenue on the Lower East Side, buried inside a strangely cut pea coat and swinging a bulging shopping bag. She invited me to come home with her to have supper and meet Nikos, her captive sailor. We walked back together to her apartment on Houston Street, where Nikos was waiting, genial, short, genuinely a sailor, right up to his round, pompomed hat. What his story was, I never found out; he didn't speak a word of English. But somehow he was communicating with Riley, for not only was he in her apartment and his duffle bag on her bed, but she had brought back what he wanted: onions, beef, tomato paste, garlic, a lemon, and two bottles of Greek wine.

While we took off our coats (she, of course, was wearing his) and Riley found her corkscrew, Nikos put together supper, slicing the meat and onions, finely mincing the garlic, setting the oil sizzling in a pot. Riley and I settled in around the kitchen table with the wine, and once he had it all cooking on the stove, Nikos joined us. We stayed there, waiting for it to cook, because the kitchen was where the warmth was, passing around the first bottle of retsina, drinking it out of little orange juice glasses, which were the closest Riley had to wine goblets. The kitchen gradually filled with the aroma of onion and meat and garlic; the windows steamed over; our stomachs grumbled and growled.

It took a long time to cook. Or at least Nikos insisted (by tastes and speculative gestures) that it was coming along but not—yet—ready. Soon, soon. Riley got out her guitar and picked out "Gypsy Rover" and "Sweet William." Nikos sat leaning back in his chair, his legs stuck straight out ahead, his thumbs tucked into his trousers, smiling nonstop. I got drunker than I knew on the retsina, powerful stuff on an empty stomach but a wine you can grow to like, even with its touch of old sneaker. Whatever it did to my head, the retsina unshackled my tastebuds: this onion stew filled up my mouth as no stew ever had before, fragrant, swimming with flavor, but surprisingly, strangely delicate. Nikos had made enough for six and we ate every bit, scraping the pot with our spoons, our bowls with chunks of bread, finishing with it the second bottle of wine.

After supper, Nikos made coffee, throwing the grounds right into the boiling water, spurning Riley's battered aluminum percolator. We sat around sipping it, while Nikos picked up the guitar and began playing fast little jazzy numbers, nothing folkloric, sweat breaking out on his forehead, beating time with one foot. Then he began beaming at me again with that nonstop smile, shaking his head up and down, and I took the hint and staggered off into the night, my stomach full, my head swimming, my nose still full of the scent of onions and beef and of Nikos, a not at all unpleasant combination . . . as if I had spent the evening in the lair of some feral but friendly, culinarily inclined beast.

Years later I encountered the recipe—or near enough to it to bring the dish back to mind—in Elizabeth David's *Mediterranean Food*. But when I made it, there was something wrong, not the few minor things that were easily corrected (she makes no mention of the lemon, for example, or the herbs, and Nikos used tomato paste, not puree, though that may have been a finer point of misunderstanding between him and Riley), but something major. The dish was fine made the way she directed, but it didn't ignite my memory; it was the same, but not the same at all.

It took me a long time to figure out what was wrong, because the error (if error it is) fell in with my own naïve culinary inclinations: she calls for too much meat. Nikos had used no more than a pound of beef to make his *stifádo;* he cut it into thin strips, not the large cubes that all the recipes call for. The result, as he made the dish, was an onion stew flavored with beef, not the other way around, the mouth focusing on a succulent, tomato-coated, beef-flavored mess of onion. . . .

Stifádo

1 pound good beef chuck or
flank steak, cut free of fat
and gristle
Juice of 1 lemon
¼ cup olive oil
3 pounds yellow onions,
peeled and cut into large
chunks

5 or 6 cloves garlic, minced
1 6-ounce can tomato paste
½ cup red wine (or water)
Oregano, marjoram, or rosemary
Coarse salt and freshly
ground pepper

Slice the beef into narrow strips, as if you were going to stir-fry it or make beef Stroganoff. Pour the lemon juice over the meat and then stir it in to coat every piece.

Heat the olive oil until it begins to sizzle in a large, heavy pot with a firmly fitting lid. Put in the beef and, stirring constantly, cook it until it is browned on all sides. As soon as this happens, toss in all the ingredients, including a generous pinch of one of the herbs, and a generous pinch as well of salt and a good grinding of pepper. Stir all this together well, cover the pot firmly, and turn down the heat as low as it will go. The *stifádo* must cook very, very slowly for 4 to 5 hours. Watch the pot—no steam should visibly escape the lid. Listen to the pot—no sounds should emerge, no hissing, sizzling, roiling.

At the end of the third hour, open the lid, gently stir the contents, and taste the stirring spoon for seasoning, adding more salt and pepper as needed. The onions should be reddish golden, not brown, soft but intact, not reduced to mush. Continue to cook for another hour or so at the same low temperature, or until all the liquid has evaporated, leaving off the top of the pot for the last 15 or 20 minutes if this is necessary. Serve with wine and plenty of good bread and butter. (*Note:* I give the dish as I remember Nikos making it and as I myself like it. Cookbooks sometimes call for twice the beef [cubed], half the onions [small white, not large yellow], and for vinegar instead of the lemon juice [or neither]. Some Greeks season *stifádo* with cinnamon and others with coarsely torn Kalamata olives: I find either a good choice.)

(Serves 4)

Fish Muddle

❋

Fish muddles are popular in the coastal plain particularly when the rock [i.e., rock-fish] are running in the Roanoke. A muddle is a stew made of various kinds of fish seasoned with fried fat meat, onions, potatoes, and peppers; at least it starts off that way.   *—The WPA North Carolina Guide*

The Otranto Club boasts of its pine bark stew . . . [which] contains no pine bark, but is a highly seasoned concoction of fish in tomato sauce. On his visit to Florence in 1909, President Taft sampled it and pronounced it good.
                                        —The WPA South Carolina Guide

Esse quam videri [to be good rather than to appear so]
                                        —STATE MOTTO OF NORTH CAROLINA

American cooking was once a patchwork quilt of tiny, idiosyncratic cuisines, where each separate community worked its personal touch on what were then our common foodstuffs—mostly game, pork, poultry, corn, and the produce of the kitchen garden—making a wealth of related but dissimilar dishes with homely names like holy pokes, huffjuffs, and Baptist bread.

When we all got connected together, these dishes were merged and homogenized, subtle distinctions were first muddied and then lost entirely. Take, for example, fish muddle, a stew made out of layers of fish and potatoes and sometimes onions, and seasoned with salt pork. In other words, a dish much like a chowder—a Down East chowder—except that it was made with just a little fish broth instead of milk. Unlike a chowder, you can about eat a muddle with a fork.

Even so, it was still chowder's poor cousin, and while once made up and down the Atlantic coast (including by the fishermen of Cape Ann, who put in crackers), it has now almost vanished from the map. It clings stubbornly to life only in the small towns lost in that mazy network of swamps, creeks, and shallow bays that is the North Carolina coast.

Even there it is not as familiar as it once was. Not half a century ago, it was mentioned with a fondness equal to barbecue in books written by Tar Heels about their state. Like barbecue (and also like chowder) the making of a muddle—preferably out-of-doors on beach or riverbank—was an occasion for a large number of people to come and eat and make merry together at no great expense. Now in North Carolina, as everywhere, people are prosperous enough to afford more expensive eating. Barbecue has endured—pork is not now the bargain it once was—but the muddle hovers on the verge of extinction.

I expect—good as it is—that it would have tumbled right over into oblivion even in North Carolina if it weren't for *South* Carolina's inordinate pride in its own pine bark stew. Tar Heels describe their state with appealing false modesty as "the valley of humility between two mountains of conceit," those being Virginia and—especially— South Carolina, the affectations of the latter state's populace being gently mocked in much the same tone Vermonters aim at their genteeler-than-thou New Hampshire neighbors. It would be a gross libel to call Tar Heels the Yankees of the South, but they do have a little in common with the Green Mountain Boys.

This difference can be seen not only in the nature of the fish stews of these two Southern states, but also in the language with which they like to define them. For, while pine bark stew strains toward bogus epicurianism and boasts of its social connections—even the endorsement of a president (though one memorable only for his girth)— the muddle is a simple, honest dish, about which boasting is nigh impossible, which is the whole point. Tar Heels are equally content to wordlessly set the pine-board cabins of their yeoman citizenry against the plantation manses of the gentry to their south. If you don't get the point, they shrug, too bad for you.

Perhaps the greatest contrast between the two fish stews, however, is the flavoring. Except in its wildest extrapolations, pine bark stew has no pine bark in it, but—worse enough—douses innocent fish with catsup, tomato soup, and Worcestershire sauce. (In recipes sanitized for export, fresh tomatoes are used, but I've never seen a native version that called for them.) Fish muddle, on the other hand, depends on a simple but compelling combination of potato and salt pork, augmented by regional flavorings of celery and hot pepper. This seasoning alone might not be enough to distinguish it from chowder, but that and its stewlike consistency, moistened with a richly fragrant broth, gives it a distinctive, savory identity, one well worth preserving.

Fish Muddle

1 or more fresh rockfish (striped bass) or other lean, white-fleshed fish, such as red snapper, haddock, or whiting, that—when cleaned, scaled, and beheaded—will yield about 2 pounds of fillets*

For the court bouillon:
The fish head (if desired)
2 bay leaves
1 large onion, sliced
1 carrot, cubed
1 stalk celery with leaves, cut
up

7 or 8 peppercorns
5 drops Tabasco sauce (or to taste)
Salt

For the muddle:
¼ pound (approx.) salt pork, cut in small dice
6 scallions, finely chopped (including some of the green part)
2 large stalks celery, finely chopped
4 medium potatoes, peeled and finely diced
Salt and freshly ground pepper

For the garnish:
Minced parsley
Lemon wedges

Clean and scale the fish, cutting off its head and tail. Place the fish and, separately, its head, with the other ingredients for the court bouillon in a large pot. Cover with cold water and simmer until the meat falls from the bones. Take pot from heat and let cool. Remove

*If you prefer, you may substitute fresh, boneless fillets, lessening the work of preparation but also losing some flavor. Use two pounds of a firm, white-fleshed fish (such as cod or haddock). Gently poach the fillets in the court bouillon until they begin to flake apart, remove from heat, and continue with the recipe above. You may also substitute an equal or lesser amount of good olive oil for the salt pork.

the fish and pick out all fish bones from the meat, including any tiny ones. Set meat aside. Strain the broth, discarding its contents. Return it to the pot and reduce over high heat to about 1 cup.

Meanwhile, fry out the fat from the diced salt pork, starting it in about a tablespoon of water. When the cubes are getting brown and the fat is rendered, add the scallions and celery and sauté until soft and translucent. Pour in the reduced broth and the diced potatoes and simmer until the potatoes are just soft, about 15 minutes. Then gently stir in the fish and simmer for an additional 10 minutes, tasting for seasoning, adding pepper to taste and salt if necessary. Ladle the muddle into soup bowls, garnishing each serving with parsley. Serve at once with lemon wedges and Texas sweet corn flapjacks (see page 21).

Pasta in a Paper Bag

⊛

Miracle of miracles, I suddenly found one day that my local super-market had a full bin of real chanterelles, flown in from France and only $4.95 a pound. I brought home a bunch, and then a few more bunches after that. A gentle sauté in butter was sufficient at first, but I grew more ambitious, and initially without much success. They were tasty but not special in scrambled eggs, one recipe recommended to me—the textures and flavors too similar to really get along. Put in a bacon and potato dish from Jane Grigson, they did better, but the dish was still not as redolent of that mushroom's wonderful but fragile fragrance as I wanted.

Pondering this on the walk back from the market, a voice out of nowhere whispered "Alitalia" in my ear. An obscure reference, to be sure, and it took me the rest of the walk to cipher it out. You may remember, way back some ten years at least, an advertisement that airline ran in places like *Gourmet* magazine, showing a burst paper bag full of spaghetti and seafood, and copy that started with the declaration: "Unless you've been to the Trattoria di Ciccio in Amalfi, you don't know how spaghetti should taste."

That was because, unlike you or me, di Ciccio baked his sauce (made of clams and olives) in a paper bag, producing not just "spa-ghetti with sauce on it . . . but spaghetti with sauce in it." After that ad, I recall, Craig Claiborne did an article in which he concocted a seafood pasta recipe along that same idea. I was disappointed: *The New York Times* should have flown him to Amalfi for the *real* one. If a wonderful new way of making pasta isn't news, what is?

❧

Happily, the technique itself is not hard to decipher; even simpler is its rationale. There are some sauces, the familiar meat and tomato one, for example, and pesto, too, I think, where you really want the contrast of the pungent sauce with the bland mass of pasta, but there are other sauces that just don't seem able to stand up to such dilution. Some are delicate and some are not, but what they have in common is that your mouth wants their flavor to permeate the pasta, where instead it seems to slide away from it.

With the paper-bag method, the pasta is cooked in the ordinary way until it is almost done, then mixed with the sauce and put in the oven to bake. Since the bag is collapsed around its contents and sealed, the flavor of the sauce completely penetrates the pasta.

There is also a second advantage. Because no moisture escapes, the cook has the opportunity to get a maximum amount of flavor from a minimum of undiluted sauce, particularly important when only a small amount of the flavoring ingredient is really wanted, as with anchovies or herbs. It is a process that—after a little experimentation—has worked so well I've gone on to use it for a few other unlikely-seeming but terrific-tasting sauces, should fresh chanterelles have not yet reached your own neighborhood.

THE BASIC METHOD.   One advance in paper-bag cookery in the last ten years is the Reynolds ovenproof bag, one of which was successfully used, washed, and reused over and over in this adventure. Have it or a sturdy paper bag open and ready; I set mine inside an oven-ready pot, as a precaution against accident. Preheat oven to 375°F. Cook the spaghetti (in this instance, better store-bought than homemade) in salted water for 3 minutes less than directed by the package: a test strand should still be tough-textured, with a faint crunch of "spine" in the center. Drain but do not shake dry. Immediately pour the pasta into the waiting bag, pour the sauce over the pasta, and close the bag tightly. (An advantage of the Reynolds bag is that you can knot it.) Put the bag, still in its protective pot, into the oven and bake for the time given.

Pasta with Chanterelles in Mushroom-Flavored Olive Oil

1 pound spaghetti
¼ cup mushroom-flavored olive oil*
1 clove garlic, crushed
½ pound fresh chanterelles (or *porcini*), cut—stems and all—into bite-size pieces

2 tablespoons finely minced parsley
Salt and freshly ground pepper

Preheat oven to 375°F. Prepare the bag and cook the pasta as directed above. While it is cooking, heat the oil over low heat in a small sauté pan. Add the garlic, the mushroom pieces, half the parsley, and salt and pepper to taste. Sauté just until the mushrooms become translucent, about 5 minutes. Remove from the heat. Drain the pasta, reserving ½ cup of the pasta water. Put the pasta in the waiting bag, add the sauce, and add the reserved pasta water. Close the bag firmly, put it in the oven (in an ovenproof pan or pot), and bake for 15 minutes. Remove bag from oven, carefully empty its contents into a serving dish, mix well, and sprinkle the remaining tablespoon parsley over the top. Serve at once. Cheese is not necessary. (*Variations:* A little minced prosciutto is traditional; so are a few dried red pepper flakes.)

(Serves 4)

*This is simple to make: Put ⅛ ounce of dried *porcini* mushrooms into a small jar and fill with about 1 cup olive oil, making sure the *porcini* (or cèpes) are well covered. Cap the jar and set on a shelf undisturbed for a month or two. After that, remove the mushrooms as needed: you will find them softened, eventually to the point where they will need no preliminary soaking for use. In exchange, they will leave the olive oil with a superb mushroom flavor, which bestows on this dish deliciously woodsy undertones. However, a good virgin oil will do just as well.

Pasta with Snails in Butter and Wine

½ pound spaghettini
4 tablespoons (½ stick) sweet butter
1 shallot, minced
1 can of 24 snails, drained

½ cup dry white wine
2 tablespoons minced fresh basil or minced parsley
Salt and freshly ground pepper

Preheat oven to 375°F. Prepare the bag and cook the pasta as directed above. While it is cooking, heat the butter over low heat in a small sauté pan. As soon as the butter is melted, add the shallot and sauté over low heat until translucent. Add the snails, wine, and basil or parsley. Heat until wine begins to steam (but not boil) and remove at once from the heat. Taste for seasoning; be generous with the pepper. Drain the pasta without shaking and put in the waiting bag. Pour in the sauce, close the bag firmly, put it in the oven (in an ovenproof pan or pot), and bake for 15 minutes. Serve at once with the rest of the wine, a salad, and good crusty bread. Again, cheese is not necessary.

(Serves 2)

Pasta in Creamy Garlic Sauce

¶ You will find your favorite *aglio e olio* sauce spectacularly good baked in a paper bag—pungent to the highest power. Here is something entirely different, a garlic sauce both subtle and richly mellow.

6 tablespoons olive oil
12 cloves garlic, peeled
1 pound spaghetti

¾ cup light cream
Salt and freshly ground pepper

Heat the olive oil gently in a heavy pot. Put in the garlic, reduce the heat to as low as possible, cover, and cook, turning them occasionally, for 1 hour or until tender and lightly browned. Don't let them scorch. Remove from the heat to cool. Preheat oven to 375°F. Prepare the bag and cook the pasta as directed above. While it is cooking, scrape the garlic and as much oil as possible from their pot into the jar of a blender or the bowl of a food processor fitted with the metal blade.

Blend, and once the garlic and oil is amalgamated into a paste, pour in the cream. Stop processing as soon as the cream is well blended with the oil-garlic mixture. Taste for seasoning, adding salt and pepper to taste.

When pasta is ready, reserve ½ cup of the pasta water. Drain the pasta without shaking and put in the waiting bag. Immediately add the reserved pasta water. Add the sauce, close the bag firmly, put it in the oven (in an ovenproof pan or pot), and bake for 15 minutes. Remove bag from oven, turn pasta into a serving bowl, and mix well. Serve at once, passing around the pepper mill. Grated Parmesan could be served with this; a few dried red pepper flakes might also enhance it.

(Serves 4)

Readers interested in this technique might want to turn to Craig Claiborne's attempt to replicate the di Ciccio recipe in *Craig Claiborne's Favorites, Vol. 2* and to another seafood pasta recipe for a paper bag (though not the di Ciccio one) in Leslie Forbes's *A Taste of Tuscany*.

Succotash

❀

Now, this latter is a curious bit of lore. Why would anyone bother
to freeze already dried vegetables? How—unless they were Eski-
mos—could such a tribe expect that the mixture would stay frozen
and not get soggy and spoiled by the inevitable winter thaws?

But as flawed a bit of historical imagining as I take this to be, it
does touch a nerve of mythic truth. Take away the idle tomahawk
and you have succotash as most school-aged children know it and no
doubt believe it was so given us by the Indians: right out of the deep
freeze. In fact, I'd be willing to hazard that few of my readers have
ever tasted this delicacy—for such it truly is—except defrosted, and
then without anything like happy anticipation either.

Until recently, there were only two standard frozen vegetable mix-
tures—carrot cubes and peas, and baby limas and corn—both equally
horrible. I'm no fan of frozen vegetables of any persuasion, but what
makes these mixes especially awful is that each combines a quick-
with a slow-cooking vegetable, all subtleties sacrificed for a flat-fla-
vored compromise. But it was standard American fare, and regularly,
all during my childhood, I received a salutary dosage. I didn't care
to look succotash in the face after that for many, many years.

Even so, what gave the frozen food industry the courage to reduce
succotash to a mouthful of two-tone cellulose was the common knowledge that the dish had been pretty much done in by its native cooks.
Yankee eaters like good food, even good Yankee food, but only if
they can't find something cheaper. There are exceptions to this, now
and then, but the fact remains that they take far more pleasure in

talking down the grocer's price for a dented can of baked beans than they choose to find in the real bean pot.

And the same is true with succotash, a dish ruined by nothing but plain indifference. I can prove this by simply quoting the standard recipe given by Fannie Farmer to New England cooks for over half a century, as brief as it is blasphemous:

Succotash: cut hot boiled corn from the cob; add equal quantity of hot boiled shelled beans; season with butter and salt; reheat before serving.

There is so much wrong here that it takes the breath away, but the revealing flaw is calling for the kernels to be cut from boiling-hot cobs: even cooks with hands heat-hardened from wood-burning stoves would balk at that. What I suspect is that this is a pro forma disguise that fooled nobody: Yankee families were treated to last night's leftover corn on the cob as this night's succotash, congratulating themselves on their frugality even as they gnawed away.

So it is, while Southerners form societies to preserve the perfection of black-eyed peas and argue vehemently the merits of ham bone versus pickled pork in red beans and rice, the mention of succotash stirs less excitement in the Yankee heart than finding a dime in a pay-phone coin return. The best New England can offer by way of chauvinistic boasting about the stuff comes from the diary of a Vermont farmer, whose single culinary reference for an entire year was a laconic "This day I din'd upon Succotash" (quoted by Evan Jones in *American Food*).

Perhaps succotash is just too easy to make to establish a claim on Down East pride: all that need be understood is that it is a quintessential summer dish. To be eaten at its best it requires just-picked sweet corn and equally garden-fresh shell beans. In New England, the traditional bean is the cranberry, mottled in brilliant red and white. It is still found in farmer's markets in season and, when young and sweet, cooks as quickly as the corn, bringing the dish a wonderfully delicate flavor. Elsewhere, limas remain ubiquitous. For four people, shell about one and a half cups' worth of the beans and set aside. Now shuck and scrape enough corn kernels from raw ears to make two cups of corn, saving as much juice as possible (this will be four to six ears, depending).

Boil up the scraped cobs in unsalted water (salt toughens beans), add the beans, lower the heat, and simmer until they are soft but not mushy, which, depending on the type and youth of the bean, can take from three to fifteen minutes or more—only tasting will tell. When done, quickly pour off the water, pluck out the cobs from the pot, and pour the shucked corn and its juices in with the beans. Add a generous gob of sweet butter, salt to taste, and a generous grinding of pepper. Stir gently over the heat until the corn has cooked in its own juices and the butter has completely melted. Serve at once. Feeds four as a side dish and two as a meal.

Some cooks add a cup of cream to the dish and cut down on the butter. The dish is richer but not better for it. Other cooks want to put in salt pork or bacon, and with this I do have a quarrel: it is sneaking salt into the beans again. Succotash can also mean a slow-cooked pot made of dried beans and parched corn, a tasty variation on the theme of baked beans. Here, salt pork makes sense: it does no harm when added an hour or so into the cooking.

However, to show I am no strict constructionist except in the matter of proportion and cooking times, consider the following, my own working of a recipe originally from Molly Finn's *Summer Feasts:*

Succotash with Fresh Tomatoes and Basil Butter

1½ cups freshly shelled cranberry beans or other shell beans, about 2 pounds in the pod
¼ cup minced fresh basil
4 tablespoons (½ stick) sweet butter
1 medium red salad onion, chopped

2 cups sweet corn kernels (cut from about 5 or 6 ears), liquid reserved with kernels and cobs reserved
3 or 4 medium dead-ripe tomatoes, coarsely chopped
Salt and freshly ground pepper

Simmer the shelled beans in unsalted water with the corncobs until soft but not mushy, checking often so they do not overcook (depending on the youth and kind of bean, this will take from 3 to 15 minutes or more). While the beans cook, use a knife to work and scrape the basil into the butter until it is nicely amalgamated. Place the onion in a small serving bowl. When the beans are just soft, they are done. Quickly drain off the cooking water and discard the corn-cobs. Combine the corn kernels and their liquid with the beans, add the basil butter, and season to taste with salt and pepper. Return to the heat and cook just until the corn is done and the basil butter barely melted. Pour into 4 bowls, strew the tomatoes over, and serve at once, with the chopped onions passed for diners to add as they wish.

(Serves 4 as a side, a feast for 2 or 3)

There is no dignity in the bean. Corn, which in my garden grows alongside the bean and, so far as I can see, with no affectation of superiority, is, however, the child of song. It waves in all literature. But mix it with beans, and its high tone is gone. Succotash is vulgar. It is the bean in it.

—CHARLES DUDLEY WARNER (1828–1900)

Ultimate Cheesecake
(With a Note on Lindy's)

❁

Perhaps the worst culinary temptation to ever lure a cook astray is the misguided belief that there is, somewhere, the perfect recipe for a favorite dish, best of the best, against which all other versions pale by comparison, and that the cook's only task is to find it. More cookbooks have been bought in vain because they promised the hopeful the consummate chocolate chip cookie, the nonpareil of pot roasts, the quintessential cassoulet or carrot cake, only to have the purchaser discover—too late—that each of us tastes the world with a different tongue.

Perfect dishes do appear now and again in this all-too-imperfect world, but perfect recipes, never. It took me a long time to learn this. For years I kept a special file of "best" recipes, not because they had worked well for me, but because their composers assured me that there was nothing in the world that would ever come close to them. I always felt it was not my place to judge these recipes; if anything, it was they who judged me.

The prize of this collection was an article by Craig Claiborne, called "The Ultimate Cheesecake," published in *The New York Times Magazine* many years ago. I suspect I still have it, somewhere down at the bottom of the recipe drawer, the newsprint brown now and the edges tattered. I used to take it out now and again and read it longingly, but I never made the recipe. The "ultimate cheesecake" required a special pan . . . hazelnuts carefully roasted in advance . . . and three hours in the oven, two baking and one resting. It was one of those things that stood just on the other side of the line we draw between efforts we'll make and efforts we'll consider making . . . sometime.

In fact, that recipe had the unintended effect of convincing me that cheesecake-making was the province of heroes (or bakeries), not me. The ultimate was beyond me; the rest not worth making. So, for years, I sat on my hands, until, by chance, a slice of this ultimate cheesecake happened to come my way. I didn't like it. To my palate, those carefully toasted hazelnuts left behind the same peanut-butter overtones that for me plague most nut-flavored versions, and I found the texture strangely resistant to the tongue.

Mind you, this is meant as no slur on the Claiborne recipe. My point is that "ultimate" recipes are something you earn, not find. He built up his perfect cheesecake in response to the promptings of his palate, not mine: I could savor his pleasure in it through his prose, but not, as it turned out, in my mouth. If I were the better reader, I would have let this enthusiasm inspire me to chase down my own dream cheesecake instead of clinging to the ignoble expectation that he had done all the work and all I had to do was skim the cream.

Ironically, as it turned out, cheesecake-making was not at all the arcane mystery that I had made of it. Most cheesecakes are easier to make from scratch than other cakes and hardly more expense. In fact, this is so much the case that my first rule in baking them is this succinct negative: the more elaborate the recipe, the more you should distrust the result.

Simplicity is the cheesecake's only secret. It may be feathery light or lusciously thick; it may be made of cream or cottage or ricotta cheese. But, to be true to itself, it must have as the foundation of its flavor and texture the delicate, sweet-and-sour presence of fresh-churned cream. The challenge to the cook is to coax out the very best from a few simple but very good ingredients, not to mask them with fruit glazes, praline, nuts, chocolate, or heaven knows what else.

Genuinely classic cheesecake recipes have no other flavors added than a dash of vanilla and a little fresh lemon (or mix of citrus flavors). That citrus tang is there simply to prod the tastebuds into noticing the delicate flavor of the dish itself, just as it does in a cup of tea or on a fillet of sole. The taste itself should fall just at the border of the placeable, whether lemon, a dribble of cognac, a few drops of orange or rose water, or a grating of nutmeg. A vague rumor, enough only to set the tongue to wondering.

Why, then, the mob of monstrosities that clutter the cooking pages? Well, for one thing, it's called a cake, and cakes without frosting sell no cookbooks. For another, those gorgeous concoctions covered with photogenic fruit preserves, flavorful-looking swirls, stripes, or layers, are all designed to whet appetites in eaters for whom the cheesecake was never intended: *sweet-toothed* eaters.

Outside of New York City (where no rule holds for long), cheesecake is the traditional steakhouse dessert, perfect punctuation to a meal of meat. Not that cheesecake and beef are natural complements, but those with an intense craving for the well-marbled (and well-salted) sirloin often have a compensating lack of interest in sweets. They want only a final, tasty, unctuous mouthful to round off their meal.

This is a minority position. To most people, dessert means a slice of cake or a handful of cookies, not the cheese board and the fruit bowl, just as the words "apple pie" summon up a vision of vanilla ice cream, not the once-familiar wedge of Cheddar. The after-dinner savory is out of fashion; those of us who yearn for it must wait a discreet span of time before reaching for the salted nuts, while our opposites suck smugly on their little green mints. Cheesecake has become a battlefield between these two parties, half spoiled for both: too sweet for one and too rich for the other—and a universal cause of heartburn.

Not that a good cheesecake isn't sweet, but it should be no more sweet-seeming than a cold glass of milk. It is exactly this clean, fresh, dairy taste that makes a cheesecake so refreshing to the palate after a heavy meal, no matter how richly concocted it may be. After all, it takes only a thin slice to leave the mouth happily savoring the lingering traces of its creamy passage.

Instead . . . well, let's take a quick run through some of the usual crimes committed in its name. First, the graham cracker crust. There's no such thing as a graham cracker, only the graham cookie. The crust is too sweet and coarse-tasting a container for its gentle contents, and it is the contents that have been forced to yield. Most cheesecakes can stand without a crust: the pan needs only a dusting with fine cake or bread crumbs to give definition to the cake's edge.

Chocolate is out of place in a cheesecake because its cocoa-butter richness drowns out all the sour notes of the cheese, however much it melds with the taste of the cream. Save it then for your mousse or *pots de crème*, where no sour taste need intrude. Nut oils have the same problem; they work against the flavors in the dairy fats to muddy each other's subtleties, resulting in a flat, peanut-buttery taste.

Finally, there's that omnipresent fruit glaze. Fruit and cheesecake are a wonderful combination, as you'll discover if you toss strawberries or raspberries in a little sugar and serve them fresh on the side. It's the excess of sugar that throws our tastebuds off-balance; what the mouth notes is the taste of the glaze, combining it with the texture of the cheesecake. It tastes good—if the glaze is made with real fruit—but half the pleasure of the cheesecake is completely lost.

The ultimate cheesecake? Rich, delicate, subtly flavored . . . as my tongue imagines it, a litany of all the pleasures of which cream is capable, impossibly enhanced. And each cheesecake maker works toward this fantasy goal in his or her own way, playing sour cream against heavy cream against *crème fraîche*, cottage cheese against farmer cheese against ricotta or even goat cheese, cream cheese against Neufchâtel or some other fresh cream cheese. Or perhaps simply changing the texture by altering the ingredients themselves—whipping the cream or separating and then beating the whites before folding either into the mixture—working out an ever-shifting set of variations in harmony and counterpoint.

Happily, cheesecake invites such play. Unlike a real cake, where exact proportions are essential for success, the underpinnings of cheesecake chemistry is a simple egg custard; there need only be enough eggs present for the mixture to set (and since the egg presence enhances the smoothness of the cheesecake's texture, there is usually more than enough). Once a general sense of proportion is fixed in the mind, an equal bulk of one kind of cheese or cream can replace another without much worry of a resulting fiasco, though taste and texture may not turn out exactly as the cook intends.

This freedom has resulted in any number of cheesecakes worthy of an enthusiast's acquaintance, far too many for me to supply recipes for here. In the ones that follow, I want only to convince you that commitment to the simple combination of a few high-quality ingredients—freshest sweet cream and sweetest butter, real lemon juice and grated peel, truly choice cream cheese (the best is made in small batches without vegetable gum)—can produce, without trauma or exorbitant expense, so many subtly differing possibilities of ultimate delight.

THE RECIPES

PREPARING THE PAN. These recipes all call for a springform pan, simply because it is easier to unmold than a standard pan, but a heavyweight cake pan will also serve. Generously butter the bottom and sides (2 tablespoons for a large pan). Then, if you wish, a coating of crumbs or very finely chopped nuts can be added, using ½ cup to coat the inside of a 7- or 8-inch pan, or 1 cup for a 9- or 10-inch one. Shake the crumbs gently, turning the pan for an even coating. (*Note:* If your springform pan, like mine, is old, it may leak a little with very liquid batter. Simply wrap foil tightly around the outside of the pan.)

PREPARING THE BATTER. Preheat oven. Have all ingredients (especially cheese and eggs) at room temperature. Mix ingredients one at a time in an electric mixer or food processor (fitted with the metal blade), periodically scraping down the bowl. Proceed as follows: Cut cream cheese into chunks and beat until soft and creamy; beat in sugar bit by bit (superfine blends most easily); then the eggs, one by one, followed by any remaining ingredients. Fold in beaten egg whites or whipped cream (if either is used) at the very last. Beat in each ingredient just enough to thoroughly blend—don't overbeat. Finally, rotate the pan in several quarter turns to settle batter and release air bubbles.

BAKING. Cheesecakes bake best at lower temperatures and for longer times, rather than vice versa, with slightly higher temperatures required when the batter is very moist. The temperature given here is 300°F, but you may find you get better results at a cooler 250°F or a warmer 325°F—which is the recommended range. Cooking times will also vary even at the same temperature, given the varying heat-retentive qualities of different ovens, so doneness is best tested by simply giving the cake a soft shake. The cheesecake is done when there is still a faint, jellylike quiver to its center ("just set"). It will continue to cook after you take it from the oven, so don't let it overbake.

Remove it to a wire rack and let it rest for an hour before releasing the springform sides (the cake will itself indicate its readiness by starting to pull away). Then put it in the refrigerator to chill a few more hours before serving. Don't wrap a cheesecake in plastic wrap when you put it in the refrigerator; cover it loosely with wax paper.

A *Simple Cream Cheese Cheesecake*

1 pound (2 8-ounce packages)
  cream cheese
⅔ cup sugar

3 eggs
1 teaspoon grated lemon rind
½ teaspoon vanilla

Following basic directions above, blend the filling, prepare 7-inch springform pan (including crust if desired), and bake at 300°F in preheated oven for about 50 minutes, or until just set. Cool and unmold as directed above.

CREAM AND COTTAGE CHEESE CHEESECAKE. Follow the directions for the Simple Cream Cheese Cheesecake above, but substitute ½ pound of cottage cheese for half the cream cheese. Use small-curd cottage cheese and push it through a sieve with the back of a rubber scraper before beating it in with the cream cheese. For an old-fashioned flavor, substitute ½ cup of honey for the sugar and omit the lemon rind, sprinkling ½ teaspoon of ground cinnamon over the top before baking. (Or, even better, use orange blossom honey, and omit all other flavorings.)

Cream Cheese and Sour Cream Cheesecake

¶ This is a New England favorite, Cheesecake Windyknowe, named after a restaurant, which, like Lindy's, found immortality in its cheesecake recipe.

1½ pounds (3 8-ounce packages) cream cheese
¾ cup sugar
3 eggs
3 cups sour cream

1 teaspoon fresh lemon juice
2 teaspoons grated orange rind
Few drops vanilla
1 tablespoon soft butter

Following basic directions above, blend the filling, prepare 9-inch springform pan (including crust if desired), and bake at 325°F in preheated oven for about an hour, or until just set. Cool and unmold as directed above.

Cream Cheese, Sour Cream, and Heavy Cream Cheesecake

¶ Here, a perfectly balanced texture of rich and delicate.

1 8-ounce package cream cheese
1 cup heavy cream
1 cup sour cream

¾ cup sugar
4 eggs
1 teaspoon fresh lime juice
2 teaspoons grated lime rind

Following basic directions above, blend the filling, prepare 7-inch springform pan (including crust if desired), and bake at 300°F in preheated oven for about an hour, or until just set. Cool and unmold as directed above.

A *Cheesecake of Cream Cheese, Sour Cream, and Beaten Egg Whites*

¶ This time, feathery light . . . but still blissfully creamy.

1½ pounds (3 8-ounce packages) cream cheese
1½ cups sour cream
¾ cup sugar

1 teaspoon vanilla
½ teaspoon grated lemon rind
3 egg whites

Following basic directions above, blend the filling together, using ½ cup of the sugar. In a separate bowl, beat the egg whites until soft peaks form, then beat in the ¼ cup reserved sugar, bit by bit, until absorbed and whites hold stiff peaks but are not yet dry. Fold egg whites gently but thoroughly into batter using large spatula. Prepare 9-inch springform pan (including crust if desired), and pour in batter. Bake at 325°F in preheated oven for about 1 hour, or until top of cake is lightly puffed and top edges are golden. (Center should still be slightly soft.) Cool and unmold as directed above.

LINDY'S "FAMOUS ORIGINAL CHEESECAKE"

> The cheesecake is genuine "New York cheesecake," made according to a recipe the Mosca family secured from Lindy's before it bit the dust.
> —JANE AND MICHAEL STERN, *Roadfood and Goodfood*

This quote, lifted from the Sterns' review of Mosca's, the fabled roadhouse on the outskirts of New Orleans, shows how pervasive the Lindy's mystique has become and how far it has spread. Why else would one of the country's best restaurants brag of having obtained the cheesecake recipe from one memorable for absolutely nothing else?

Lindy's restaurant is no more. By the time it expired, its sole purpose was providing a tourist audience for people who wanted to be taken as Damon Runyon characters. And, apart from the cheesecake, memories of the menu have not endured. The cheesecake, however, has: it is the richest, mellowest mouthful of creamy sweetness that ever stuck your tongue to the roof of your mouth.

Alas, though I lived in New York during Lindy's last days, I never ate there. So I have had to depend on the kindness of strangers for the recipe—about which there is surprising unanimity. This I credit to Lindy's waiters, who, it seems, were more than willing to part with the recipe for a discreetly palmed bill. Anyway, Jim Villas (writing in *Esquire*, July 1982) records this as the method his father used to obtain it—slipping "our longtime and trustworthy waiter, Sammy, a crisp ten-spot."

Trustworthy Sammy must have done a brisk business. The secret recipe appears in several other sources, including *The World Atlas of Food*, edited by Jane Grigson, Time/Life's *American Cooking*, and John F. Mariani's *Dictionary of American Food & Drink*. Let's hope he really did know the secret: waiters aren't always privy to the pastry chef's recipes.

But we'll take this one on trust until something better comes along: the formula makes as moist and silky-smooth a cake as ever caused tongue to shiver in delight, the flavor a delicate balance of dairy sweet and citrus sour, with the faintest whisper of vanilla.

The original Lindy's is an extremely rich cake, albeit so smooth on the tongue that it takes a few bites for its cloying weight to register. Then, even while each bite registers "good, good," the total mass in the stomach registers "tilt, tilt." By increasing the proportion of cream (and especially sour cream) to that of cream cheese, this effect is lightened, though at the expense of the texture, which becomes wispier. Instead, I think, the cake is meant to be eaten in a small portion, by the tiny bite.

With that in mind, I have cut down the original to a more manageable size, and—though purists will scream—omitted the traditional sugar-cookie crust (the pan was lined with sugar-cookie dough and prebaked to a golden tint before the batter was added). Instead, I just butter my pan and generously coat it with some clean-flavored crumb, such as from slightly stale pound cake or about half a pound of pulverized choice sugar cookies (Pepperidge Farm's "Bordeaux" cookies work famously). After all, why double the time it takes to make the cake for a crust that makes a rich cake even richer?

A Version of Lindy's Legendary Cheesecake

1¼ pounds (2½ 8-ounce
   packages) cream cheese at
   room temperature
¾ cup sugar
1½ tablespoons flour

1 teaspoon grated lemon rind
1 teaspoon grated orange rind
Few drops vanilla
3 eggs plus 1 yolk
2 tablespoons heavy cream

For the crust:
   ½ cup finely pulverized dry cake or cookie crumbs
   2 tablespoons sweet butter

Preheat oven to 300°F. Generously butter a 7-inch springform pan
and coat it with as many of the cake or cookie crumbs as will adhere.
Gently pour out excess. Prepare filling by beating cream cheese until
creamy and smooth. Slowly beat in the sugar, and when well incorporated, beat in the flour, the lemon and orange rind, the vanilla, the
eggs, and the heavy cream. Pour the filling into the prepared pan and
bake for 1 hour. After 50 minutes, start to check the cake: it will be
done when its center just barely quivers. Remove to a rack and let
cool, removing the sides of the springform pan after an hour's time.
Then let cool in the refrigerator for a few hours before serving.

III

KITCHEN DIARY

Spring

JAMES BEARD died in January. To this reader, he was a generous-souled but deeply complex man with an actor's genius for putting before the world the hearty Falstaff it wanted of him. He wrote a memorable book, *Delights and Prejudices*, and many truly useful ones. He had a gargantuan appetite but also a bold one: his great gift to our cooking was this special combination of pleasable palate and restless curiosity. If neither appetite nor curiosity were ever completely appeased, it is because, like many people with perfect sensual memory, his adult life was haunted by the feast of his childhood, an acuity of flavor that nothing in later years could ever hope to match. His cooking changed with the times, but not his heart.

VALENTINE'S DAY, fifteen years ago. I was in graduate school and casually seeing a woman who drove a tiny ancient British car, a Morris Midget or such, the sort of vehicle that pulls up in the center of the circus ring and disgorges a crowd of clowns. It was older than she was and kept just this side of operative with a calculated mixture of cosseting and cursing.

This same night—Valentine's treat—we were going to see *Wild Strawberries* at the art cinema. But when she arrived to pick me up, the Midget wheezed, shuddered, and died. Clogged gas filter. By the time it was removed, flushed clean, and grit blown out of the gas line, she was a mess and we were both soaked from the slushy rain. No movie. Instead, she took me over to her place, where she took a quick shower to get off the grease, and emerged in nothing much more than shirt and underpants to cook us a compensatory dinner.

Remember, this was then, not now. Her state of undress was not an invitation but an almost innocent statement of trust, declaring she felt so easy in my company that she just wore what she would have if she'd been home alone. Young women made statements like that then. And since this itself was one giant step in my expectations, I was happy to sit there watching as she made us our supper, two steak subs.

At that time of my life, almost every kind of food was a still new adventure, and I found my eyes drawn away from her pink cleanness, captured by the grace and rigor of her method. The oil heated to a hazy film, the beef chuck cut razor thin and heaped in two huge mounds, the large-size can of Pennsylvania Dutch sliced mushrooms carefully drained and set to wait. The onion slices were thrown in, let brown, scraped to the side of the pan. The steak and mushrooms then had their turn in a sizzling cloud of steam and smoke. Turned over, turned over, turned over, the onions worked back in, the whole savory mess swung with dextrous spatula into two split submarine rolls—and topped with—the pièce de résistance!—a slathering of Carriage House brand Béarnaise sauce.

The very thought of it causes stirrings still, not all of them gastronomic. Ah, the food of love! It isn't all champagne and violins . . . not by a long shot.

ENDIVE. Salad of the season: Belgian endive pulled into leaves and carefully washed, then broken into bite-size bits and dressed with hot meat juices from a piece of sautéed chicken or pan-fried steak. Crisp and peppery and very good left alone like this, without bothering it with lettuce or onion. My only way of cooking it is to wilt the separate leaves quickly in the same meat juices or maybe melted butter. Rich people can afford to slowly braise whole heads in butter or cream, which sounds terrific, but any recipe that calls for it to be steamed or boiled should be destroyed for good. The result is a stringy, soggy, sour mess that made me hate the stuff for years—until I finally learned better.

FISH ROE. Browsing in the fish section of a local supermarket, I noticed some packages tucked in a corner marked simply "Spawn." They were salmon pink and looked more like sweetbreads than anything else. What fish they were spawn of—and once hoped to spawn into—the woman behind the counter didn't know. But at $1.79 a pound, they seemed worth a try. None of my cookbooks mentioned "spawn" and I decided to treat it like shad roe, a pricy delicacy not due on the market for several more weeks.

Most shad roe recipes direct that it be poached, in some instances beyond any conscionable limits. I don't think it should be poached at all, just given the lightest coating of flour and quickly sautéed in butter no more than four minutes to a side. This is how I treated the spawn, using plenty of butter, already flavored with a minced shallot, a few capers, a spritz of lemon juice, pepper and salt. I got them off the flame just in time; the interior still moist and pink and meltingly soft, with that delicate lobstery roe flavor, bland even, but picked up nicely by the seasoned butter—not a bad bargain at all.

SEED CATALOGUES.   My gardening is an erratic thing, thanks to a peripatetic life-style and a not-very-green thumb, but, even so, I've managed to have something like a garden almost everywhere I've lived—and when I didn't, felt the lack of one. Even now, living in a rented apartment in an almost-urban neighborhood, I have a plot—thanks to the tolerance of the landlord—in the front yard, a minuscule six feet square, out of which I draw lettuces and peas in the spring, and a mass of tomatoes and basil in the summer. (I had a brief spell as an "intensive gardener" and also grew beans, corn, and cornichons, too, but that phase has ebbed.)

Unlike many home gardeners, I can't hope to feed myself by what I grow and have no intention of reaping bumper harvests of the exact same vegetables that fill the farmer's market at give-away prices even as mine are ripening. So I look for better things. This is especially the case in tomatoes, where even the so-called vine-ripened ones are a disappointment, whether from Holland or Israel or the nearby farmer. I use French seeds and produce sultry beauties that lie so warm and firm and soft in the hand and fill the mouth with melting flavor. Not only corn, but fresh peas, too, are best when you can pick them yourself and rush them to boiling water. Corn, however, is impractical in my plot; peas, not.

Consequently, I don't feel quite the armchair traveler when I pick up my seed catalogues and sift through them for the scent of spring, the feel of soft loam crumbling beneath the fingers. I read them all, but I favor the small producers, companies whose catalogues still have the shape of an individual gardener's personality, a passion for the particular.

Here are some of my favorites from the current crop:

Suffolk Herbs is an English firm that specializes in organically grown herbs and British wildflower seeds. Their list of these, especially the latter, is impressive. But they also offer a good selection of oriental and European vegetable seeds, including a wide variety of Italian salad greens. Prices are reasonable although a minimum order is required of £5 (about ten seed packets). Their catalogue is informative but not illustrated. To get it send four international reply coupons (65 cents each at the post office) to: Sawyer's Farm, Little Cornard, Sudbury, Suffolk CO10 ONY, England.

The Cook's Garden offers the home gardener a superb selection of salad greens. Its attractive (and free) catalogue has 35 varieties of lettuce, 13 of chicory, and 28 unusual salad greens—perpetual spinach beet, good King Henry, miner's lettuce (potherb), and assorted cresses and *mâches*, plus hard-to-find vegetable seeds for such as Italian cherry tomatoes especially for drying, Provençal peas, and so on. Write them at: P.O. Box 65, Londonderry, VT 05148.

Herb Gathering, Inc. Paula Winchester is the successor to J. A. Demonchaux of Kansas City, who helped pioneer the introduction of French seeds to American home gardners, and who was my own original (and then only) source for French tomatoes, radicchio, and *mange-tout* green beans. Since Paula's own interest is herbs, she's expanded the original list to include such nonculinary herbs as sea lavender, blackberry lilies, and feverfew, but the larger part of her catalogue is still devoted to French vegetable seeds, including Welsh onion (*ciboule*), cornichons, French endive, *petits pois*, a Provençal eggplant, and much more. Write to: 5742 Kenwood, Kansas City, MO 64110.

Johnny's Selected Seeds. Albion, Maine, isn't far up as Maine goes, but far up enough to give them a claim to their specialty: seeds for farmers with a short growing season and a difficult climate, whether for commercial or home growing. Their catalogue offers seeds specially suited to cold, and accompanies them with germination guides and growing schedule charts for careful planting and maximum production. Among their specialty seeds are Rhode Island White-Cap flint, the corn that makes Rhode Island jonnycakes (see page 23) the special thing they are. Write to: Johnny's Selected Seeds, Albion, ME 04910.

Le Marché. Charlotte Glenn and Georgeanne Brennan produce a handsome and informative catalogue offering a wide range of specialty vegetable seeds, often specifically sought out in their places of native origin and so available nowhere else. They carefully explain the provenance, growing, and—sometimes—the cooking of their vegetables, including tasty recipes (their comments on preparing fava beans entirely changed my attitude toward a legume I had previously felt fit only for horses). They offer a wide range of lettuces and salad greens; various corns, including blue tortilla and white *pozole* corn from the Southwest and broom corn (for making brooms—instructions included); a wide range of sweet and hot peppers (including a fiery Thai one); and some especially superior zucchini (i.e., tender, flavorful—see page 104), one from France and the other from Algeria. They also carry a Provençal pumpkin, *musquée de Provence,* that is the perfect *courge* for Pumpkin Tian (see pages 43 and 45). Their catalogue is $2. Write to: P.O. Box 566, Dixon, CA 95620.

Vermont Seed Company. Although Vermont Seed's handsome catalogue offers a wide range of vegetables (and special gardening supplies), their specialty is beans, page after page after page of them. For example, they offer the true cranberry bean, an heirloom shelling bean that cooks in minutes and is the perfect complement to fresh corn for true New England succotash (see page 137). They also offer hard-to-find Swedish brown beans, which I think make a better baked bean than the ubiquitous navy bean, and have a whole section on cowpeas: Mississippi silver, pink eye purple hull, crimson Arkansas. In short, a real find. Write them at: Garden Lane, Bomoseen, VT 05732.

GARLIC SHOOTS. If you have a head of garlic start to sprout before you've had a chance to use it, don't throw it out. Break it apart into separate cloves and plant them in the garden or in a plant box with some good potting soil. The resulting young green shoots, called *aglio fresco,* are much favored in Italy for their flavor, especially in *frittata* and *insalata mista* (simple mixed salad).

According to Elizabeth Romer in *The Tuscan Year,* Italian markets sell them in bunches like scallions, which they resemble. She describes their flavor as "excellent, not being particularly hot and garlicky." In fact, the long, green, leafy part is quite delicate and makes a delicious salad herb where actual raw garlic might be too overpowering a presence and elsewhere—finely snipped—a more robust replacement for chives. Here is a frittata recipe with garlic shoots, adapted to my own taste from *The Tuscan Year:*

Frittata with Aglio Fresco

2 fresh garlic shoots
2 tablespoons good fruity olive oil, plus a little extra
4 eggs
Coarse salt and freshly ground pepper

Rinse the garlic shoots, shake dry, and cut away and discard any flabby remnant of the bulb. Slice the stalks into tiny rounds or slivers, including all of the green. Heat 2 tablespoons of the olive oil in an omelette pan and add the garlic, gently sautéing it until it softens and the white parts are golden-tinged. Beat the eggs, seasoning them to taste with salt and pepper. Turn up the heat and, making sure the garlic bits are evenly distributed across the bottom of the pan, pour in the eggs. As soon as the underneath of the eggs has set, turn the heat down as low as possible and let the mixture firm.

At the exact moment the top is no longer runny, turn the *frittata* out of the pan upside down onto a warmed plate. Add a little more oil to the pan, turn up the heat, and—when the oil is hot—slide the *frittata* back in, so what was formerly the top is now underneath, being crisped by the hot oil; this takes only a minute. Serve at once, cut in wedges, with a little green salad, and some good bread and fresh red wine.

(Serves 2)

AT BREAKFAST IN FRANCE.   An observation: "[It] is usual and perfectly polite to dip your roll or croissant or even bits of bread into your coffee, and then fish it out with a spoon, if you are unable to keep hold of it with your fingers. Very few British grownups can sincerely enjoy doing this, but children often do."—Pamela Vandyke Price.

. . . And its exception: "Miss Fisher . . . broke a croissant in two and dipped it with perfect naturalness into her coffee, smiling away at herself for some interior reason and not observing Henrietta's surprise. Henrietta was sure you did not do this to bread . . . she sat biting precisely into her half of roll, wondering how one could bear to eat soppy bread."—Elizabeth Bowen.

A Greek Lenten Custard of Eggplant, Yogurt, and Fresh Herbs

¶ Pureed eggplant and yogurt are a familiar Middle Eastern combination, here baked into a savory custard that will serve three or four as a light main meal or up to six as a side course.

1 large eggplant (about 1½ pounds)	1 teaspoon salt
4 eggs	Generous grinding of pepper
1 cup plain yogurt	¼ teaspoon minced fresh oregano or dill
2 tablespoons good fruity olive oil	2 teaspoons fresh lemon juice
	¼ cup finely minced parsley

Preheat oven to 325°F. Peel the eggplant and cut the flesh into 1-inch cubes. Set 2 quarts of salted water to boil in a large saucepan. Add the eggplant, reduce to a simmer, and cook until tender—about 15 minutes. Drain the eggplant well, pressing gently to remove some of its liquid. Then transfer to a mixing bowl and beat until smooth. Stir in the eggs, yogurt, olive oil, salt, pepper, oregano or dill, lemon juice, and parsley, beating until the mixture is well amalgamated and creamy.

Pour into a buttered 1½-quart baking dish, setting this on a wire rack or trivet inside a larger pan. Place in the oven and pour boiling water into the larger pan to a level two-thirds up the side of the baking dish. Bake, uncovered, for 50 minutes, or until the custard is nicely set. Let rest 15 minutes before serving.

GUESTS NOT TO INVITE TO DINNER   (I). Thomas Carlyle. "Carlyle . . . silenced everyone by haranguing on the advantage of silence. After dinner, Babbage, in his grimmest manner, thanked Carlyle for his very interesting lecture on silence."—Dinner at Charles Darwin's; source, alas, lost.

SOUP GREENS.   Early February. Outside, sullen lumps of what once was snow have taken on the grayish hue and steellike consistency of matter determined to last the millenium. Jack "the Knife" Frost rattles white knuckles mockingly against the windowpanes. The ground too hard to unearth their stash of acorns, squirrels huddle together like hobos, blowing on their fingers and conspiring against the bird feeder. Spring seems as likely to come round again as my twenty-first birthday.

Thus I linger long in the produce aisle of the supermarket, newly flooded with a burst of the year's first greens, come from somewhere far south, a crisp wave of verdure that crams the display case with not only a host of different lettuces but bundle after bundle of fresh greens—mustard, turnip, dandelion, and collard, along with kale, Swiss chard, broccoli rabe, even bundles of baby spinach. . . .

Most times of the year, I must confess, I would have slid on by. My palate turns on a salt/fat axis, not a sweet/sour one, and the mere unexpected whiff of turnip greens can flip off my appetite as quick as the snick of a light switch. But this time of year, when my green vegetable intake seems a Ping-Pong match between broccoli and frozen peas, my vitamin-starved system is aglow with desire. Suddenly, my mind is conjuring up a bowl of soup, shredded leaves floating in their own savory broth, spiced with a dash of hot pepper, tempered with a stir of olive oil or even a golden puddle of chicken fat.

Soup greens. It's worth pausing at this point to note how much good homemade soup has become an endangered species in our cooking. For one thing, Campbell's has managed to slot the whole tribe as a "convenience item" only worth serving in combination with something else—like a toasted cheese sandwich—that will hide the tin-can taste. Another thing is that good soups are often simple, and simple foods don't look like much on the recipe page, where the list of ingredients must capture our attention. And that simplicity doesn't help them when we want something easy; simple and easy aren't near the same thing, when easy means just opening a can.

To fall in with the natural rhythms of our cooking, soup has to be an ad hoc proposition, pulled out of the scraps in the refrigerator and the surplus from garden or grocer's shelf. And not for any moral reason, but because the cook in us takes secret delight in taking some random bits and pieces and coming up with a savory whole. Greens are excellent candidates for soup for just this reason. Really, for most of us, they are garbage by nature, the stuff that ordinarily we would throw away, trimmings and leavings. Imagine a plate of greens and you'll think up a pungent-smelling, acrid-tasting, slimy mass coated with bacon grease. But think of the soup pot and something else entirely opens up. After all, generations of Southerners haven't been dipping their corn bread into "pot likker" for nothing. This stuff is good.

The only way to convince yourself is to work your way through them, bunch by bunch, sniffing and (surreptitiously) chewing a taste of torn-off leaf. Here it's all personal chemistry. I was delighted to find that collards had a pleasant, herby aroma and only a touch of bitterness in the taste. Swiss chard and kale also passed muster. Broccoli rabe and turnip greens were entirely too pungent, with mustard greens hovering on the margin.

The following soups were composed on an impromptu basis this spring, right in the supermarket, one hand on the greens, the other on the bunch of scallions or the bag of black-eyed peas. Improvisational cooking has taken on the notion of a bravura performance in these days of the superchef, but real impromptu inspiration mostly springs from putting old familiars into a shape that can match both appetite and what's cheap and good at the store. I make no claims of originality, and in most cases, I just follow familiar and favored combinations. It is from these always that inspiration most easily springs.

I say all this to encourage you to follow my example more than my recipes; let your hands do their own walking in the produce bin. Just remember this simple rule: lots of a few things. Soup companies add too much of such flavor enhancers as sugar and salt to squeeze by with what is often little more than a can of flavored water, or they add a jumble of ingredients so that the soup's flavor need meet no special standard. You'll find that a generous hand with a few favored ingredients will give your soups a rich, clear flavor and aroma—and drive those cans off the shelf forever.

Swiss Chard, Mushroom, and Orzo Soup

¶ Swiss chard is an easily approachable green, mild-flavored, even delicate. Wash it carefully, then pull each leaf into bite-size bits, discarding any parts that are wilted or brown. Chop up the stems and use them as part of the soup base. The day I brought Swiss chard home, I had a bunch of mushroom stems in the fridge. Whole mushrooms, of course, could be used, or something else substituted entirely, like a generous number of carrots. (I use a little sugar to smooth the taste of my broth; omit it if it offends.)

1 pound bunch (or so) Swiss chard
½ pound mushrooms, whole or stems
1 tablespoon butter
1 onion, minced
1 carrot, cut into small dice
Pinch grated nutmeg
1 teaspoon brown sugar (optional)
Salt and freshly ground pepper
½ cup of orzo (rice-shaped pasta)

Prepare the Swiss chard as directed above. Wipe and thinly slice the mushrooms. Melt the butter in a heavy pot and sauté the onion, mushrooms, carrot, and chopped chard stems until the onion is translucent. Add 3 cups water and bring to a simmer. Add the nutmeg, sugar if desired, and salt and pepper to taste. Simmer for 15 minutes. Add the orzo and chopped chard leaves. Simmer another 15 minutes, taste for final seasoning, and serve. (*Variations:* This is an excellent soup for thickening with egg. Remove finished soup from heat, uncover, and scoop out ½ cup of broth. Let it cool while you beat together 2 eggs. Beat the broth into the eggs bit by bit. Then beat the egg-broth mixture back into the pot; the soup should now be cool enough to not scramble the eggs. Put soup over the lowest possible heat and let rest a few minutes before serving.)

(Serves 4)

Collard Greens, Black-Eyed Peas, and Rice

¶ This is a classic Southern combination, but I haven't seem them specifically combined like this as a soup. I'm sure they are—the result is transcendental. Once when I made this soup, I had a piece of bacon rind around and threw that in. Another time I had some chicken, and I pulled some skin off it, fried that up to render the fat, and served the cut-up crisp skin as a garnish. If I had neither on hand, I wouldn't hesitate to use olive oil.

1 pound collard greens	Handful of rice
1 bunch scallions	Few drops Tabasco sauce
½ pound black-eyed peas or	1 teaspoon brown sugar
1 10-ounce package frozen	Salt and freshly ground pep-
Nice bit of fatback, minced,	per
or 1 tablespoon oil	

Prepare the collard greens as directed for Swiss chard, above. (The stems aren't as substantial, but mince them up anyway; they give a lot of flavor.) Chop the scallions into small bits, including half the green part. Prepare the black-eyed peas until almost ready (they should be a little *too* chewy) as directed on their packaging. Do not overcook. Pour in enough additional water to make about a quart of liquid.

In a small frying pan, sauté the minced bits of fatback until they are just turning brown and have rendered some fat. Put both the rendered fat and the crispy bits, or the oil, into the soup pot, and with them add the chopped collard stems, scallion bits, and the rice, and simmer for 15 minutes. Stir in the Tabasco and brown sugar and taste broth for seasoning (broth should taste neither hot nor sweet, just suggestive). Add collards and simmer another 5 minutes or until they are tender (many cookbooks call for grossly overcooking collards—let your own tongue decide). Serve with plenty of hot corn bread. (*Variations:* Obviously, if your taste runs to ham hocks or if you have a ham bone on hand, such will only improve the soup. But collards do not need to be offset by such powerful flavors as turnip greens do; I thought this soup made with chicken fat just wonderful. Butter beans can be substituted for the black-eyed peas.)

(Serves 4)

Romaine Lettuce and Chick-Pea Soup

¶ Most lettuce soups are bland and creamy; this one has some tang. Without the greens, this soup can be found in Ed Giobbi's *Italian Family Cooking;* both ways it is a favorite fast staple in my own kitchen.

1 bunch romaine	1 teaspoon fresh lemon juice
1 clove garlic, minced	2 tablespoons olive oil
1 20-ounce can chick-peas	Salt and freshly ground pepper

Prepare the romaine as directed for Swiss chard, above. Again, mince the stems separately. Put the garlic, the chopped stems, the chick-peas, and the liquid from their can into a heavy pot along with ½ cup of water. Simmer gently for 20 minutes. Add the torn romaine leaves and simmer an additional 10 minutes. Now remove from the heat and stir in the lemon juice and olive oil, seasoning with salt and pepper to taste. Let rest for 5 minutes off the heat and serve.

(Serves 4)

Kale and Potato Soup

¶ Kale has two unusual virtues for a green: it can endure cold weather gracefully and can be cooked for a long time and still keep its texture. Thus, it's often matched with long-cooking vegetables such as dried beans and potatoes. The following soup is my version of the Portuguese *caldo verde.* The kale can be shredded quickly by rolling several of the leaves together, as if making a cigar, and slicing them thinly with a very sharp knife.

1 pound kale
1 pound potatoes, peeled if you choose
2 tablespoons olive oil
Salt and freshly ground pepper

Prepare the kale as directed for Swiss chard, above, mincing stalks and finely shredding leaves separately (discard any stalk that does not mince easily.) Set aside minced leaves, and add minced stalks to 5 cups of salted water set to boil in a large pot. Drop in the potatoes, cover, reduce heat, and simmer for 20 minutes, or until potatoes are tender. Remove potatoes and mash them, then return to pot and stir in well with cooking water. Add the shredded kale, olive oil, and taste for seasoning, adding salt and pepper as needed. Bring this mixture back to a simmer and cook, uncovered, for 5 minutes, until the kale is tender and the flavors well mixed. Serve with corn bread. (*Variations:* No Portuguese would frown if you added a generous handful of sliced chorizo—a garlic-flavored sausage—to the pot at the same time the kale leaves are added.)

(Serves 4 to 6)

CHOCOLATE-COVERED RASPBERRIES.   Every year in raspberry season, the St. Louis chocolatier, Karl Bissinger, shuts down normal operations to hand dip fresh raspberries in chocolate fondant. The raspberries are picked in Oregon, flown overnight to Bissinger's, where they are coated in milk or dark chocolate, then sent out express for next-day delivery. Last year a pound of these yummy little morsels was about $40—expensive but not outrageous, perhaps, when you consider the logistics and the price of fresh raspberries these days. Even so, for me, that price finally sprinkled enough grit onto the slope of slippery logic by which I justify so consummately decadent an experience to bring desire to a dead stop.

Fortunately, an alternative was at hand. Good-quality chocolate *couverture* (milk or bittersweet) is readily available in these days of home chocolate-making for the melting and dipping. My own choice was a Belgian bittersweet coating chocolate made by Callebaut, available in a 17-ounce bar, which melts easily to a rich and grainless coating consistency with the simple assist of a double boiler. (A source of supply, if none can be found locally, is S. E. Rykoff, P.O. Box 21467, Los Angeles, CA 90021).

The chocolate melted, it was held at as low a temperature as possible. The berries were dipped in, one by one, each speared at the end of a round, double-pointed toothpick, and twirled in the chocolate until completely coated. The other end of the toothpick was then stuck into an inverted styrofoam tray (the sort that supermarkets package meat in), so the covering could harden without risk of smearing. When the dipping was complete, the whole bristling tray of them moved to the refrigerator, to quicken the setting and lessen chances of spoilage.

The result was all I hoped for, not the melting swoon of sweetness that characterizes the usual fruit-flavored chocolate center, but a fresh, tart bite of pure raspberry breaking through the foil of luscious bittersweet, setting out the flavors of each in the mouth in clear detail. A wonderful mouthful, and my 17-ounce bar of *couverture* took care of a pint of raspberries, another of strawberries, and some random nibbles along the way. Or, if you're rich or just shamelessly lazy, you can call Karl Bissinger and arrange for delivery in season: 1-800-325-8881 (or write for his catalogue: 3983 Gratiot, St. Louis, MO 63110).

Summer

❁

CLAM SOUP, WITH TOMATOES AND WITHOUT. Recipes that add tomatoes to what we now know as New England clam chowder can be traced back to the last century. But so far as I can discover, there is no such precedent for Manhattan clam chowder, which is really no chowder at all in any meaningful sense of that word. Apparently it began to appear as a first course in Italian seafood restaurants sometime in the 1930s, based on a familiar Neapolitan soup but without its true character. For while *zuppa di vongole* is almost all clams, the rest being garlic and tomatoes, Manhattan clam chowder is rarely, if ever, so generous.

We may find it hard to credit that *zuppa di vongole* is a soup at all, given the lack of bottled clam juice in the recipe. It's been a long time since we Americans could afford the prodigality of calling for almost a pound of clams per person for a mere soup! Little wonder then that Waverley Root, when he gives the recipe in his *Best of Italian Cooking*, upgrades the dish to "Clams with Tomato and Basil."

Perhaps the best title of all would be "Clams Cooked in their Own Broth with a Sauce of Tomatoes and Basil," which is really what the dish is. And it is obviously direct kin—along with its tomatoless companion—to the synonymous pasta sauces, red and white, the only difference being the amount of clams. In the pasta sauces, there are far fewer of them.

Two versions of *zuppa di vongole*—clams in their own broth—are given below, one for littleneck clams, the other for small soft-shell ones. While neither version is limited to the particular clam it calls for, the sense of the preparation is, since the inevitable grit inside the soft-shell clam requires the cook to take special precautions.

Whatever the clams used, they should be given a good picking over, with any punctured or open ones discarded. They should then be rinsed well and scrubbed clean of any surface grit. Otherwise, let the basil be fresh and fragrant, the tomatoes perfectly ripe and fatly juicy. There should be good crusty bread provided for sopping the juices. This is good food.

Littleneck Clams in their own Broth, with Tomatoes and Basil

3 pounds littleneck clams, scrubbed clean of grit
3 or 4 fat, red, ripe tomatoes
⅓ cup olive oil

1 clove garlic, minced
¼ cup finely chopped fresh basil
Salt and freshly ground pepper

If possible, set the cleaned clams in a pail of clean seawater for an hour or so to dispel any interior sand. (Do not, however, set them in fresh water or water salted by you, or all those fragile briny undertones will be diluted into nothing.) At the same time, set the tomatoes in a colander in the sink and pour boiling water over them. Let them cool enough to handle and slip off their skins. Being careful to lose none of their juices, chop them coarsely, seeding them only if you wish.

Heat the olive oil over medium-low heat in a large, heavy skillet for which you have a cover. When the oil is hot, add the garlic and basil, and sauté, stirring, until the garlic just begins to turn color. Immediately add the tomatoes. Season with salt and pepper to taste, raise the heat just enough to bring the sauce to a simmer, and cook for about 15 minutes, or until the mixture begins to thicken into a sauce. Add the clams, cover, and cook for about 8 minutes, or just until the clams open their shells; discard any that do not open. (*Note:* Traditionally, this "soup" is served over *crostini*, crusts of bread toasted brown in olive oil. Do this if you wish, or simply serve good bread on the side . . . so long as no broth goes to waste!)

(Serves 4)

Although there are ways of fiddling with the above dish to make it with small soft-shell clams, the soup doesn't then fall together in the same pleasing, uncomplicated way, and I don't bother with them. Those who have access to a supply of not-too-expensive, not-too-large steamers, I think, are better advised to make this tomato-free version:

Small Steamers in their own Broth with White Wine, Basil, and Garlic

3 pounds littleneck clams, scrubbed clean of grit
1 bunch seaweed, well rinsed in and still dripping of seawater, or several leaves spinach, rinsed in fresh water and lightly shaken
1/3 cup olive oil

1 clove garlic, minced
1/4 cup finely chopped fresh basil
2 scallions, chopped fine, including the green part
3/4 cup dry white wine
Salt and freshly ground pepper

If possible, set the cleaned clams in a pail of clean seawater for an hour or so to dispel any interior sand. (Do not, however, set them in fresh water or water salted by you, or their briny flavors will be diluted.) Take a heavy skillet for which you have a cover, and cover the bottom with the damp (but sand-free) seaweed or the damp spinach leaves. Arrange the clams evenly on top of this, cover, and set over low heat. Cook *only* until the clams open, about 5 minutes, discarding any clams that do not open. Carefully remove pan from heat and let clams cool until they can be handled, taking care that none of their liquor is spilled.

Remove clams from their shells, holding them over a bowl so all liquid is saved. Pull away and discard the black neckcaps. When done, rinse the clams in their own juices, reserving them in a separate dish. Then let those juices settle until the grit falls to the bottom. While this is happening, remove and discard the seaweed or spinach and wipe the skillet clean. Pour in the olive oil and return it to the heat.

When the oil is hot, add the garlic, basil, and scallions, and cook, stirring, until the white part of the scallion has turned translucent and the garlic is faintly yellow. Pour in the wine, stir well, and raise the heat, bringing the wine to a simmer. Then add the clams and as much of their liquor as can be poured off without disturbing the sediment. Taste for seasoning, adding pepper and salt as necessary, and cook only long enough to heat through, about 2 minutes. Serve at once in heated bowls, dividing the clams and broth equally. Serve with the rest of the wine and with a loaf of good crusty bread for mopping up the juices. (*Note:* Again, traditionally, this dish is served on *crostini*, slices of slightly stale bread toasted golden in garlic-flavored olive oil. In this instance, I personally prefer to eat the dish with a fresh loaf of sourdough.)

(Serves 4)

ROBERT H. ROBINSON, shellfish devotee and sympathizer with man's endless search for the exactly right tool to deal with them, is the author of a book I have admired for some time, *Left to Your Own Devices*, a volume devoted entirely to implements for opening shellfish, with directions for their use, all illustrated with great idiosyncratic wit. It is the definitive work on oyster breakers, stabbers, and knives—the clam digger's dagger, the conch conker—not to mention various crab saws, knives, and pickers. Alas, the book may have proven too overspecific to attract a general public, for it has gone out of print.

Happily, this has not discouraged Mr. Robinson, who simply broadened his scope. His *Essential Book of Shellfish* is almost as implement-oriented but at the same time more practical, with explicit directions for getting the most from a lobster, opening the most stubborn of oysters, or relieving some of the tedium of picking a crab. Plenty of professional illustrations and recipes—a good deal for $6.95.

He has also published *The Shellfish Heritage Cookbook* ($7.95), in which classic shellfish recipes have been worked into what is really a unique collection of curious and quaint shellfish prints taken from a wide range of historical sources. No surprise that he has turned several of these into a charming and sometimes humorous collection of notes and postcards. These are illustrated in his catalogue, but you will have to order some to realize how nicely colored they are, mostly in antique tints. Summer clammers, shellfish lovers, and those who delight in culinary history will find them just to their taste. For catalogue and free sample, write: Shellfish Series, P. O. Box 469, Georgetown, DE 19947.

THREE SUMMER SALADS

POTATO SALAD. We are so used to thinking of potato salad as a fixed constellation in the culinary firmament that it almost comes as a shock when the words are reversed into a "salad of potatoes," and it dawns on us that we might do something else with them besides drowning them in mayonnaise, chopped pimento, and hard-boiled egg.

For one thing, they make a splendid foil for fresh herbs that are a little too pungent to eat as a salad by themselves. Fresh-boiled potatoes sprinkled with minced rosemary or oregano or thyme, dressed with some good olive oil and a little wine vinegar make good company with a dish of olives and a glass of wine. And no harm will be done if you add to this some minced anchovy fillet, even dressing the result with some of the olive oil in which those fish were (or should have been) packed.

Or, instead of the anchovies, turn a whole can of oil-packed tuna over 10 or 12 small boiled Bliss potatoes, peeled and cut in quarters, and you have a light summer meal. Season it with minced scallion and parsley, dress it with olive oil and lemon juice, salt, and a generous grinding of pepper—tuna salad transformed into magnificence!

Thin slices of boiled, peeled potato also make the perfect foil for fresh-picked baby peas, podded and added raw or boiled just long enough to flush a more vivid green. This salad is enhanced still further by the presence of a buttery (as opposed to bitter) lettuce, such as Bibb or Boston, and can be dressed simply with a dribble of oil, a few drops (really) of a good wine vinegar, and salt and pepper to taste.

Good as this is, it is a combination that also works well when lightly touched with a good homemade mayonnaise, into which, perhaps, a spoonful or two of minced fresh basil has been worked, or perhaps an equal amount of watercress or mint. Add to all this a chopped hard-boiled egg—it will easily make itself at home—and we've worked our way full circle, back to the familiar potato salad, but now only one of many potato salads, and with a fresh, new face.

GREEN BEAN SALAD. Any gardener worth his or her salt produces more green beans than the neighbors know what to do with; unlike the fabled zucchini, this is no vegetable of a thousand uses.

But as Italian cooks have long known, it makes a super salad, the only secret being to serve it with the beans still warm from their cooking. They should be young and sweet, newly picked and plunged, trimmed and washed, into boiling salted water in an uncovered pot. Cook them only until *just* tender (6 to 8 minutes) and drain well. Toss them in only enough olive oil to give them a gloss, and sprinkle with a little fresh lemon juice, salt, and coarsely ground pepper. Serve at once with your best bread and sweetest butter.

This simple classic is sometimes augmented with paper-thin slices of red salad onion or a whisper of garlic. The salad can also be strewn with fresh minced herbs—parsley, mint, or basil—but, please, not grated cheese. (*Note:* Obviously, broccoli can be treated much this same way, and often is. But so can small, tender bulbs of fennel—or "anise" as it is sometimes marketed—diced up as you would celery, including all but the base of the bulb and a bit of the feathery leaves. It should need no cooking or, like the broccoli, no more than a par-boiling—just enough to heat it through.)

TOMATO SALAD. To my mouth, tomatoes and lettuce are not a happy combination. In a sandwich with bacon and mayonnaise, yes, but not in a salad. I want to write that they taste too much the same; that's what my tongue tells me, even if my brain says that they have nothing in common at all. All I know is that their flavors simply don't work well together without a host of intermediaries or some chef's trick to pull the thing off. Even Greek salad is better without any lettuce, and an argument could be made that this dish, too, in its best and purest form, never contained lettuce in the first place.

So, let there be lettuce salads and tomato salads. We know all about the former; lettuce has been having a renaissance lately. But tomatoes, conversely, are facing a rough time, and it might be a good thing to remind ourselves what a good thing they are, just sliced thick, set out flat on a plate, and sprinkled with olive oil and seasoned with a grinding of pepper, a pinch of salt.

And, to take it one step further, a pinch of fresh herb. Parsley would do, I suppose, but there is a special affinity between tomato and basil, tomato and thyme, tomato and oregano—you can't want for choices. This time, after adding the herb, dribble the slices with some fruity olive oil, shower them with pepper, and let them sit for a good hour or so in a cool place (but not the refrigerator) before serving them. Salt them only when you pull up your chair to eat; otherwise it draws out their juices and makes them flabby.

The most popular Mediterranean tomato salad, found from Spain to Turkey, is a combination of roughly cut chunks of tomato tossed in a bowl with small pieces of sweet onion (a red salad onion will do nicely, although a specialty onion like the Vidalia is a special treat here), dressed with a good fruity olive oil and some freshly squeezed lemon (or lime) juice, and that grinding of pepper. This, too, should be put aside for an hour or so to let the flavors mingle . . . and salted only at the last moment.

This tomato and onion combination is also a salad that herbs will enhance—big torn pieces of basil, a fragrant sprig of oregano. The Portuguese add a generous amount of minced watercress and a tiny pinch of minced fresh coriander. The Greeks mingle a little basil and oregano with a lot of fresh mint and stir that in with a handful of black brined olives, again, all dressed with olive oil and a few drops of lemon juice or good wine vinegar. (I don't give specific proportions here because individual tolerances to fresh herbs vary so enormously. Mix them tiny pinch by tiny pinch into your mixture of tomatoes and onion—or tomatoes alone—until you find the balance that suits you.)

The final ingredient to this most perfect of salads is a portion of cheese. The standard Greek salad should not blind you to the fact that crumbled feta and tomatoes mix well together by themselves, enhanced perhaps wth a few black olives and a pinch of parsley or oregano. A slightly more complicated version adds slivered bell peppers as well.

Equally successful is the popular Italian combination of tomatoes, basil, onion, and mozzarella. To prepare this salad properly, the ingredients should all be at room temperature, and mixed together with olive oil, a little crushed garlic, and a generous amount of torn fresh basil. Season with freshly ground pepper (but, again, hold the salt until just before serving) and let the mixture marinate together in a cool spot in the kitchen (but not in the refrigerator) for an hour or two. Served with a loaf of bread and a bottle of simple red wine, it is feast all of itself.

Finally, if there is no time to let this mixture mingle together for the required hour, prepare it thusly. Preheat the oven to 350°F. Slice the tomatoes as thinly as possible with a razor sharp knife. Then slice the cheese the same way (mozzarella can be cut in thin slices if you dip the blade of the knife in boiling water between slices). Cut your loaf of bread in half lengthwise. Set one half aside for some other use and layer the other with the sliced tomatoes, the mozzarella, and, alternatively, a basil leaf or a ring of sweet red onion. When the half loaf is covered, dribble it with olive oil in which a little minced garlic has been mixed, and grind some pepper over all. Bake it in the oven just until the bread is crusty and the cheese melted—no more than 10 minutes. Serve at once, cut into wedges, with salt and olives at the side.

GARLIC SOURCE.   I wrote Jalapeño Ltd. looking for a source of dried chili peppers; I found instead an importer of the best Mexican garlic. If your local sources can provide only mingy, two-to-a-box, withered midgets, you may welcome a source for fat, juicy, pungent ones. (They also sell pigtails of 25 bulbs, strung in a 34-inch queue, for $15.95.) Besides garlic, they offer a unique collection of spiral-bound Texas cookbooks: *Calf Fries to Caviar, The Bounty of East Texas; Best Little Cookbook in Texas; Mrs. Blackwell's Heart-of-Texas Cookbook,* and lots more. Write for their price list: 112 Lemonwood, San Antonio, TX 78213.

Speaking of garlic, it's well into elephant garlic season. These monster bulbs are each large enough to fill a fist—a single clove can be the size of a regular whole bulb—and yet their flavor is surprisingly delicate. Willacrik Farm offers excellent ones, whole or broken into cloves, either giant or baby (3 inches in diameter or less). They also carry an attractive English terra-cotta garlic cellar for $14. In my experience, the separate cloves are the better buy and are as durable as the bulbs. Peel a bunch and crowd them into a small ovenproof dish, tucking a few fresh rosemary leaves among them. Dribble with olive oil, grind some black pepper over, and sprinkle with coarse salt. Lightly cover with foil and bake in a 375°F oven until they are fragrant and soft, about 45 minutes. Then carefully spoon them out for spreading on hot buttered toast. The best bedtime snack there ever was. Write to: Willacrik Farm, P. O. Box 599, Templeton, CA 93465.

BLACKBERRY ROLL.

> Blackberries—fresh and fine,
> I got blackberries, lady,
> Fresh from de vine,
> I got blackberries, lady,
> three glass fo' a dime,
> I got blackberries, I got blackberries, blackberries.
> —Street cry, New Orleans blackberry woman

Blackberries are a difficult fruit. They need a perfect summer to ripen properly: if it's too dry, they're sour and seedy; too much rain and they get bloated and flavorless. But just when you've almost written them off entirely, the right summer comes along and they're suddenly glistening in the brambles, all black and shiny and full of pungent flavor. Except by the roadside handful, they're not really an eating fruit—nor do they make a memorable preserve. But they glorify a pastry. Nothing ever became a pie crust better than that violent scarlet juice, oozing freely from a fresh-cut blackberry pie. The current regime, with its lust for order on the pie plate, dumps in cornstarch by the tablespoon to contain this anarchy, transforming that glorious flood into turgid purple sludge. Better by far, then, the following Southern rolled pie, whose layers discipline the flow of natural juices—at least until each eater gets a fair share.

Southern Rolled Blackberry Pie

6 cups blackberries
1½ cups sugar plus ¼ cup
¼ teaspoon salt

1 tablespoon fresh lemon
  juice (optional)
1 tablespoon milk
1 tablespoon sweet butter

plus
  2-crust pie pastry made from your favorite recipe (or see page
  92)

Preheat oven to 350°F. Wash and pick over the blackberries carefully, draining them well. Put them in a large bowl and mix with 1½ cups of sugar, the salt, and—if they taste a little flat—the lemon juice. Roll out the pie crust on a floured surface into an oblong sheet, rolling the pastry as thin as possible. Spread some of the sugar-berry mixture across one end of the sheet, fold the pastry over, spread more berries, roll again, and so on, continuing until all the berries are used up and the pastry is rolled into a bundle. Brush the final seam with milk and seal firmly; crimp the edges carefully so that the juices do not escape. Put this roll in a buttered baking pan or cookie sheet (with rim), seam side down. Brush the exposed surface with milk and bake for 30 minutes. Melt the butter and mix with the remaining ¼ cup sugar. Baste the roll with this several times while it bakes for another 20 minutes. Serve warm with heavy cream or vanilla ice cream.

GUESTS NOT TO INVITE TO DINNER (II). Louis Pasteur. "He minutely inspected the bread that was served him [at the dinner table] and placed on the tablecloth everything he found in it: small fragments of wood; of roaches; of flour worms. Often I tried to find in my own piece of bread from the same loaf the objects found by Pasteur, but could not discover anything. This search took place at every meal, and is perhaps the most extraordinary memory that I have kept of him." (Adrien Loir, quoted in René J. Dubos's *Louis Pasteur*.)

LIME RICKEY. The lime rickey is to the Boston area what the chocolate egg cream is to New York City—a local phenomenon that, despite passionate fans, resists transplanting to most anywhere else. It is a temperate offspring of the gin rickey, a turn-of-the-century version of a gimlet without the sugar: "Juice one lime; leave half of the pressed lime in glass; one lump ice; one wine glass Tom gin. Fill with siphon" (*The Cocktail Book*, St. Botolph Society, 1925). The secret to the drink is the addition of that crushed lime half, its bitter oils giving the drink its memorable bite. (Modern bar guides call for only a twist of lime, meaning, most likely, bottled lime juice as well—a total swindle.) Remove the gin and add lime syrup and you have the lime rickey as thirsty summer patrons of Brigham's or Bailey's know it—an icy soda glass bubbling over with fizzy tartness, a grown-up thirst quencher. Patrons with a sweeter tooth call for a raspberry lime rickey, which may originate from what that same bar book calls a "circus rickey," (the same recipe plus a tablespoon of grenadine), with raspberry subbing for the more expensive (and exotic) syrup. A real lime rickey, however, should be made of nothing but fresh limes and pure lime syrup.

Lime Syrup

4 limes
2 cups superfine sugar

Grate the rind from the limes and *then* squeeze them, straining the juice. In a saucepan combine the sugar with 2 cups water, bring the mixture to a boil over medium heat, and stir until the sugar dissolves. Add the lime rind and simmer for 10 minutes. Let the syrup cool until it is lukewarm and strain it into a jar, pressing hard on the rind with a spoon. Stir in the lime juice. Will keep in the refrigerator for 2 to 3 weeks.

(Makes about 3 cups)

To make a lime rickey, put some ice in a large glass, pour in ¼ cup lime syrup (or to taste) plus the juice of 1 tiny lime or half a medium one. Toss in the squeezed half and fill the glass with seltzer, stirring only enough to mix. Drink at once.

CURE FOR THE UNWANTED GUEST.   Every recipe file needs such a remedy. This one I found while enjoying Diana Kennedy's personably quirky *Nothing Fancy*. It was given to *her* by a Mexico City veterinarian. To make it, you will need 2 cups pure cane alcohol (or vodka) and 1 pound garlic, broken into unpeeled cloves and then lightly crushed. Process both ingredients in a food processor fitted with a metal blade until they form a coarse paste. Put in a jar, cover, and let age in a cool, dark cabinet or closet for a month. Then gently pour the liquid into a bottle and discard the residue. The dosage is 10 drops before breakfast: the cure should take effect immediately, but if not, repeat as necessary. The same dosage for circulatory problems and parasites. It does not cure bad breath.

FRONTIER COOPERATIVE HERBS.   There are many reasons to rejoice in the existence of this cooperative, and not least is the wide range of herbs and herbal products that they offer. Their price list of herbs and spices alone runs to almost three full-size 8½-by-11-inch pages. Not all of the herbs are for culinary purposes, of course. A few years ago, reading Richard Bradley's *The Country Housewife and Lady's Director* (1736), I came across an entry on "dog-grass": "This should be put to a dog, at any time, when he is sick, and he will eat it greedily, and cure himself; but for want of this Help, which favourite Lap-Dogs in London want, they lose their briskness." Useful stuff, for dogs, and this catalogue has it. (Note, however, that Bradley calls it "one of the Gardener's plagues, and in every garden too much"; the catalogue describes it as "a noxious weed.")

Still, you get the idea: they cast their net wide. Among the useful herbs for cooks that they offer are black current leaves, which give dill pickles a special flavor and are used by the British for a delicate frozen ice; raspberry leaves, which make a refreshing herbal tea, quite different from the flavored black tea; gumbo filé for Creole cooking; Mexican oregano for seasoning many Southwestern dishes, including chili; and lemon grass, a common flavoring in Southeast Asian dishes (it also makes a pleasant herbal tea—they give the recipe). Herbs and spices, moreover, are not the only products they sell: dried vegetables, sea vegetables, seeds for sprouting, bulk teas, organic coffee, medicinals, extracts, and essenial oils are also carried (plus brand-name lines of herbal products).

Equally important as this variety is their concern for finding organically grown herbs and then seeing that they are processed in ways that do least damage to their flavor. The first is especially important because many of our seasonings are imported, and pesticides forbidden in this country are still sold abroad—and lavishly sprayed on products destined for this country to ensure they are pest-free. Also, because our national interest in herbs has until recently been a latent one, inexpert processors often adapt machinery not really suited for the job to process them; it mangles rather than cleanly cuts, or else overheats the herbs and destroys the flavor.

It seems too much to ask that they also have excellent prices, but they do. Black currant leaves, a hard-to find product, which a New York City store offered me at $4.29 an ounce, is sold by them (to nonmembers) for about $6.12 a *pound*—and raspberry or blackberry leaves go for a quarter of that. On all items I have checked, savings have been similar.

Individuals can order from them, but there are advantages in joining with friends to form a "buying club" and getting a Coop membership. For one thing, you may not need a whole pound of St. John's wort, that weight being the smallest amount they will sell of herbs and spices (minimum order is $20 or you have to pay an extra service charge); for another, your savings will be greater. Price list and membership information is free; their excellent catalogue, $2.50. Write to: Box 69, Norway, IA 52318.

Autumn

❁

POTATO DEVIL.   The Potato Devil® is an earthenware double pot, the top half identical to the bottom, in which potatoes are baked on top of the stove. It is a common item in many European kitchens but virtually unknown (and until recently unavailable) over here, since we have ovens that do the same thing. However, as utility bills continue to rise, cranking up the oven to bake a clutch of potatoes has begun to require a little more justification, unless there is a roast to put in with them.

And even the roast is no longer such a sure solution. I doubt that I'm the only cook who has found that those stultifying Sunday dinners built around a massive piece of meat no longer summon up the automatic appetite they once did. This is in part because lighter cooking styles have come into favor the past few years and also because fewer of us have the time these days to spend Sunday afternoon prone and wheezing on the sofa. Thus, with the handwriting on the wall for the baked potato cooked by traditional means, we can only thank heaven for the Devil.

I could step into parentheses here and fill up the page with a paean to the potato; it's enough to say that it's the only vegetable that can make my mouth water just by reading about it. And the baked potato is the very summit of potato cookery—baked, that is, without aluminum underwear, in its very own natural skin, crackling crisp on the outside and moist, soft, crumbly within.

These are my standards. The good news is that the Potato Devil actually does what it promises, baking potatoes of all sizes and persuasions to perfection on the top of the stove. The Devil serves as a tiny clay oven, baking the spuds without recourse to liquid, and the doubling design allows the pot to be turned over a few times during baking, guaranteeing an even cooking and helping to crisp the skins.

But equally attractive is its simple, homey look. Nothing could be further from high-tech styling than this plump, fragile, unglazed pot: the interior soon becomes speckled and blackened, while the heat from the gas flame (or electric coil) gradually bleaches the top and bottom. After a few years of use, the casual visitor will take it for a family heirloom—or a theft from some archaeological dig. (The top of mine is branded with a crisscross design, all that remains of a potholder I put under the Devil to protect the dinner table: the Devil burnt its way through it and a second one to leave a plate-size scorch mark on the varnish. Be warned.)

The importer brags that it cooks faster than the oven, something I haven't noticed, though I put it over a higher flame than they recommend. But it has more impressive, unmentioned virtues. Baking potatoes in a small, enclosed space allows you cooking options not possible in an oven. For example, you can generously sprinkle the potatoes with herbs such as sage, thyme, or rosemary—or poppy or caraway seeds—and find the spuds impregnated with those flavors by the end of the baking. Or you can make salt potatoes by throwing in a handful of coarse salt, which is impaled in the skin as the potato cooks. And if a garlic head is broken apart and the individual (unpeeled) cloves mixed in with the potatoes, the garlic emerges tamed into a soft and fragrant pulp, the potatoes crisp and garlicky.

Enough already to recommend it to any potato lover, but I've saved the best news for last: its ability to impart a delicious fireplace flavor to the roasted spuds. This is a natural occurrence—the heat of the pot chars the skins of the potatoes where they come into contact with it—but this effect can be greatly enhanced by adding some smoldering wood chips.

This discovery was serendipitously inspired by a bag of mesquite chips left over from barbecue season. I disconnected the nearest smoke detectors and fired up about eight chips (not chunks) of mesquite, setting them right on the gas ring. I let them burn for a few minutes to work up a good char (the smoke they gave off was negligible) and then, using a pair of kitchen tongs, quickly tossed them right into the Potato Devil, where a dozen or so tiny red Bliss potatoes had just started to bake. (Speed is of the essence here, since the chips stop burning once they leave the fire.)

The flames are snuffed once the lid goes back on; the Devil is filled with mesquite smoke. The results greatly exceeded my expectations. Mesquite smoke, it turns out, does some extraordinary things to the taste of potato, something you can tell as soon as their aromas start to mingle in the kitchen air. I just sat down with butter, salt, and pepper, and devoured the whole batch on the spot. The Devil transformed the tiny red Bliss potatoes (not a kind you would think of roasting in ordinary circumstances) into little lumps of creamy softness, their taste set off by the faintly resinous notes of the mesquite and the appetizing aroma of smoke and char. Sheer heaven!

The French also use the Potato Devil to roast chestnuts (be sure to poke a vent hole in each or they'll go off like little grenades), but further experimentation discovered that it was also an interesting way to roast eggplant. Here, the technique is different; that vegetable should be cooked over the lowest possible flame for several hours, to gently extract its excess juices without burning it to a crisp. As the time passes, the eggplant collapses into a fragrant, flavorful pulp, enhanced, again, by the use of smoldering wood chips.

Eggplant is often roasted over embers in Mediterranean countries for the added flavor of the smoke before being made into a flavorful spread or dip. This simple preparation has as many names as variations, but the following is a tasty example.

Eggplant Spread

6 to 8 baby eggplants, each pricked twice with a fork
¼ cup olive oil
1 clove garlic, finely minced
4 scallions, minced (including the green part)
2 teaspoons minced fresh oregano or ½ teaspoon dried
1 tablespoon minced parsley
1 teaspoon capers, drained and minced
Juice of ½ lemon
Salt and freshly ground pepper to taste

Roast the eggplants over lowest possible heat with smoking wood chips in the Devil, turning the pot every half hour, for 3 hours or until the eggplants have completely collapsed. Or, instead, roast each eggplant directly over a gas flame or on a charcoal grill, turning constantly, until the skin is charred all over and the flesh soft. When cool enough to handle, cut in half and scoop out the flesh, discarding the seeds. Blend thoroughly with the remaining ingredients and serve with warm wedges of pita bread, on which it is eaten, dribbled with a little additional olive oil.

(Yields about 1½ cups)

To order: The Potato Devil is available by mail from The Wooden Spoon, Inc.: Box 852 – Route 6, Mahopac, NY 10541; toll-free telephone: 1-800-431-2207. Call or write them for the current price (about $15) and postage charges. Mesquite chips are now widely available by mail order. One source is Turkey Hill Farms, RD 1, P. O. Box 163, Red Hook, NY 12571. They also offer cherry, hickory, and applewood chips, plus a mixture of maple and corncobs. Write for their current price list.

GRAPE LEAVES.   Almost any recipe for stuffed grape leaves results in some of the leaves being left over, too few for another batch but too many to simply toss out. Minced small they can be used as a potherb, a savory addition to any soup made with greens or cabbage. More attractively still, Elizabeth David suggests using them in a mushroom casserole to provide a tasty bosky pedigree to ordinary white mushrooms. Use a shallow heavy casserole with a cover that will comfortably hold the mushrooms. Line it with grape leaves and brush them with a film of olive oil. Then arrange the mushrooms over the leaves (cut away the stems of the large ones) and sprinkle with a little salt and pepper, a few minced garlic cloves, and then a little more olive oil. Lay a few more grape leaves over all this and cover the dish. Bake in a low (300°F) oven for about 45 minutes, or until the mushrooms are tender and flavorful. Serve hot.

According to Jane Grigson, villagers in the Vas Vendômois region of France wrap grape leaves around leftover ends of cheese and bake these in the communal bread oven to make a flavorful snack. You can do the same, setting the wrapped bundles seam side down in an ovenproof dish (a pie plate will work just fine) and baking in a preheated 400°F oven only long enough for the cheese to soften, about 15 minutes.

These bundles can be further enhanced by dipping each bit of cheese in olive oil and then sprinkling it with a fresh herb—thyme or rosemary, say—and freshly ground pepper before wrapping. A surprising range of cheeses can be prepared this way—Cantal, Gruyère, Fontina, Asiago, Kassari, even Montrachet. With care, they can also be done on the barbecue grill on an oiled rack, cooked about 4 minutes to the side.

The packets should be carefully unwrapped and the molten cheese spread on slices of good crusty bread. The grape leaves, however, in both this and in Elizabeth David's recipe above, are discarded, not eaten.

DAUDET ON MADAME ZOLA'S COOKING.   In the chapter on dining with Zola in Jane Grigson's *Food with the Famous*, she repeats the famous—if vulgar—quip by Daudet that he found the hazel hen he was served at that novelist's house as tasting of the "scented flesh of an old tart marinated in a bidet." But Grigson explains that this comment, ungracious though it may be to Madame Zola's culinary efforts, isn't entirely off the wall as a *description,* since hazel hens (shipped frozen to France from Russia) "taste strongly of the pine cones on which they feed." Q.E.D.? Not for me: having been told this much, I want to know a lot more. Or is it self-evident that old Parisian tarts (or their bidets) should taste of pine cones? And if they do, how does Jane Grigson come to know this? Sometimes a little explanation leaves one in far worse confusion than no explanation at all.

A FRESH PORK AND APPLE PIE.   This vision sprang to mind when I found some inexpensive strips of pork tenderloin right after admiring the new crop of apples in the fruit bin. The exact seasonings required some serious mulling over; I finally decided on lemon, parsley, and fresh ginger. (My first impulse, however, was for fresh sage, walnuts, and scallions. If that seems the better choice to you, the transposition should be easy enough to work. Let me know how it turns out.)

Pork and Apple Pie

1 teaspoon minced fresh ginger (or more if you want a more pronounced ginger presence)
1 lemon
1 tablespoon minced parsley
3 pie apples (Granny Smith, Jonathan, Northern Spy, etc.)

¼ cup flour
Salt and freshly ground pepper
2 tablespoons butter
1½ pounds lean pork (ruthlessly trimmed of all gristle and fat)
¼ cup white wine or French apple cider

plus
2-crust pie pastry made from your favorite recipe (or see page 92)
1 egg for glaze (optional)

Preheat oven to 350°F. Line a 9-inch pie pan with part of the pie dough and roll out the top crust with the rest. Grate enough rind from the lemon to measure 1 teaspoon and mix this in with the ginger. Combine with the parsley in a saucer and set aside. Squeeze the lemon and put 1 tablespoon of the juice in a large bowl, reserving the rest for some other purpose. Peel and core the apples and cut the flesh into small dice. Toss pieces as they are cut into the bowl with the lemon juice, coating them well so that they don't turn brown.

Put the flour in another bowl and season with 1 teaspoon salt and ½ teaspoon pepper. Melt the butter in a large skillet over medium heat. While it is heating, cut the pork into ½-inch cubes. Immediately toss these into the seasoned flour to keep them from sticking together. When the pan is hot, spread these coated pork cubes evenly in the skillet (after shaking off any excess flour) and sauté, turning often, until they are crusty and light brown. Transfer these to the bowl with the apple pieces, and repeat the process, if necessary, with any remaining pork cubes. (Do all this quickly. Otherwise, despite the flour, the raw pork cubes will clump together and will not easily separate.)

Add the ginger, lemon rind, and parsley mixture to the sautéed pork and apple bits, and toss until well combined. Barely wet this mixture with the cider or white wine and adjust seasoning, adding more salt and pepper to taste. Fill the bottom crust with this mixture, packing as full as possible. Cover with the top crust, crimp shut, and prick or cut ventilation holes for steam. Glaze with a beaten egg if you wish, then bake the pie for 40 minutes. Let cool before serving; the pie should not be cut until it has cooled about half an hour or so, but it should be eaten warm.

(Serves 6)

GUILTY PLEASURES DEPT.   Marinated some chicken thighs in some soy and "Cajun garlic sauce" and sautéed them in a little olive oil. Since the meat was to be eaten cold later, I peeled off the skin— fried up a crispy char-spotted brown—and made myself a chicken-skin po' boy. Broke open a chewy sub roll, spread it with some mayo spiced with hot sauce, laid in a few lettuce leaves and scallion slivers, and crammed it full of those crusty, garlicky-tasting, succulently greasy chicken skins. Oh, boy! As I put away what should have been my caloric intake for the year, I started planning my New Orleans chicken-skin po' boy shack. You go in, pull an icy Dr Pepper out of the cooler, and wait in line at the counter. Your turn comes, the chef plucks some crackling skins off the mesquite grill and tucks them in a roll. And for an extra 50 cents you get it topped up with French fries— the baddest, most notorious New Orleans po' boy ever: the fried-potato chicken-skin po' boy! Move over, Chef Paul Prudhomme!

COOK'S BOOKS.   My cookbook collection sits in one corner of the living room, next to a large, comfortable chair. Because it takes a very persuasive volume to get me to bring it into the kitchen, my shelves are weakest on fat recipe omnibuses and strongest on the personal, the thoughtful, the different, and—hence, often—the obscure.

Many were found scouring remainder tables and rummaging the dusty alcoves of local used bookstores, but not a few have been acquired right in the above-mentioned armchair, treasure-hunting through the temptation-packed catalogues issued by Michael and Tessa McKirdy, from their home-based Cook's Books, of Sussex, England. Only cookbooks with character need apply.

In the two years or so since I discovered them, I have come by a shelf's worth of happy acquisitions, starting with Dorothy Hartley's wonderful *Food in England*, Rena Salaman's discursive *Greek Food*,

Lesley Chamberlain's exploration of *The Food and Cooking of Russia*, and Florence White's modest-sounding classic, *Good Things in England*. Some of these were hardcover, some paperback, some old, some new. Some came from their catalogue, others were specially ordered or patiently searched for. One was supplied from their personal library. And with unfailing good cheer, a sense of genuine interest and care.

It seems hard to ask for more than that, but their catalogue is always a source of serendipitous interest and includes the literate cover sheet, "Notes from the Dean," which is pursuing an annotated bibliographic listing of twentieth-century food writers (in alphabetical order, now up to F. Marian McNeill, author of *The Scots Kitchen*). I find their prices, for a specialty catalogue, to be more than fair despite the pound's recent gains, and the McKirdys' wide net seems to ensure inclusion of something affordable for almost any taste. For a copy of their next catalogue, write them at 34 Marine Drive, Rottingdean, Sussex BH2 7HQ, England.

PUMPKIN.   If it weren't for jack-o'-lanterns, we would hardly ever see a pumpkin. Pies are about the only thing we do with them, and many people make theirs out of a can. This is a shame, both for the pie (see Mary Randolph's wonderful recipe on page 269) and for the squash: its sweet, rich flesh can be turned to much good advantage. I've already given a recipe for a pumpkin tian (page 43); now here's a delicious Jamaican specialty (made there from the related West Indies pumpkin) that's just in time for Halloween. This recipe was worked out from several sources, but especially Sheryl London's versatile volume, *Eggplant and Squash*.

Meat-in-the-Moon

1 3- to 3½-pound pumpkin
1 tablespoon olive oil
1 medium onion, minced
1 clove garlic, minced
1 pound lean ground beef
1 cup cooked rice
1 tablespoon chopped roasted cashews

1 teaspoon fresh oregano or ½ teaspoon dried
1 or 2 dashes Tabasco sauce
Salt and freshly ground pepper
2 tablespoons (approx.) melted butter

Cut away the pumpkin top as if making a jack-o'-lantern and set aside. Scoop out and discard the stringy parts and remove the seeds. Gently lower the pumpkin into a pot of boiling salted water, tipping it so it fills inside, and parboil for 15 minutes. At the same time, heat the olive oil in a skillet and sauté the onion and garlic until the onion just turns translucent. Add the beef and cook, stirring, until it is browned and crumbly. Remove from the heat and drain away excess fat (leaving about 1 or 2 tablespoons). Mix in the rice and cashews, and season with the oregano, Tabasco sauce, and a generous grinding of pepper, salting to taste.

Preheat the oven to 350°F. Carefully remove the pumpkin from the water and drain completely. When cool enough to handle, pat it dry inside and out with paper towels. Pack the beef and rice mixture into the pumpkin and cap with the reserved top. Set in a buttered baking dish, brushing the outside of the pumpkin with the melted butter. Put in the oven in its baking dish, and bake for 45 minutes. Remove and let cool for at least 15 minutes (the contents will be *hot*) before slicing to serve. Cut it like a pie, giving each eater his or her fair share of pumpkin. (*Note:* While making this dish, you can transform the pumpkin seeds into a tasty snack. Boil them in salted water for 20 minutes, then, after shaking them dry in a colander, spread them out on a cookie sheet and toast them in a 300°F oven for about 30 minutes, or until toasted and crisp. Sample them as the end of the cooking time approaches, so they don't overcook.)

(Serves 6)

FRENCH CUISINE, ANOTHER VIEW. "Rosemary? You're a French girl and you don't know rosemary? God Almighty, what do you usually eat?"

"Food." She shrugged. . . . "What the hell do you think? Whatever they got in the supermarket. Jean didn't care: he liked tripe and beans, that was all. I do the special offers; you know, a free glass if you buy the big soap box. Those and the competitions—you can get really good things on them." —Nicholas Luard, *The Robespierre Serial*

IRISH WHISKEY CAKE. Recently, almost every gift food catalogue in the country has been carrying one version or other of the Irish whiskey cake originated by Downey's of Philadelphia, essentially a sponge cake drenched with John Jameson, and much resembling in its way a baba au rhum, being moist, soft, and very boozy indeed.

I was immediately struck with the idea of an Irish whiskey cake (it's a liquor I favor anyway), but not one like that. I wanted something moist—yes—but also dense and rich, something much more like a torte. So I replaced the walnuts in the original with pecans for a nicer balance of flavor with what is really a subtle-flavored liquor, added some lemon for zest . . . and came up with a cake with a dense and crumbly texture, a spirited aroma, and a delicate nutty taste, not at all dominated by whiskey flavor. A fine tea or coffee cake, served plain or perhaps lightly dusted with confectioners' sugar, it also makes a distinctive dessert at dinner, each slice anointed with freshly whipped cream.

Irish Whiskey Cake

1 lemon
¼ cup Irish whiskey
¾ cup (1½ sticks) sweet butter
½ cup white sugar
⅓ cup brown sugar

3 egg yolks
1¼ cups (about ¼ pound) pecan meal*
1 cup flour, sifted
1 teaspoon baking powder

*Pecan meal is available from Sunnyland Farms (minimum order 3 pounds). Write to: P. O. Box 549, Albany, GA 31703. You can make your own by grinding pecan bits into as fine a powder as possible. Be careful using a food processor to do this: it is easy to end up with pecan butter instead.

About 3 or 4 hours before making the cake, thinly peel the lemon (removing as little of the white pith as possible) and set this zest to macerate in the Irish whiskey for at least 3 hours, reserving the rest of the lemon for some other purpose. Afterward, remove the peel, mince a scant teaspoon's worth, and return to the whiskey, discarding the remaining pieces.

Preheat the oven to 350°F. Cream the butter, both the sugars, and egg yolks together for several minutes, until the mixture is silky smooth and lies luscious on the tongue. Pour the lemon-flavored whiskey with its minced peel into the pecan meal. Stir this together and beat into the cake batter until well blended. Sift together the flour and baking powder and stir into the batter. When this is well incorporated, scrape into a buttered and floured 9-inch (preferably springform) pan. Gently smooth the batter with a spatula and put into the oven to bake for 1 hour. Then turn off the heat and, the oven door put ajar, let the cake cool in the oven for 15 minutes. Remove, release the sides of the pan, and put the cake on a rack to cool. The cake tastes even better the next day: it does not need refrigeration and will keep in a cake tin for at least a week.

(Serves 8)

APPLESOURCE.   One happy sign of America's interest in its own good food is the resurgence of the apple, our national fruit. Not so long ago, even in the height of apple season, the supermarkets thought it daring to offer a few Rome Beauties or Jonathans with the paraffin-glossed piles of Red Delicious and Granny Smiths. Things are much better now, but we still have a long way to go before we can match the fruit markets of a century ago, through which a spectacular pageant proceeded from as early as May right into the winter: Early Strawberries, Golden Sweetings, Yellow Boughs, Summer Pippins, Pearmains, Belle-Flowers, Beswicks, Red Astracans, Seek-No-Furthers . . . names as pretty as poetry and now almost forgotten, every one.

But Tom Vorbeck's Applesource is making a heroic effort to change all that. From his own orchard in Chapin, Illinois, and from other specialist suppliers in Kentucky, Indiana, Michigan, and California, he offers us a chance to taste not only many of those old apples, but an astounding variety of new ones. The aromatic Black Gilliflower, Calville Blanc, a French dessert apple, the drab, flame-tinged Cox's Orange Pippin, with its subtle but lingering aftertaste . . . by my count nearly one hundred different varieties.

Applesource offers special tasting packs (which I've tried—every apple was perfect and delicious, the varieties as various as grapes, good in many different ways), or you may also pick specific varieties. Prices are reasonable: the tasting packs are $15 for twelve—two each of six varieties; slightly more when you specify your own choices. Write for their informative brochure: Applesource, Route 1, Chapin, IL 62628.

Winter

❀

AGED SARDINES.   Another almost vanished culinary art, that of aging sardines. Once, not so long ago, or so the story goes, down in every gourmand's cellar sat a carton of sardine cans. This, unlike its companion case of Château Latour, the *bec fin* faithfully rotated every few months to give each fish its fair soak in the virgin oil in which it was canned, and thus bringing it to the peak of perfection. Well, just in the past few months, I've stumbled across several mentions of this subject in various reading, and I'm naturally eager to share it all.

First of all, Patricia Wells reveals in her fascinating *Food Lover's Guide to Paris* that sardine-aging is once again the rage of that city. This means that you can already find them in exclusive New York food stores at astronomical prices. And somewhere in Maine a firm of young entrepreneurs is putting up the "new American cuisine" sardine, grilled on mesquite and hand-packed in date-stamped tins, filled to the brim with extra-virgin olive oil and lesser-known Provençal herbs.

Naturally, with sardines as with wines, some dates are better than others: we must not only learn to inquire if a sardine is vintage, but *what* vintage exactly. How do you tell the good sardine years? In *The Official Foodie Handbook* (a delightfully mean-spirited send-up of the current, and especially current British, food scene) we learn that Oscar Wilde's son, Vyvyan Holland, started London's first sardine-tasting club in 1935 to answer just this question. (Dad was a hard act to follow.) He said the best *they* ever tasted was a 1906 Rodel. Not many of those still around, I'll wager, but he does have some useful pointers for the contemporary taster: Brittany sardines in Midi olive oil are the best combination, especially the early spring catch that is canned in April. However, it isn't the sardines who have a good year but the oil they're packed in. You tell a good olive oil year by how the Sauternes have done that same year (but remember the sardines, canned in April, will be dated the year after).

Well, the last great year for Sauternes was '75—before that, '71 and '59. The problem is that they don't tin sardines like they used to: nowadays the recommended aging time is four years, not forty.

So, alas, we can only imagine it . . . gathered with our fellow gourmands around the table, palates cleansed, nostrils flared, butter knives at the ready, while the sardine steward cranks the key on a thirty-year-old can, the interior of which has melded into something so richly mellow that at the first tender pat of the blade the fish crumble into a single, buttery, piscatory mass, awash in a fragrant oil. . . .

WORST EXCESSES OF THE '80S (TO DATE). *Kiwi fruit.* Its promoters claim it tastes like a strawberry, an apple, a grape—and so it does, only not nearly as good as any of them. An insipid, expensive fruit with a phony, cutesy name—I say it's a Chinese gooseberry and I say to hell with it. *Calphalon cookware.* In my personal experience, while it may have all the features they claim for it, there's an important one they forgot to mention: food sticks to it like crazy. What good is the heavy weight and the even heat distribution if you have to scrape out the bacon with a chisel? *Paul Prudhomme.* Okay, a wild and crazy guy, a genius in the kitchen—just forget the cookbook. The recipes are overelaborate, the dishes hokey without his personal touch, and nothing at all like real Cajun home cooking. What this country needs is *Chef Paul Prudhomme's MOTHER'S Louisiana Kitchen.*

CHICKEN IN A BLADDER. In *An Omelette and a Glass of Wine,* her collection of essays reviewed elsewhere in these pages, Elizabeth David quotes a certain Madame Barattero's assertion that it is difficult to poach chicken, however carefully, without having it turn out *un peu delavé*—"a little washed out" in flavor. Indeed it is, and often dry in texture as well. That lady's solution (after stuffing the bird with "a little foie gras and slices of truffle"!) was to tie it up in a pig's bladder before immersing it in the poaching liquid. There it was simmered to perfection, removed, and let cool—still in the bladder—the flavors undiluted, the juices, those that escaped the chicken itself, solidifying into a "clear and delicately flavored jelly." Another advantage is that a tenderer younger fowl can be used than is usually poached: the flesh is meltingly tender and, because its juices are not diluted in cooking water, equally full of flavor.

No recipe is given, Elizabeth David correctly assuming that few of us have pig bladders at hand. But I did have one of the ovenproof roasting bags that I use for pasta-making (see page 131). My fowl being no *poulet de Bresse,* it deserved no sliced truffle nor foie gras and got none; instead it was stuffed with a simple mélange assembled as follows. Two shallots were minced and sautéed in a lump of sweet butter, along with the chicken's liver, about a cup of sliced, fresh mushrooms, and an equal amount of chopped sweet, fresh fennel (stalk and leaf). This was removed from the flame the moment the shallot was translucent and the liver done. The liver was cut into bits and returned, and this entire mixture was tossed with about a cup's worth of stale French bread that had been broken into small bits and freshened (but not to sopping) in a fresh white wine.

After as much loose fat was pulled away as could be, the bird was rubbed inside and out with a generous pinch of coarse salt already mixed with bits of fresh tarragon and coarsely ground pepper. Then its cavity was filled with the stuffing. The bird was then placed in the bag, which was knotted tightly shut after as much air as possible was forced out (or rather drawn out via my lungs). A large pot of water (sufficient to cover the bag) was set to a simmer and the bag lowered in. When the water was returned to just less than a simmer (the surface just quivering—it must *never* boil), the pot was covered and let to cook for about 1½ hours, or until the leg moved freely when tested through the bag.

This was then carefully removed from the pot, the bird lifted from the bag and set on a platter, and the liquid poured through a strainer. The fat was skimmed off and the juices—which made an excellent jellied broth—were set in the refrigerator to cool. The meat itself was eaten warm, served with the stuffing and a little of the broth, the remainder of both being saved to be put to various uses. However, the chicken can be cooked without the stuffing and, when cool, simply set in the refrigerator (the juices separate) for later use.

Afterword. Recently, I received a letter from Barbara Tropp in which she shared her own foolproof poaching method, given in her really superlative *Modern Art of Chinese Cooking.* That book should be consulted for the fine details, but it essentially entailed seasoning the bird and lowering it into simmering water. The heat was then turned off and the chicken left to cook to perfection in the slowly cooling water.

I adapted this technique to the chicken in the bag (with a few touches of my own) to absolutely astounding success. The bird emerged from the pot as juicy and tender as can be imagined and full of its own flavor. If you want to try it, I suggest omitting the stuffing entirely to avoid possible bacterial spoilage; instead, generously rub the bird with seasonings (I used a mixture made of tarragon, garlic, and salt and pepper stirred into olive oil). Tie it in the roasting bag as directed above, again drawing out as much air as possible (otherwise the bird will float on top of the poaching liquid, not in it).

Bring a good amount of water to a boil in a large, coverable pot. As soon as it does, remove the lid of the pot and wrap it in a dish towel. Gently lower the bagged chicken into the roiling water, cover the pot with the towel-wrapped lid—pressing down firmly to ensure a tight fit—and turn off the heat. The towel acts both as a seal to help keep the lid fitting snugly and as an insulator. Check to make sure that there are no wrinkles or folds where lid joins pot that would let heat escape.

That's all there is to it. The chicken will be perfectly poached in about 3 hours, or when the side of the pot is no longer too hot to touch. (Using Barbara Tropp's direct-immersion technique, it cooks in 2 hours, but I allowed an extra hour because of the bag's insulating properties—no problem, since with this method it will not overcook. It can even be left in a few hours longer if you are out.) Remove it from the water and either eat or refrigerate as directed above.

PRIVATE STOCK.   Marie Carey, who does a food show for San Diego's public broadcasting station, and Robert Menifee, "world traveler and raconteur" (a position I've widely applied for to no avail), have together published a small but sprightly spiral-bound collection of their favorite recipes, appropriately titled *Private Stock*.

Most of the dishes they offer are nicely thought out, attractive, well flavored . . . and spiced with a subtly challenging note. Sitting down to dinner with them, one imagines one of the duo catching the eye of the other while saying to the guest, "Now, I know you're going to think you won't like this," and out comes the tureen of Louisiana turtle soup, the platter of grillades and grits, the bowl of *macque choux* (a mélange of corn, squash, tomatoes, and chilies), or the plate of tomato pudding. Of course it turns out terrific. After the first polite and tentative taste, you end up mopping your plate. Chalk one up for Carey/Menifee.

Private Stock is, in fact, a book of plate moppers—dishes that, however simple, demand to be served to company . . . rich, satisfying, and with just the right amount of swag. This recipe for pork-stuffed onions, for instance (slightly adapted to my own taste), meets all those qualifications: for ease, surprise, delight. (This book is available by mail from Cobble and Mickle Books, P. O. Box 3521, San Diego, CA 92103-0160, for $6.95 postpaid.)

Pork-Stuffed Onions

8 medium or 4 very large
  onions
1 pound ground pork
¼ cup minced cilantro
2 cloves garlic, minced
½ teaspoon dried oregano
1 teaspoon salt

½ teaspoon freshly ground
  pepper
½ teaspoon cayenne pepper
2 cups fresh French bread
  crumbs
4 tablespoons (½ stick) butter

Boil 2 quarts of water over medium heat. Drop in the onions and simmer for 8 to 10 minutes, depending on their size. Carefully remove and set in a colander to cool. Then cut off the root ends and pull away the skin. Slice away a cap at the top and scoop out the center with a spoon, being careful not to puncture them. Mince and reserve half a cup of the scooped-out onion.

Preheat oven to 350°F. Heat an ungreased skillet over medium heat and, when hot, add the pork, breaking it into bits with a wooden spoon. Cook it, stirring occasionally, until it begins to turn brown (about 10 minutes), add the reserved minced onion, herbs and other seasonings, incuding the salt and pepper. Stirring constantly, continue cooking until the pork is brown and the onion translucent. Turn this into a bowl and mix in 1½ cups of the bread crumbs.

Stuff the onions with this mixture and then top them with the remaining ½ cup of bread crumbs, dotting them with the butter. Set into a buttered baking dish and bake for 20 to 30 minutes, depending on size.

(Serves 4)

PEARS AND TOASTED HAZELNUTS IN WHIPPED CREAM WITH ARMAGNAC,   a simple but elegant dessert. You need only be blessed with perfectly ripe pears—about half a pear per person, more if the pears are small. Pare them, core them, and cut them into small dice, and then toss them in a small amount, 2 tablespoons or so, of Armagnac or Calvados. Let the pears macerate in a small covered bowl in the refrigerator for an hour or so.

Crack a handful of hazelnuts and toast them the lightest tint of brown in a preheated oven (or toaster oven) set at 400°F, tossing the pan occasionally. Let them cool and chop them fine. At dessert time, whip some heavy cream (about 2 tablespoons per person), sweetening it with a little honey. Gently stir the fragrant bits of pear all through the cream and divide it among the requisite number of dessert dishes. Lightly dust with the hazelnut bits and serve. (The nuts, of course, can be omitted for eaters who do not care for them. They will be quite happy with the pears and cream alone.)

THE FART IN COOKING.

> *Chew your food properly. Your digestion depends on it.*—Slogan decorating the childhood home of Claude Lévi-Strauss

Americans, more than any other culture on the earth, are cookbook cooks; we learn to make our meals not from any oral tradition, but from a text. The just-wed cook brings to the new household no carefully copied collection of the family's cherished recipes, but a spanking new edition of *Fannie Farmer* or *The Joy of Cooking*.

No doubt this has its good points, but the drawbacks are many. Not only is our nation's cooking far more homogenized than needs be (a benefit mostly to giant food conglomerates), but it is robbed of the lip-smacking appreciation of the sensuality of eating, something very few cookbooks are able—and no basic cookbook even attempts—to share.

The cookbook is more than an organized repository of recipes: it is a bible of refinement and economy, the worst two bugbears to find on any pathway to a good time. Its historical place has been to preach (under the guise of nutrition and tastefulness) submission of the body pleasurable to the socially acceptable to a nation composed of immigrants, many initially innocent of Protestant-ethic prudery. Almost always, therefore, the cookbook belongs on the shelf, not next to the *Kama Sutra*, but beside Emily Post.

An index of the subversion of pleasure to good manners is the

submersion of the rough sort of humor that would otherwise link eating
with the other things earthy and real. Italians, for instance, prepare
such dishes as Nun's Thighs and Nipples of the Virgin, names that
would strike sheer terror in the heart of even the most adventurous
American housekeeper. Even the homely but tasty English dish, Toad
in a Hole, has not found many friends on this side of the Atlantic,
let alone the similarly named but more obscene-sounding French dish,
poulet à la crapaudine.

It is entertaining to watch the ways American translators shy before
such uninhibited fare—as in the instance of the common French
dessert or snack, *pets de nonne,* or "nun's farts." Under that sobriquet
it is easily found in France and has been for some time, a crispy-
brown fried nugget powdered with confectioners' sugar. But the name
is too embarrassing for most cookbook writers (look for it in vain in
Julia Child or Elizabeth David), and those that do mention it either
bowdlerize the name or retitle it entirely.

Thus, in the translation of Robert Courtine's *Real French Cooking,*
pets de nonne damnée ("farts of a damned nun") is transmogrified into
"doughnuts (almond)"—and Helen McCully's recipe for the pecul-
iarly named *pets de nonne au fromage* (which is cheese—the nun or the
fart?) is rendered as "cheese fritters."

Or else the scandal is alluded to without being named, as does Roy
Andries de Groot: "This irreverent name for a light-as-air, very re-
strained little deep-fried fritter has been shocking diners for almost
300 years." More likely, on its home turf, the name *hasn't* shocked
any diners for at least 300 years, but the curious reader who knows
no French will have only the faintest clue as to what the fuss is about
from his translation, "the puff of a nun from Chamonix."

So far as I can tell, only two writers, Anne Willan and Richard
Olney, have been willing to call a spade a spade, though Olney makes
the odd observation that while they were called *pets de putain* ("whore
farts" . . . or "tart's farts") early in the nineteenth century, the name
was changed to the current one to make them "more respectable."
Surely the movement was in the opposite direction—to increase the
shock and hence the humor. (He provides conclusive evidence to
disprove his own theory: the largest of the tiny puffs is attributed to
the Mother Superior.)

In her *French Regional Cooking,* Anne Willan bites the bullet: "The
name has no polite translation; they are, quite simply, nun's farts."

However, when *Time* magazine reviewed her book (November 23, 1981), the admiring and amused reviewer couldn't help but mention the dish; his editor, likewise, couldn't help but blue-pencil it: ". . . the fritters from the Alps known as *pets de nonne* (the name suggests they are gaseous)." Which, of course, it doesn't at all; the famous fact-checkers at that magazine were defeated by a centuries-old bit of whimsy.

It might be argued that the reason for our delicacy in this matter is that America is a multidenominational society: in France, where most of the population is, or pretends to be, Catholic, no one need worry about being thought a bigot. However, in many American households, the nether end of the turkey or roast chicken is known as either "the Pope's nose" or else "the parson's nose," and I have never noted that this cognomen fell along strictly denominational lines.

More to the point, I think, is our terror of ever hinting at the table at the ultimate terminus of the food that passes through our body—as witness the frantic soaking of kidneys, which serves less as a means of removing all possible hint of their bodily function than as a kind of baptizing them into their new life as a food. And likewise with things sexual: no bull's pizzle ever finds its way to the national menu, vanishing instead into dog food factories. Even the innocuous oxtail is a hard ingredient to lay a hand on, as are "Rocky Mountain oysters," a prime ingredient of the sheepherder's version of son-of-a-bitch stew.

Surprisingly, the French phrase *pets de nonne* does appear in an 1869 American cookbook, Pierre Blot's *Hand-Book of Practical Cookery*. After that, however, the name vanishes for a hundred years. The fritter, however, did not. Whether because of this introduction or another, it became a familiar American dish in the latter part of the nineteenth century. Eric Quayle, in *Old Cook Books*, erroneously attributes it to an "old American recipe" under the name of "nun's sigh" and states that this "American soufflé" is "still a favorite dessert in the more exclusive and expensive restaurants in New York and other East Coast cities." Not that I can afford such places, but I doubt this very much.

So, how does one make a nun fart? Why, load her plate with cassoulet . . . no, no, no. The devil made me write that. Actually, the recipe is simple and good, and for the hell of it, I'll throw in one for the Breton fart, too. Lionel Davidson (the noted thriller writer and author of *The Rose of Tibet*, *Murder Games*, and *Night of Wenceslas*) says this is so named because of the flatulent sound it utters in the oven. Go ahead and listen, but it is no more than an oven-made version of the original.

Nun Farts (Pets de Nonne)

6 tablespoons (¾ stick) butter
2 teaspoons sugar
Pinch salt
1 teaspoon grated lemon rind
4 eggs
1 cup flour (sifted)
1 teaspoon vanilla
1 teaspoon dark rum (optional)
Oil for deep-frying
Confectioners' sugar

Combine the butter, sugar, salt, and lemon rind with 1 cup water in a saucepan and bring the mixture slowly to a boil. When the butter has completely melted, remove the pan from the heat. While the pan is heating, break each of the eggs into a separate custard cup or similar small dish and have these ready. When the pan is removed from the heat, add all the flour at once, stirring, first carefully, then, when the flour is absorbed, vigorously with a wooden spoon.

When you have a compact, thick paste, turn the heat to medium high and return the pan to it. Cook this mixture for 3 to 4 minutes, stirring constantly and scraping the sides and bottom, until the batter clings together in a solid mass, leaving the bottom and sides of the pan clean, and takes on a glossy look. Turn off the heat and remove the pan from the stove.

Beat in the vanilla, and the rum if used, giving the batter a chance to cool a little. When it has, make a well in its center, pour in 1 egg, and beat this into the mass. When it is incorporated, beat in another egg and proceed until all the eggs are used. The resulting pastry should be flexible and soft, firm enough to hold its shape and not at all runny. Set it aside and let it rest for about 45 minutes, or for the duration of supper.

When ready to make the fritters, fill a deep skillet or deep-fat fryer two-thirds full of oil and heat to 360°F (not too hot, or the exteriors will brown before the center is cooked). If you are using a deep-fat fryer, do not use the basket, but a slotted spoon or wire mesh skimmer instead. Drop the batter into the hot oil a teaspoonful at a time, dipping the spoon into the oil after each scoop. Don't overcrowd the pan, since they puff up to about four times their original size. Nudge them to roll over, so that they color evenly on all sides. When golden brown, drain on paper towels and sprinkle with confectioners' sugar. Serve hot.

(Makes 40 fritters)

Pet de Breton. This recipe makes 1 large fart. Make the batter with the same ingredients the same way as explained above, including the 45-minute rest. Preheat oven to 375°F. Pour the batter into a large greased pan (a 10-inch or so heavy cast-iron frying pan works well for this) and set in the oven. Bake for an hour. Remove, sprinkle with confectioners' sugar, tear apart, and eat as soon as it's cool enough to handle.

ROASTING YOUR OWN.   Only a few years ago, we coffee drinkers seemed presented with a renaissance. Coffee stores blossomed every-where, offering fragrant, fresh-roasted beans from every port of call on a caffeine-addict's dream tramp-steamer manifest: Haiti, Jamaica, West Africa, Sumatra, Hawaii. All that was needed was a rebirth of the coffeehouse for a return of paradise. It was not to be. Whether because of the erratic zigzags of the coffee market, the turn of the chic to wine and the health-conscious to herbal teas, or just the natural American resistance to paying big bucks for beans, suddenly it all changed. The wealth of variety vanished, replaced by ersatz exotica like "Tip of the Andes," mimicry like "Kona style," or, worst of all, the endemic plague of the flavored beans, brandy and hazelnut, Swiss chocolate cherry. . . . Equally depressing has been the trend of the few remaining spe-cialty roasters to dark-roast all their beans to the European style. The taste for coffee slowly percolated up through Europe from its starting point in the Middle East, and the closer you return to those origins, the more you still find coffee drunk black and thick as sludge, with caffeine enough to knock a mule to its knees. Silken-textured and drenched with flavor, this style of coffee in its many Mediterranean versions is a ceremonial drink, meant to be slowly savored with due regard—like whiskey neat. And because dark roasting demands beans that can stand up to the strongly bitter, caramel taste characteristic of a dark roast, a pungent, even coarse-tasting bean is preferable over a delicately flavored one.

Our own taste in coffee is very different. Drunk in England and later in this country in competition with tea, it evolved into a tealike brew: fragrant, full-flavored, and with a brilliantly clear liquor. Coffee firms sought out the fragile, expensive beans that produced such a cup to perfection, and roasted them just to the point where their own flavor bloomed, unmarred by any hint of scorch.

In short, there are beans to roast dark and beans to roast light, and what I object to is our specialty roasters' recent insistence on submitting superbly delicate beans to a treatment for which they were never meant. I recently came across some fancy Kona roasted black, all its special flavors burnt away. The sheer waste—and snobbish ignorance—of it upset me enough to get me thinking again about roasting my own. So, when Melitta recently introduced an electric hot-air roaster, I decided to give it a try.

Alas, I can't recommend it. Green coffee beans have a markedly sour odor that roasting draws off; otherwise, the coffee itself will taste too much of it. The beans must be heated at over 400°F to get rid of it; the Melitta machine—or at least the two I tested—got up to only about 325°F, enough to turn the beans brown but not get rid of the sour tang. It was also too noisy for me in the morning, like fifteen minutes with a hair dryer running in the kitchen.

But inspired by the two pounds of green coffee beans I purchased at the same time as the machine, I tried roasting a batch in my toaster oven. They turned out well enough to keep experimenting, and I've come close enough to perfection, thanks to what's turned out to be the near ideal implement for the job: a Chinese metal dim sum steamer tray (like a round cake tin but only six inches in diameter, and with a perforated bottom), purchased in a Chinese grocery for about one twelfth the cost of the electric coffee roaster.

I preheat the toaster oven to 450°F, spread 3 scant scoops of beans (5½ tablespoons—enough for 4 cups of coffee) over the bottom of the steamer tray, and set it on the oven rack. I give them a good shake every 30 seconds or so until they start to brown. When they start popping (like popcorn, but without the vigor), I shake them every 15 seconds until perfect (about 6 minutes, all told). I then toss them into a colander to cool them down and shake away some of the chaff. Then I grind them and make a pot of brew.

Is it worth it? If you already grind your own beans, it's certainly worth considering. It's only a little more work and coffee from fresh-roasted beans is not only better but more interesting; you'll catch little flavor notes that have long evaporated out of the roasted beans you bring home from the store. Since I have time in the morning, I have happily worked a daily roasting into my breakfast routine; I love the aroma, the busywork, the absolute and stunning freshness of the brew.

The bad news: roasting your own beans produces a distinct aroma, the same one you may have noticed gracing the neighborhoods of coffee-roasting businesses. It is a wonderful thing to sniff on a cold winter's day as you pass outside, but consider a bit before you decide to live with it; it can cling to the drapery as tenaciously as cigar smoke. More seriously, overroasting the beans forces their volatile oils to the surface, *where they may ignite.* You *must* watch the beans carefully, especially when dark-roasting them.

Not everyone, I realize, has a Chinese grocery handy, but I got pretty good results using a plain metal roasting pan. (The toaster oven tray itself is not a good substitute, because the beans need vigorous shaking to roast evenly.) And while not every toaster oven is large enough to accommodate such a pan, an alternative would be to preheat your oven to 500°F and roast the beans there in a wire colander (which will have to be devoted to that purpose, since it will soon turn black). However, the method described in most coffee-making manuals, where the beans are roasted on top of the stove in a covered pan with an oven thermometer inserted, is, in my experience, a joke.

Actually, the most serious problem the neophyte roaster will face is finding green coffee beans to roast. Few coffee dealers roast their own, and few of those are willing to sell green beans. Here are three solutions, should no one sell them in your vicinity. (If someone does, they should give you a discount: not only are you doing the work, but since the roasting drives out moisture, a pound of roasted beans contains about 15 percent more beans than an unroasted one.) Don't hesitate to stock up, by the way; kept dry and cool, green coffee beans have an almost unlimited shelf life.

The Melitta company offers their own blend green at $4.70 per pound ($5.65 decaffeinated) plus a single $1.50 shipping and handling charge for any amount of beans (Customer Service Department, Melitta Inc., 1401 Berlin Road, Cherry Hill, NJ 08003). Nescafé Royal beans, a mixture of high-grown beans from Costa Rica, Guatemala, and Kenya, are available at 17½ ounces for $6.50 plus a single $3.50 handling charge (item 4510 from The Chocolate Collection, P. O. Box 217, Paradise, PA 17562). But before ordering, write and make sure these are still available. Catalogue companies drop such esoteric items easily, and coffee prices these days are very volatile.

My own solution has been to purchase them from a local firm, The Coffee Connection. They sell green any coffee they roast and at a 15 percent discount, including such premium ones as Kona, Jamaica Blue Mountain, and Celebes Kalossi, as well as less pricy African and Latin American (plus four decaffeinated) beans. For their current list and mail order information, write their mail order department at 342 Western Ave., Brighton, MA 02135, or phone: (617) 254-1459. VISA and MC accepted. They also sell these beans freshly roasted and a prime selection of teas, both premium—such as Golden Nepal black and Japanese Sencha green—and special grade—such as Namring Darjeeling (first flush). Good stuff.

In a word, coffee is the drunkard's settle-brain, the fool's pastime, who admires it for being the production of Asia, and is ravished with delight when he hears the berries grow in the deserts of Arabia, but would not give a farthing for a hogshead of it, if it were to be had on Hampstead Heath or Banstead-Downs. . . .
—THOMAS TRYON, *The Good Haus-Wife Made a Doctor* (1692)

IV

TABLE TALK

Fat Cook, Thin Cook

❀

Only a person who had spent loving hours hovering over a serious
stove in pursuit of a serious feast could have developed such an
intense personal bouquet as now permeated his entire presence.
The man was wearing his menu. There was the salty, vivacious
ozone of flat Brittany oysters . . . the unctuous continuo of foie
gras in a single, suave bass note; the powerful benthic aroma of
a lobster . . . and, over all, the principal melody line, familiar
even to a visiting American, the chestnut-stuffed turkey. . . .
With his stately tummy, his prosperous countenance, as round
and red as a ballon of Beaujolais, he could have been a butcher
or stockbroker. . . .   —RUDOLPH CHELMINSKI

The kitchen monk . . . considered me thoughtfully. "One must
feed the corpse as well as the spirit," he observed in a heavy
Provençal accent, and grinned seraphically. He was thin as a
fencepole, with the marks of asceticism like the marks of an
axe over his long face and frame. He disappeared into an echo-
ing pantry and came out with plate after plate balanced on his
arm. . . . I was told simply, *"Mangez, mais mangez, tout-ce que vous
voudrez!"*   —RICHARD HOLMES

Cooks come in two classic sizes, just like clowns: fat and thin. But
while the most appealing of clowns is Pierrot, pale, lean, and dreamy,
with cooks, at least until recently, the popular one was the fat one.
Built solid as a side of beef, with bloodred complexion and well-licked
lips, wiping his pudgy pink fingers on a greasy apron, he embodied
appetite itself, with eyes eternally larger than the stomach.

He understood. "Eat!" he encouraged and eat we did, not because
his heft was proof of his capabilities (when the truth is told, I think,
the thin cook holds the edge on quality) but because he cast no cold
eye on the largeness of our hunger. In fact, he (or she, for sex is no
issue here) assuaged our guilt. No matter how much we put away,
we never rose from it looking like him. If *he* was gluttony, then our
own most outrageous gorging was almost a golden mean.

Fat cooks are an inclusive fraternity: all are welcome at their table. The more who eat with them the better; they increase the pleasure of their own lips by the smacking of ours. Nothing delights them more than matching flagon to flagon, than some competition as to who gets the last chop on the platter—and wipes it clean of gravy with the last bit of bread.

His cooking is characterized by its ease of swallowing, the way each bite demands another to fill its place. Not that he isn't finicky enough about flavor, but for him the taste of food is in good part its richness, the ecstatic slide of pleasure down the tongue. The celebrator of fullness, he is the fat cook not only because of his personal avoirdupois but also because he writes his signature with butter on a dish already heavy with suet and cream.

Cooking for the fat cook is an extension of his appetite. He has already sat down to dinner when he lights the stove; he will have eaten a whole meal before he serves it forth. The whisk, the stirring spoon, go automatically into his mouth, not the sink, the few bits of buttery onion left in the sauté pan swept up deftly by his thumb. I knew a cook who would actually prepare an extra portion for himself to eat before he came to table, so that the remaining servings could be equally divided without the worry he might not get the larger share, and for a long time I thought this sort of greed was the motivation for stove-top tasting—a reward for doing the work, a head start on the rest of the diners.

But, on further reflection, I think this greed the exception, not the rule. The fat cook will carefully trim away the suet and gristle from a roast or some chops and then, instead of discarding it, rub the bits with garlic and salt and fry them up as a solitary hors d'oeuvre. If there were a general demand, he would be delighted to prepare and pass around a whole plateful. But he knows better, as he also knows that no one wants the broccoli stalks he crunches or the carrot ends, the sweet tips of the corncobs. They are his by popular surrender, not private fiat.

And what of the thin cook? M. F. K. Fisher, in "I Was Really Very Hungry," one of her most disturbingly haunting culinary writings, recounts how she once stopped for lunch in an old country mill a famous

Parisian chef had turned into a restaurant. It was off season and she was all alone in the dining room. Only wanting something simple to eat, she found herself the unwilling recipient of a magnificent feast, cajoled and bullied by the waitress into trying taste after taste, each more spectacular than the next, but in relentless total pushing her a terrifying distance past surfeit.

Monsieur Paul, the master chef who prepared—for this solitary foreigner—these masterpieces, remained anonymous behind the kitchen door. He never appeared, even at the end of the meal, to receive his applause and perhaps even share a glass of brandy with his fortunate victim. Although the author calls the waitress mad, she was but handmaiden to the cook. If mad she was, the madness didn't stop with her. And that afternoon she pulled off an astounding feat—that of being high priestess to a private god before a reluctant cult of one.

Monsieur Paul. I imagine him as the thin chef carried to the ultimate extreme, a cook whose appetite can only exist in the mouths of others. Unlike the fat cook, who uses other appetites as a foil, an amplifier for his own, for the thin cook, other people *are* his appetite. Only at that amount of distance can he allow himself to take pleasure in his cooking.

Thus the kitchen of the thin cook is entirely different from that of the fat cook: a place of immaculate order. Each ingredient is scrubbed, pared, polished into a tiny jewel, all coarseness fined away. If, in the fat cook's kitchen, the best-fed mouth is his own, in the thin cook's kitchen, it is that of the garbage can; into it tumbles the oddments and scraps, the less-than-perfect. Utensils, pots, counters are scoured clean as soon as they are used. It is as if the taste of what remains is concentrated by the essence of all the flavors that are flung away.

And where the fat cook feeds his appetite as if he were stoking a furnace, the thin cooks strops it with denial until it holds a razor's edge. He watches over his simmering pots with a fierce scrutiny but tastes them hardly at all, and then only enough to wet his tongue. He eats nothing in the kitchen; he knows his flavors by denying them to his mouth. His desire—and it is often realized—is to taste his dish only in the startled, delighted mouth of the one he feeds. Or, like Monsieur Paul, merely in the rumor of its acclaim.

If the fat cook cries out "Eat, eat!," the thin cook demands we taste. "Try this," he says, offering a sliver of duck pâté dotted with glistening morsels of truffle and crackling bits of fried skin. And when we do, he is with us just for that moment when the flavor explodes across the tongue. For the thin cook, pleasure ends the split second anticipation becomes reality. If he had his way, he would never swallow anything.

It is the thin cook who is in fashion today, except for a few militant rebels led by that king of fat cooks, Paul Prudhomme. The thin cook is artist, not artisan (just as is the thin clown, Pierrot, who nowadays almost never appears at the circus but has become instead the persona of the mime). In the best restaurants today we find on our plates only a few limpid slivers of moist and milky veal, spun round with a tracing of succulent sauce, accented with a few perfect ovals of baby carrot, a graceful arch of herb.

Each mouthful is so poignant, however, that our appetite, if not assuaged, is at least abashed. To be hungry before such food is as vulgar—as seemingly wrong—as feeling lust before the Venus de Milo. The thin cook invites us to use hunger, not satisfy it, to deny it even as we tempt it until our senses are pushed toward epiphany.

Nothing puts off a thin cook's appetite more than watching people actually devour his food. At best, he is happy in the company of others who, like himself, want only to taste and then quietly exclaim. But mostly he eats alone, after all the others, something simple and plain. Ironically, this is the one thing the thin and fat cook have in common: both eat more alone, the thin cook because it is the only time he can eat, the fat cook because he cannot imagine a meal for less than two, and, when sitting down to it, he plays both parts with gusto.

Stan Laurel, Oliver Hardy—you're fond of one and think the other's a goof or a bully. The same with the thin and the fat cook: we immediately take sides. They are myths, of course (although some cooks come surprisingly close to bringing them to life), masks we put on hunger to humanize it, the way clowns reduce life's random carelessnesses to harmless buffoonery.

Appetite can torture us with revulsion even as it fills us with delight, set guilty feelings astir as easily as visions of sugarplums. So, between appetite and self, we set the cook as gatekeeper, turning to the fat one when we are most at ease with it, the world our oyster. But we embrace the thin cook when we feel vulnerable, suddenly frightened of this act of eating, the world too hard, too awful to bite. The thin cook's hypercaution, his peckishness, his dizzy excitement over tiny tastes perk up even the most neurasthenic appetite.

There's no possible reconciliation: at any moment—maybe always—we feel kin to one or the other. But remember that, like Stan and Ollie, fat cook and thin cook feel for each other not antagonism, but a mysterious mutual—if barbed—affection. They are two different masks, but that which wears them is one.

In Defense of Picnics

❀

The Rat brought the boat alongside the bank, made her fast, helped the still awkward Mole safely ashore, and swung out the luncheon-basket. The Mole begged as a favor to be allowed to unpack it all by himself; and the Rat was very pleased to indulge him, and to sprawl at full length on the grass and rest, while his excited friend shook out the tablecloth and spread it, took out all the mysterious packets one by one and arranged their contents in due order, still gasping, "O my! O my!" at each fresh revelation.
—KENNETH GRAHAME

The most-read and most fondly remembered book of my childhood was Kenneth Grahame's *The Wind in the Willows* (the edition with Arthur Rackham's illustrations, please!). That story starts, as those of you who know the book instead of the Disney travesty will remember, with a picnic. The Mole, on the lam from spring housecleaning, encounters the river, the Water Rat, and the rowboat in a series of dazzling revelations and is swept away by all three to an ecstatic afternoon and the beginnings of a new life. At the center of all this, like some benign totem, is the picnic basket.

I mean, naturally, the classic picnic basket, the one made of wicker with all the necessary accouterments: the straps for plates, cups, and silverware; the different leather compartments to hold the wine bottle, saltcellar, and pepper mill. You can still purchase them at such posh British emporiums as Fortnum and Mason, Ltd. and Harrods, but it is now most often received as a wedding present—exclaimed over and then tucked away in the back of the storage room, a lifelong encumbrance too valuable to give away, too classy to hock, and too cumbersome to use.

This is all very sad and it shows, if nothing else, that there should be some sort of gift-giving event at the beginning of the amatory hunt. For that is the only time such a basket would nowadays be fitting and useful. What better way to win a heart than to spend a lazy summer afternoon in some shady and secluded country spot, a stream meandering by at the foot of the grassy slope, a few fleecy clouds floating overhead, and a bright red-and-white checkered cloth spread out, upon which sits the champagne, the fat wedge of *pâté de campagne*, the strawberries and cream?

In fact, writing down these lines awakens a memory of a picnic some eighteen years ago at Tanglewood in the Berkshires. Then a graduate student, I had no wicker basket and no funds to procure one, but I had enough for a visit to a local shop that carried a profusion of Japanese paper goods. Out of my knapsack that evening came a paper tablecloth of azure blue, followed by plates of that color in an even deeper hue, and other, smaller ones in a bright Kelly green, plus napkins of lavender—a regular little symphony of that end of the spectrum—followed by real wine glasses carefully wrapped in tissue.

I could tell I had already won her heart, at least for the evening, even before the food was displayed, a flute of French bread and an assortment of uniquely wrapped cheeses—one in vine leaves, another in cracked peppercorns, the last in grapeseeds. There was a little crock of sweet butter, a heap of glossy cherries, and a bottle of white wine.

We sat back on the grass far enough from the orchestra shed to have some space for ourselves, and lay on our backs watching the stars as strains of Mozart and then Mahler flowed past. My own regret that night was that I hadn't yet learned how to drive—otherwise, the presence of the friend who navigated us there and back again wouldn't have been required—and I might have been able to blow up the sparks of that evening and ignite them into a warm little blaze. It didn't happen—but the evening was its own pleasure enough.

No one would have a problem imagining the *romantic* possibilities of the right picnic at the right moment, but that, I think, is as far as most people's interest will carry these days. Discounting family outings, which aren't the same thing at all, most of us seem to have let picnics slide out of our lives altogether. That picnic shared by Rat and Mole, after all, was one that cemented a friendship, and what two (at least male) friends today would be caught setting off with a wicker basket between them? We can imagine them prowling the coast roads for the best fried-clam shack or hiking off to some wilderness stream to catch and cook up a pan of trout. But the essence of picnicking is *not* doing something. There is just no male model these days for drifting downriver in a rowboat, watching time and tide flow by, talking of nothing in particular, the oars adrift in the oarlock. Unless, of course, the boat is full of booze. Getting drunk together in any circumstances is an always acceptable male pastime.

This is not because we are fiercer than we should be but tamer than we want to admit. After all, what has replaced the picnic generally is the day's hike into the mountains with wilderness gear (a little more professional than really necessary), stuffed with survival rations of the sort that are meant to be eaten while spiked to the North Face of the Eiger. Friends that would once carry a picnic basket on an excursion up Mt. Monadnock (as tame a mountain as they come) now make an expedition of it, handing round the jerky, trail mix, gorp, and freeze-dried ice cream. Even the kids have their scaled-down sleeping bags and Rover his own doggy backpack.

I'm sure this is good healthy fun, and as the hikers clomp past me as I lie sprawled on the grass, tucked in front of a good view with an *al fresco* repast on the cloth before me, I give them all a friendly salute with my wine glass. But I think I detect in their return nods a shadow of censoriousness, a hint that they feel they are participating in some higher calling than my landscape browsing. Well, I retort (to myself), if there's too much Kenneth Grahame in my makeup, there's too much Lone Ranger and Tonto in theirs.

The picnic basket versus the backpack: two essentially incompatible visions. It's the difference between a brisk, invigorating ten minutes in the shower and a lazy half-hour in a warm and sudsy tub; both get you clean, but the pleasure each offers is markedly different. Your basic hiker-showerer believes that the best sort of pleasure is the direct consequence of virtuous action: the honest sweat from a trot around the neighborhood, the release that follows when cramps are kneaded out of knotted muscles after a scramble down a rockslide.

On the other hand, the average bather-picnicker has a more serendipitous vision: he prefers to be surprised by grace. For him, there is nothing like the gentle amazement in the paradox that something as pleasurable as a bath can get you clean, too . . . or in waking up from a postprandial snooze to find a family of raccoons rummaging through his leftovers. He is the happy recipient of small rewards he knows he doesn't deserve and treasures all the more for that fact, since they prove that life has other laws than those of strict cost-accounting.

The backpacker, on the contrary, sees existence's superfluous bounty as a snare; his is a horror of dead weight, and nothing fills him with more dread than putting into his knapsack something he might not absolutely need. His ultimate dream is to enter the wilderness with only a good knife and a hank of string—and to emerge a month later unscathed. The picnicker's wildest fantasy is to produce on the top of some unscalable precipice a whole roast chicken and a bottle of vintage Burgundy, and a real cloth spread to set them out on.

These are obviously irreconcilable differences. A little further into *The Wind in the Willows,* Mole makes an excursion all his own into the fearsome Wild Wood. After a nightmare flight (accompanied by the ostensibly rescuing Rat), he tumbles into the Badger's den, finding there the epitome of all that is comfortable and homey. The night ends with the two friends taking a long winter's snooze before a chuckling fire as a bitter storm rages without. If Rat and Mole had been made of sterner (i.e., the *right*) stuff, they would have dug themselves into a snowbank, lit their primus, climbed into their down-filled sleeping bags, and warmed themselves on thoughts of their tough moral fiber. These aren't two different endings; they are two different stories.

Am I getting too philosophical? Well, then, ask yourself when *you* last climbed up to the attic (if you're lucky enough to have one), not to clean it, but to just step outside yourself, watch life sail past outside and listen to the quiet heartbeat of things. If all you hear when you reach the top of the stairs is an inner voice nagging you to go do something productive, you had better stick to backpacking. But if you are suddenly overwhelmed by the simple delight of finding yourself on the other side of things for a moment, hunt out that lost wicker basket and meet me for the afternoon. There's hope for you—and for picnics—yet.

Truly Awful Recipes

❋

Question: What do the juice of one lemon, a quart bottle of Heinz catsup, a quart of Schweppes ginger ale, and two medium heads of (coarsely chopped) cabbage have in common? Well, whatever you think, it seems hard to imagine that the answer is that they're all part of the same casserole recipe. But, as a good friend informs me, those ingredients form the basis of a dish that's all the rage of his grandparents' Florida retirement community. You mix all these ingredients together, add meatballs (made from three pounds of lean ground beef, three eggs, and a minced onion) and simmer the result for an hour (covered) and twenty minutes (uncovered). People are crazy about it when he makes it and beg, plead, threaten for the recipe. Try it, he said, you'll love it.

There are three possible responses to a recipe of this type: outright disgust, hypnotic fascination, and a complex mixture of the two. Maybe I speak only for myself, but I think it's not unusual for even good cooks to nurture close to their hearts a recipe or two about which they're justifiably ashamed but not quite able to shake out of their repertoire. In my own case, for example, there's a chocolate cake made from Duncan Hines devil's food cake mix, instant chocolate pudding, a bag of chocolate chips, and a cup of sour cream. Rich, moist, and fairly oozing chocolate flavor, it's been my most regular contribution to office party and family picnic dessert tables for many years.

Truly awful recipes, like perpetual motion machines and no-diet weight-loss schemes, are recognized by what they promise: something always a little too good, too easy to be true. Recipes that conjure instant elegance from dross: scrumptious canapés from biscuit mix and processed cheese; creamy casseroles from canned soups and celery salt; magically moist chicken from flavored bread crumbs and Hellmann's mayonnaise.

A confidence trick, then . . . but that is only the start of the story. Like any truly brilliant swindle, they thrill us most when we know we're being taken but just can't help ourselves. The other side of the coin, of course, is that when they *don't* work, there's no magic there at all: the flavors cloy, the texture gums the mouth—one damning first bite and the rest is gingerly pushed to the side of the plate. The really and truly vulgar is a surprisingly personal thing.

Recipes like this almost never appear in cooking magazines anymore and not that often in the local food pages. But they have a fantastic underground currency, as anyone who takes even a peripheral peek into a spiral-bound community cookbook will attest. It's hard to open a page of a fund raiser without landing on Velveeta, crushed Ritz crackers, or Lipton instant onion soup mix—sometimes all in the same recipe. And any unbiased observer would have to admit the direct line between these dishes and the living pulse of American cooking.

I used to think that the reference to specific brand names (my friend swears that the above dish is no good at all without the Schweppes) meant that they originated in some corporate test kitchen. Now, after more reflection, I'm not so sure. I can't imagine Schweppes or even Heinz having the chutzpah in these culinarily self-conscious days to offer a dish of such sheer, unabashed vulgarity. Instead, I suspect those names represent "good taste." Made with store-brand catsup and no-name ginger ale, the dish takes on a pathetic note of poverty or—worse—stinginess. But while no cook would be oblivious to its economy (with two heads of cabbage and three pounds of ground beef, it must feed a herd), the top-of-the-line brand names give it a deluxe veneer.

Outside of this, the brand names in themselves are irrelevant. This dish has no special appeal to ginger-ale buyers or even, probably, catsup lovers, though any of those may like it. Its appeal comes from somewhere very different, as you will understand if in some unhallowed crevice of your subliminal appetite you did feel a little disquieting tremor. These recipes, somehow, excite.

One clue is that they increase in appeal when exchanged hand to hand with a glowing personal recommendation. It was an officemate who first got me to try the cake recipe, creating in the tension between the intensity of her praise and the humdrum ingredients a sense of complicity, like getting a spell from a witch. Really, she says, I know you won't believe this, but just cook up a mess of earthworms, stir in this toad water, and a sprinkling of cobweb—your guests will absolutely rave.

Magic, then, but a complex magic. Remember, this isn't your run-of-the-mill sort of shortcut with canned onion rings: we're talking strips of Wonder Bread spread with Cheez Whiz and rolled in Bacos. Truly *awful* recipes. The prominent presence of all highly processed foods in these recipes can't be by accident. At some pretty conscious level, these dishes are intentionally, even gleefully, hostile to the dictates of culinary good taste. Every reputable cookbook ever written defines good cooking as based on the taking of good honest ingredients and carefully and respectfully preparing them. Here, instead, unnatural ingredients are nonchalantly tossed together to everyone's delight.

Really, if they like it (and here's why the friend's recommendation is essential, to show that the dish works with your peers), your guests won't be the least offended when you reveal what they just ate. On the contrary, they'll most likely be delighted. How clever, they say, happy to be in the know, relieved at not having to do justice to what otherwise would have been your sincere effort to please. In certain circles, these dishes represent a kind of social tact. But there's still more to them than that.

Cleverness—this kind, anyway—is no virtue; it's more like gossip—relieving accumulated social pressures by a symbolic act of revenge, getting even. Who do these dishes get the best of, if it isn't those who eat them? Imagine picking up the phone and calling—say—Richard Olney or Madeleine Kamman to share this great recipe. You wouldn't be able to squeeze out the words. Just too shame-making. And that is exactly the magic power of the dish: where it is, those exacting culinary perfectionists are not. It creates an instant sense of tribal bonding. "Relax," it says for its maker, "I'm no Julia Child either. Like you, I hate to cook—but do I love to eat!"

The friend who phoned me with this recipe worked for several years in a good restaurant. He's far and away the better cook than I. But he has a jaundiced view of the cooking world and, like many people, is just as happy not having Pierre Franey peering over his shoulder every time he picks up a frying pan. A recipe like this (steering completely clear of cookbooks and cooking magazines) represents his way of sending such ghostly presences fleeing from the kitchen.

From the few of them that I've met, professional food people are the sort of overachievers whose eyes automatically light up at the mention of a new technique for hand-stretched strudel dough. As for myself, well, I have my good days and my bad days. During the latter, sometimes, I just don't give a damn. On those rare evenings when I feel an irrational but irresistible desire to heat up a panful of frozen, batter-dipped chicken wings, I know it isn't the food I crave. I just want—for the night—to shove all the company the hell out of the kitchen.

As for the chocolate cake recipe: 1 small package instant chocolate pudding; 1 box Duncan Hines Devil's Food cake mix; 1 12-ounce package chocolate chips; 2 eggs; and 1¾ cups sour cream. Mix it all together and scrape it into a buttered and floured Bundt pan (or facsimile). Bake 50 to 55 minutes in a preheated 350°F oven until the cake springs back when pressed lightly. (A cake tester will still emerge sticky; this is a very moist cake.) Yummy . . . but, hey, don't tell where you got the recipe.

Loving to Cook

❀

And when people say flatly that I *must* love to cook, since I not only write about food but make it, I wince a little, I cringe, invisibly. Why must I "love" it, just because I do it as well as I can? Are they really saying that I love myself? —M. F. K. FISHER

Love to cook. It's hard to get the phrase out of the mouth sounding right; directed *at* us, it's even faintly accusing. Cooking is work and while we can still like doing it, even the smallest sign of this pleasure seems to goad others into reminding us that they do not. When someone brightly notes, "You must really love to cook," most often they aren't so much interested in my answer as telling me, "Lucky you. I have to, you don't."

Well, yes, lucky me. Even so, if I do love to cook, it isn't the way I love eating pistachio nuts or sleeping late. For one thing, I casually admit to adoring both those things as easily as I do them. But admitting that I love to cook—*that* sticks in my craw. Cooking, I say defensively, is something I just do. Please don't mistake me for some kind of enthusiast.

How come? Well, to start, loving to cook implies mastery of same, and there I'm strictly a noncontender. This always seems hard for some cooks to grasp, but loving to cook is not necessarily loving to cook *well*. M. F. K. Fisher writes nicely about this in the first issue of *The Journal of Gastronomy*, confusing love for cooking with the power that comes from mastering it: a power over oneself, the people around us, the brute stuff of the world itself. Sometimes the power is real, sometimes not, but its relation to cooking is really only conterminous: we could as easily be talking about racing cars, writing books, raising kids, or anything else people get to preening about.

Loving to cook. My mother used to say, when I declared love for fried chicken backs, Charles Addams cartoons, or summer vacation, that you can't love something that can't love you back. Reciprocity: that's what made loving different from just liking. There's something to that idea, but really, I realize now, she was trying to protect me from the fickle human heart: we end up, so often, loving just those who can't—or won't—love back.

And there it is. If we mostly mumble and look pained when brought to confess a love for cooking, it's because we have the grace to remember all too well the times that love bored, depressed, even hurt. We might not know what love is, but we know what it does: puts us right up to the sharp edge. The crumpled pages that litter the floor, the Rapidograph pounded into the drawing board, the handful of tempura batter flung at the hungry interloper complaining about dinner's delay. "Love to cook?" we mutter. "To hell with yez."

Only, giving up on the page, the drawing, or the dish, we don't, can't, give up on being writer, artist, cook. Sometimes we think we can, just as we believe—after some absolute and irretrievable break— the heart forgets the lover. Then one night we wake up in the dark, covered with sweat and sadness, knowing that those feelings are all still there, only locked in a small box whose key we will never find again.

Love is only incidentally concerned with feelings of reciprocity, mastery, or even pleasure. We know it by a sudden sense of vulnerability, from the necessary but still almost unbearable touch of some stranger's heart against our hand—a touch, however ill the fit, that we never want to let go.

And it's here that loving and cooking intersect. Cooking, after all, before it ever became a craft, a hobby, or just another family chore, is what happens from when the hand first closes on what we mean to eat to the moment it puts it in the mouth. That time can be a few seconds, or minutes, hours, days—a span mirror image to the inner passage we call digestion, with eating the communion that connects them, making the flesh of the world the flesh of ourselves.

Cooking isn't only a deeply central part of our flirtation with the world, but also of our image of the world's flirtation with us. In our kitchens, we clean and anoint its body with oils and perfume, making it comely and sweet with such craft as we possess, though we have so wrapped this act in the language of sanitation and skill that we almost forget that this is the pivot of a cook's real calling, except, perhaps, inversely in the old slanders of cooks as slatterns and sots, the Bacchae of a merely secular humanism.

Buried, maybe, but not lost. To call yourself cook at all is to feel something of that tremor of the heart, some vulnerability to the attraction to the world as flesh, a feeling both of tenderness and terror. Eating is an amazing and a frightening thing, an act both of sustenance and contamination, a lust for connection and closing with corruption. Little wonder our feelings about it are so elusive and complex.

Our appetite, turned loose on the world, would eat it all; our fears, if we ever wholly listened, would starve us to death. And the balance between them is no mediation but an endless tug of war. Fear jerks and we slink off and suck dry toast; appetite hauls back and we bolt raw oysters, feast on mushrooms plucked on impulse from the reeky woods.

To cook is to lay hands on the body of the world. Those who do it just because they must have learned to keep their distance, their fingers numb, an easy task these days, with that flesh so weakened and so much put between. But to love to cook is to feel—to want to feel—that flesh itself, to be open and vulnerable to what the touch entails, a tremor of connection to the heart of what we eat.

An act of not just love but of loving. We come closest to feeling this when we cook for just ourselves. The more others intrude, the more complex and confusing the calculus; turned loose in the kitchen alone, we feel an intimate connection that seems almost illicitly intense, exactly why so many won't cook for themselves at all and others escape by taking the emblem for the thing itself, poaching an egg in consommé to take a true but finally passive comfort in its warmth and mouth-ease.

We, real cooks, want more. Satiety is an end only after we have used it as a means—putting hands, eyes, nose, and mouth to play, pulling out of scraps and crusts something messy, greasy, crunchy, good. Only in such privacy do we dare such intimacy, rubbing appetite right up against that razor edge where it lives most fiercely, the very border where our terror threatens to topple it into disgust.

This is the secret desire that the real cook clutches close to heart and what makes cooking mean more than any mastery: to tease the tongue and calm the fearful heart, to bring our appetite to where the eggs are eaten loose, the meat served rare and juicy, the cheese not parted from the mold—to lay our tongue against the palpitation of the world's own body and not faint dead away.

That is where love is and what cooking is about.

Intimate Cuisine

❀

Something has happened to supper.

I don't mean *dinner*, that special, slightly formal meal that we have friends over to and sometimes sit down to ourselves on special occasions, but the plain and casual feed that awaits us at end of day. I still look forward to it, but when I actually pull up to table, there's been a hesitant feeling somewhere inside me, a sense that something was no longer right.

All this must have been edging around in the back of my mind for some time, but I only became actually conscious of it the other night, watching one of those television ads where the family waits with bated breath for Dad's approval of a potent replacement for some or other thing Mom once made from scratch. But my sense of disquiet had nothing to do with the product. I realized I didn't believe in supper anymore, at least not that kind of supper.

With that realization came a sudden, happy feeling of relief. My relations with that meal have been troubled for a long, long time. I've always believed that home cooking means food simply and inexpensively made from cupboard staples. But I'm also aware that it mostly isn't—and how tempted almost every cook is to fall back into the waiting arms of the crowd of convenience foods that fill the supermarket shelves.

Not, of course, that some of those aren't better than others. Still, the fact that many cooks feel that they have no choice except to make meals scraped out of cans or defrosted from the freezer means that we are forced into playing a role we don't yet fully understand. After all, why should we—any of us—feel compelled to go on making more and more compromises in making a meal that shouldn't, and never did before, require it? We pay so much; we get so little back.

The usual argument, of course, is that these meals save us labor or time. But good, simple food from scratch can be set on the table almost as easily, so easily, really, as to make no difference. But—and this is the really important point—that food isn't the same as "supper" at all. When I cook for myself, I could easily make that kind of meal. But in my relationships, almost always, it hasn't seemed quite enough.

Instead, as best as I or the other could, we compromised or worked harder than was fair or sensible, to put real supper on the table.

The reason for this compulsion, I now realize, came from a sense of civility, of what in a family we sense is due the others. If that due is not paid, even for the best of reasons, it generates a sense of tension, of things not being right. The problem, however—for me, at least—is that this same unease has crept into ordinary supper as well.

What struck home so hard watching that television ad was the realization of how much we all eat supper as though we already were on television. Supper is such an incredibly public meal. Just as we were—many of us—brought up to wear clean underpants in case we got hit by a bus, we've also been trained to eat supper—to think of supper—as if at any moment the neighbors might shove their easy chairs up outside the picture window and settle down to watch the show.

Now, admittedly, this sense of public scrutiny was the flip side of the family's sense of self-esteem. It provided part of the cement that held things together. "Let them look!" it said. "They'll see us all around the table behaving ourselves, eating good stuff off polished plates, and none of us talking with our mouths full."

Nothing is wrong with this. It's just that the strain of providing this kind of theater in our current relationships is starting to tell us something. It's not so much that we don't want this at supper, but we hunger for something else very much more. And that hunger springs, not from the stomach, but from the heart.

Supper, after all, is our most social meal and, of all the day's contacts (apart, at least, from acts of love), perhaps the most needingly personal one. And it isn't simply the growing impersonality of the food needed to make our familiar supper possible that distances the eaters at the table from one another, but the very shape of the meal itself.

Food, we need to remember, is communication as much as nutrition, and the message isn't simply what we pay for it, the care we put into making it, or even how nicely we serve it forth. It's right in there with the slices of boiled beef, mashed potatoes, green beans, lump of squash. That plain and homely food is awash with messages for us, talking all the time.

Only it's no longer saying what we need to hear. Its generous servings still speak of prosperity, its quality of good taste, its nutrition of education and concern, its very division into neat portions on the plate of respectability. But these aren't the things we now need most to say to each other. Outside in the world, things have changed. A public sense of family esteem no longer holds relationships together. Couples—married or not—and whole families, for that matter, now have to work hard to provide this for themselves.

The way that they work at this is to establish a sense of personal closeness, of a special caring and understanding that only comes from carefully nurtured attentiveness to each other's private self. What we now want to celebrate at supper is not civility but intimacy, and to do that, we have found an entirely different cluster of manners. Now we need a new way of eating—a new cuisine—to display it.

Intimacy . . . food. Brought into conjunction, our imagination immediately conjures a romantic occasion: caviar, dim lighting, a special vintage wine. And that's okay, I think; the intimate eating I have in mind flows from our desire to capture the special closeness such meals provide and bring it into the unromantic eating of the every day.

To accomplish this sense of needful privacy, intimate food must work in a very different way from the old-fashioned supper, which, even when painfully modernized, works best when it is—in form, if not content—almost identical to what is being eaten next door. Intimate food strives for another effect. Relaxed, uncomplicated, personal, it provides an oasis from our public selves and the pressures of outside demands by pushing the public world away. Mood matched to mood, candles are lit and shutters pulled shut, this time before—not after—the meal.

Because of its very personal qualities, intimate food may seem at first to share something of the unkempt carelessness of the solitary eater. A whole meal might be made of only appetizers, the meat served on, not with, the salad, the dessert eaten first. But, in fact, there is a style to this eating that springs directly from the claims of intimacy, twisting convention into off-centered patterns that mark them as our very own.

First, this is a cuisine of accommodation. Often, both partners work and neither wants to put the other to the task of an elaborate nightly meal. Supper must come together simply and easily out of what is at hand and by whoever has the chore or gets home first. And, since our days now follow eccentric rhythms, accommodation also means bending to meet the appetite that had no lunch, waiting for a suppertime that is suddenly delayed, or hurrying when the eaters must rush out directly after. Pasta, for instance, has become a mainstay of this kind of cooking because it can be so fresh, so quick, so adaptable to all these things.

Next, I think, it is a cuisine of spontaneity. Not that every meal must be impromptu, but there is always the sense that it springs, like good talk, from real attention and not a stock response. Politeness now demands not graciousness but mutual understanding, and supper has become a place where this is most pleasurably displayed. The golden melon on the fruit stand, the impulsive splurge on the first asparagus of the season, the sudden mutual craving for spareribs—intimate eating presupposes on both sides a willingness to meet a mood and join in, something that can't be done unless little risks are taken, desires voiced, contact made.

This, by the way, is also why one of the first reactions to this kind of eating is a feeling of vulnerability: we are too used, every one of us, to this idea of supper as something that is served us, from which we take our pleasure as we want, even to the point where one or the other must play the servant, at least before sitting down. But in intimate eating, it is not the stomach who is king, and especially not any particular stomach.

So, also, intimate eating is a cuisine of less. While there are many reasons for a general concern about overeating, in this instance it springs particularly from intimacy's need to share. And while no one can deny the satisfying closeness that comes from occasionally shared bouts of gluttony, in the long term it becomes a sort of mutual bribery, a substitute for something else.

Here, instead, selectivity has replaced surfeit as the accepted form of pampering: a few succulent slices of Westphalian ham for the slab of roast pork; the lustrous single chocolate truffle for the hot fudge sundae. Less on the table means the more we need—or should—offer the other in the pleasures of ourself.

Since I write this as an exercise of unfolding understanding about something whose outlines I can only just begin to trace, all this is nothing more than an act of tentative, sympathetic imagining, not at all an attempt to establish a code, a set of rules. This is a cuisine, after all, if I have grasped it at all right, that means to keep bending rules to find breathing space somewhere on the other side.

Even more tentatively do I offer the following thoughts on what its food is actually like. Obviously, just as almost any dish from any of the world's cooking has been adapted to fit the confines of the familiar, public supper, intimate cuisine will also pull dishes from the standard repertoire and put them to its own use. But not, I think, to the same use. It is this shift of meaning I have tried to convey in what follows, rather than specific recipes. The recipes, more or less, will be the same. The difference lies somewhere else: there can be no intimate cuisine unless feeling makes it so.

BREAD AND BUTTER. The simplest way to give some sense of what makes intimate cuisine different from our familiar, public one, is a supper of bread and butter, with a little something to give it savor. This is a meal that would seem too Spartan to anyone eating alone and no supper at all to anyone expecting his or her "supper." But it can be exactly the meal two people might have when they want appetite to enhance connection, even as it pleases itself.

I don't, here, mean a sandwich. Those, for all their virtues, are about as public as food can be, existing to be eaten while the eater is involved in something else. The meal I have in mind is put together as it goes along and eaten with attentive pleasure, not something put up in the kitchen for hasty eating, the eyes glued to television or a book.

The bread is cut by hand in satisfactory slices, not too large nor too delicate, each worth a couple of bites but still small enough so that we eat only what we really want. At its simplest, the meal might be a loaf of terrific pumpernickel, say, a chunk of sweet butter, and a dish of coarse salt, all served with some beer to wash it down. But it could also be expanded to include some radish cut into coin, or slivers of scallion, or leaves of romaine, which are delicious with butter and a densely-flavored loaf.

Hungrier eaters could set out a plate of choice sardines or oil-packed tuna (served as is, not mixed into a salad)—or even raw oysters, which make a great match with sweet butter and light, unseeded rye. Of course, any cheese or cold meat would work fine, too, but the balance of the meal should always lean in favor of the bread, not the savory: it is to be eaten for itself, not allowed to become a shovel.

THE GOOD VEGETABLE.   Another contrast between intimate and public eating is the use of the vegetable. Previously, it has been almost entirely forced to play a supporting role, the "& etc." on the menu. This has so much been the case that it now seems like a little culinary cripple, unable to go anywhere without clinging to a slice of meat. Too cheap, too numerous, and hence too common to have any power on the plate, its sole, dubious status was its claim of being good for us.

But the same qualities that made it a loser before now shove it to plate center, opening a large and wonderful realm of simple, quick meals, none of which requires any new recipes, only a different appreciation of our own appetite. One of my most fondly remembered summer feasts was a huge platter of just-picked corn on the cob, served in generous but solitary splendor on a country porch with nothing else but butter and salt and pepper. It was an especially happy occasion, I remember, because we all felt together that it was exactly what we wanted and exactly all we wanted.

In the same spirit, supper could be made of a platter of tiny, stove-top roasted potatoes, served with coarse salt, butter, tiny pickles, and, maybe, a bit of Cheddar. Other obvious examples are ripe tomatoes served in their season with fresh basil and lots of freshly ground pepper, or a head of sweet fennel or Belgian endive, served raw with a dipping bowl of fruity olive oil infused with a little garlic.

But apart from this, there are many vegetable dishes that we don't often get to eat because they require too much work to include in a larger meal, but not too much when made just for themselves. Almost any good vegetable cookbook takes on a new look when its dishes are considered as the main course, letting the day, not the meal, balance our nutritional needs.

FRIED EGGS.   The poor egg. First, except for the occasional omelet and the ubiquitous soufflé, it was declared too light for supper and banished to the breakfast table. Now it's considered too heavy for breakfast and thus has pretty much vanished as an entree entirely.

But eggs find an immediate place in intimate cuisine, even if only made occasionally, since, like pasta, they are quickly made and are almost infinitely adaptable, whether scrambled, poached, or baked. But I remind you of frying eggs because that, more than any other method of egg cookery, seems so unsuitable to supper, and yet works so well as intimate fare. Properly prepared, they are neither tough nor greasy, and are unexpectedly delicious, fried, say, in olive oil and slid onto a bed of roasted sweet peppers, or in butter and served on shredded lettuce that was heated just to wilting in the same pan.

DUCK HASH.   This dish is emblematic of my imagining of all that can be good about intimate cuisine: easy to make, cheap, with enough of a quirky spin to take it out of the common domain and make it part of the family. Hash is a dish more fondly remembered than much made these days, since we rarely have the surfeit of leftover meat that is its reason for being. But the carcass of a roast bird will usually yield enough picked meat to make a wonderful one, especially if the eaters are willing to let the proportion of meat drop to a more reasonable level.

My own favorite for this process is duck, in part because there always seems to be so much meat left after a meal of it and partly because its rich taste and unctuous fat make an especially fine hash. Any ad hoc preparation does fine, but my own favorite is to mince an onion and fry that in a mixture of the duck's own fat and some butter until it softens, then to add a generous cup of small cubes of parsnip. These are cooked together until the parsnip is soft and tender. A cup or so of already cooked pecan rice (or any rice) is stirred in, and when that is hot, all the picked duck meat. Serve when the rice gets a little crusty, moistening it with a little cream, if you like, or, better, with stock made by simmering the picked bones in a little plain water.

(Serves 2)

Duck hash, because of its impromptu nature, has more in common
with a supper of fried eggs or boiled potatoes than it does with ordinary
hash, because it owes nothing to the obligations that ordinary hash
does to its rituals of making. It—like all the above foods—invites,
even requires, discussion between the eaters, a joint assent and understanding before it can become a supper. And that's just what
intimate cuisine is all about.

American Cooking: Notes on a Scandal

❀

Today one hears a lot about "American cuisine" and I think it is high time we took proper pride in it.   —RICHARD NELSON

The recent flurry in the food world over the discovery by *The Washington Post* that a substantial portion of the award-winning *Richard Nelson's American Cooking* was lifted from an Italian cookbook and—most blatantly—from Richard Olney's *Simple French Food* (Nelson discovering to his discomfort that that book was not about simple French food after all, but simple Olney food) has ignored what to me is the most remarkable aspect of the whole business.

Shift this scandal to France. There would be screams of rage, yes, but not so loudly from the plagiarized authors as from an outraged public: how dare this man foist off the cooking of two other nations as French cuisine? Even if he had dared borrow recipes from some other province and claim them for his own, he had better not ever show his face in the local bistro again.

Nelson claims the offending recipes were brought in by his students, which, if so, shows he either has no idea what Americans cook or just doesn't care: it's "American cooking" if he puts it in his book. And he's right: even when the provenance of these dishes was exposed, no one questioned the legitimacy of his title. And that to me is a truly fascinating thing.

Fascinating, first of all, for the unexpected perspective it gives us on the current cookbook madness. Nelson is a well-known cooking teacher and, until the scandal, his book was critically acclaimed as one of the year's best of what was a very large crop. No one can be oblivious of the enormous number of cookbooks published these days. Publishers seem to think that there is nothing less than infinite space on top of the refrigerator. But to me, even more disturbing is the number of excellent cookbooks issued every year that those reviewers call "essential for the serious cook."

These are good cookbooks, every one, but how many even truly excellent cookbooks does a cook need? Thirty? Sixty? Ninety? If we really do think of these books as somehow necessary to our cooking, perhaps it is time to wonder what "excellence" means in reference to cookbooks at all.

Make no mistake—I find these books highly desirable myself. Picking one up in the bookstore, the familiar rationalizations run through my mind: I need a really good baking book . . . my cooking is weakest in interesting vegetable dishes . . . this is really the definitive work on some particularly desirable cuisine—South Side Chicago, maybe, or the waterfront of Marseille. Behind the rationalizing, though, is a poignant and almost irresistible pang: I feel—truly—that my life will not only be made richer by this book, but that now having seen it, if I don't get it, my life will somehow become poorer. So, I buy.

It's at this point—the purchase—as you may know, that the problem begins. The book is excellent, yes, but the author and the cuisine remain on one side of the page and I on the other. All I get are the recipes. And what I've found—and it's been a painfully long time learning—is that recipes without the author, without the cuisine to which they were once a living, seamless part, die. Or, rather, become no more and no less than any other recipe.

This is why Richard Nelson, however knowingly, could take all those "simple French" recipes and call them "American cooking": recipes reduce any subject to the exact same common denominator. Whatever the name of the book or the origin of the dish, the process of constructing it from the cookbook is identical: you start at (1) and proceed until you reach "serve at once." Then you eat.

The only analogy I can think to compare to this process is painting by number. The "excellent" cookbook writer patiently traces in small detail some fine old masterpiece and gets us to go buy first-class artist's colors to fill it in; your worst cookbook writer copies big-eyed little girls holding big-eyed little puppies, and calls for poster paint. But the results have one thing in common: they are both copies.

What we keep finding out again and again is that recipe cooking is to real cooking as painting by number is to real painting: just pretend. The problem is that we don't seem to be able to grasp it. We keep trying—with a different cookbook.

Of course, this kind of cooking does produce food, sometimes very good food. The problem, the reason why these cookbooks finally don't give us what we crave from them, is that, however appealing the subject, we the cooks are always treated the same, demoted into a kind of robot, assembly-line workers in our own kitchens. Recipes are made by breaking down a complex relationship of smell, touch, taste, and instinct born of intimate familiarity into a series of minimal commands containing none of those things.

This is why, maybe, so much cookbook writing is so relentlessly cheerful and encouraging, with everything made to sound so wonderful and easy. Out of them speaks the professional voice of the diet counselor or aerobic workout instructor, people paid to jolly us into doing something—whether or not it might be good for us—that goes against our instinctive grain. What we truly want is to touch on something deeper, but all that's being offered us is . . . this.

The real question, then, is not only why we have become a country of recipe-following cooks, but why it is so hard not to be one. Other nations, of course, have their cookbooks, but none depends on them so entirely as we do to image the very shape of our cuisine—the truth, by the way, and a very ironic one, of Richard Nelson's book title.

The single largest reason for this state of affairs, I think, is that the price it costs to live now is paid for in the coin of experience: we have time for less and less of it. The sort of long, leisured absorption that nurtures a genuine sense of place, a close familiar bond, or the slow growth of an original thought is our most precious commodity: such as we have we can only niggardly spend.

Few of us, really, can afford to spend much of it in the kitchen. I don't mean time to make the stew; I mean time to think it, to give it complete and unbegrudging attention. Instead, mostly, we summon up a set of prefab building blocks and let them fall together. The result is good enough.

How lucky we are, then, to have those few who do pay the price, who hold those blocks in suspension until they work a fit as fine as the joints in a Hepplewhite chair. These writers give us recipes because we demand it, but it is in the prose with which they situate them that we hear the hum of that devoted attention that made this food be. This is art. We know because it touches us beyond hunger: it makes us feel.

Simple French Food is one of a very short list of books that makes us think cooking through the sheer artful force of its example. Like a poem, it affects us with the impact of actual presence, shoving us mercilessly toward revelation. There is nothing remotely comparable to this in *Richard Nelson's American Cooking*. That is why had I been the judge, I would have awarded Richard Olney the decision, but only a farthing's damages.* His book was unharmed: all Nelson took was recipes.

---

*In fact, Nelson's publisher settled out of court for $50,000.

Perfect Food

❀

I am sad for those who cannot see that a brown-spotted two-foot-
high lettuce, its edges curling and wilted, is ugly and offensive.
It is a fundamental fact that no cook, however creative and capable, can produce a dish of a quality any higher than that of its
raw ingredients.   —ALICE WATERS

Also a leaf or two of lettuce, which she cut up daintily. Louisa
was very fond of lettuce, which she raised to perfection in her
little garden. She ate quite heartily, but in a delicate, pecking
way; it seemed almost surprising that any considerable bulk of
food should vanish.   —MARY FREEMAN, "A New England Nun"

Sometime last summer I happened into a downtown Boston department store when a demonstrator was putting a new food processor
through its paces. Whole zucchini slid down the feed tube, frag-
menting into perfect slice, shred, dice, bright green piles of which
were heaped on the counter before us. A lemon followed after, sliced
so thin that each successive piece glistened faintly through the trans-
parent film of the one before. The thick slicing blade was then set
in place, a whole fat ripe tomato was dropped in, swallowed, and spat
back in thick, perfect slices, red as fresh meat and oozing seed and
juice.

Without pausing for us to digest our wonder at this feat, already
exclaiming about some entirely different virtue of the machine, the
demonstrator swept it all—lemon, tomato, zucchini—into the black-
bagged trash can at her side with one deft scoop. I felt a sudden pain,
a moment of anguish, then revulsion. Not even because there are
kids who go unfed in that city every day (some of whom, in fact,
wander unwelcome in that same department store), but because all
this had somehow touched my appetite.

I don't mean that it made me hungry. Like a well-fed cat that has
just caught a mouse, I wanted to play with these things, touch them,
poke them around a bit in a pan. Even as I watched them tumble

through the blades, a dish was involuntarily shaping in my mind, the zucchini set to simmer in a crude tomato sauce, seasoned with the lemon and basil and coarse bits of pepper. Toward the processor itself I felt nary a tinge of interest. But the lemon, the zucchini, the tomato—I would have gladly taken *them* home.

But what about the others around the demonstration table, the ones not coveting the garbage? What was it that held them so engrossed? It was, I think, the effortless force of that machine, its sheer voraciousness. "What an appetite it has," I imagine them thinking, not consciously perhaps, but at some deeper level of realization. "How much it likes to eat!" And I envision them, these happy purchasers, alive with a fresh, new hunger, coming home with bags of groceries to slip down the feed tube, one blur after another—green peppers, sausages, mushrooms, grapefruit, cabbages. "You liked that? Good! Try this . . ."

Who can blame them? Our very prosperity has conspired against our cooking by stealing appetite—not out of our stomachs, perhaps, but out of our eyes, our hands. How can they be hungry, even curious, when they can be so easily satiated? What else *do* we know but perfect food? We grumble, maybe, if we can't get the cream of the cream, but the ordinary stuff, the broccoli, potatoes, apples, onions, spinach, lemons are plucked from their bins identical in their flawlessness, smooth, clean, fresh, entirely admirable. And the effect of so much perfection is to deaden. After a certain point, we might as well be fondling tennis balls or plastic sponges.

This is why the food processor exists at all. Our hands have lost their hunger; they no longer care to taste these things. Let the machine do it, then, we think, and its anonymous, furious appetite jars us, whets lagging desire, makes us hungry again. Not that the food that passes through its maw becomes any more desirable: what excites us is the mindless, frantic gnawing.

This need for a prosthetic appetite is expressed in a subtler way by those who refuse to cook with anything less than absolutely perfect ingredients, foods so stripped of the rough nub of reality that they are already cuisine, arriving in the kitchen wearing appetite on their sleeve. It is really the utter vulnerability of such food, not culinary ecstasy, that thrills the unhungry to the point where they can bear to eat. "See," they say to themselves, stroking the head of a perfect baby lettuce, "it's such a sweet little thing, so delicate, so yummy. Won't you try a tiny bite?"

Watching one of these cooks hovering indecisively over a pile of carrots, seeking the bunch a tiny bit more perfect than the rest, one can't help feeling that there's something truly disturbing, almost anorectic, about this, more than its obvious and silly snobbery, its fear of offending the Calphalon cookware by steaming grungy parsnips in it.

And the least worst that it does is transform cooking into playing at cooking. Somewhere entirely outside the purview of these cooks and their perfect foods are people who have no choice but to make do with what they can scrounge up. Among them are cooks who can coax out of scrofulous old potatoes, flabby turnips, and sinewy bits of meat such performances that you or I would hardly imagine possible. It is a cooking that no one with constant, unlimited access to perfect ingredients will ever duplicate, because having the best means never needing to look, touch, or smell.

These lovers of perfect food will not, I know, understand what I mean. They often do pause to lift that flawless bunch of carrots to the nose or pose them, ferny tops *en brosse,* on their worktables. But the aroma that greets their nostrils, the perfection that caresses their eyes, because it asks for nothing and gives nothing, serves only as a mirror for its admirer. The cook who must carefully sniff the gamy shank of lamb or pick suspiciously through the pail of bruised berries is drawn to connection by necessity. Their scrutiny is genuine and the repayment is in kind: such stuff tells us things that perfection can never share.

This isn't to say that real cooking requires the spur of dubious materials. What I imagine as the counter to anesthetic perfection is what to the kitchen gardener is a common experience. They glory in what is perfect in their crop, but they feel attached to all that they planted, tended, protected, plucked. These are, after all, their children too.

And the hand that happily sorts these things, gouges away the soft spots and digs out sprouting eyes, that rubs off scabs and flings small, salvageable bits into the soup pot, is a hand once again an extension of the tongue. Our appetite should always be larger and more curious than our hunger, turned loose to wander the world's flesh at will. Perfection is as false an economy in cooking as it is in love, since, with carrots or potatoes as with lovers, the perfectly beautiful are all the same; the imperfect, different in their beauty, every one.

V
COOK'S BOOKS

CAROL FIELD
THE ITALIAN BAKER
(Harper & Row, 1985, 448 pp., $19.95)

If the Frenchman is not now the greatest bread eater, who, in comparable Western countries, is? No doubt the Italian . . . it would be my guess that among all the industrialized Western countries, it is in Italy that the greatest proportion of bread is homemade. Get out of the cities and into the countryside—and you come upon that precious product of the past, homemade bread. Here it is still the staff of life.   —WAVERLEY ROOT

The peasants of Sicily, who have kept their own wheat and make their own natural brown bread, ah, it is amazing how fresh and sweet and *clean* their loaf seems, so perfumed, as home-made bread used all to be before the war.
          —D. H. LAWRENCE, *Sea and Sardinia* (1921)

One afternoon when I was about twelve or so, my grandfather, inspired by one of those whims by which he guided his life and confounded the opposition, popped me in the car and drove us to a local Italian bakery. I had never then been to a bakery, but I already knew that they were big factories where the bread was mixed in vats and came tumbling off conveyer belts wrapped in plastic bags.

This bakery, however, was nothing like that at all. It was simply a single huge room with a makeshift counter in front and a huge brick oven in the rear. Men dusty with flour were pulling big chunks of dough from a bowl and slapping them into loaves. Others used long wooden paddles to scoop the baked bread from the oven and slide it onto the counter, where it was put into plain paper bags seized eagerly by waiting customers. By the time our turn came, that wonderful aroma of bread, so sour and salty and clean, had aroused a terrible hunger.

It must have done the same to my grandfather, for when our turn came, he gave me the loaf to carry (still hot to the touch inside its bag) and took me to an Italian grocer where he bought a chunk of salami . . . and we proceeded to eat the two sitting right there in the car. I don't know what pleased me more—the wonderful chewy bread with a fragile crust that exploded into fragrant crumbs, or the astounding revelation that things like bread and salami could just be eaten as is, without being carefully sliced, spread with mayonnaise, and made into regulation sandwiches.

Many years later, I went back to look for that bakery, but, of course, it was gone. And so, too, to my mind, is really good Italian bread. I don't expect this is true everywhere, but it is in Boston, which still has a strong ethnic Italian community served by many bakeries. The bread is honest and good, but it is not nearly as good as it could—or should—be, and this is a sad thing.

Part of the problem, I think, is that the real genius of Italian cooking is its triumph over adversity. Unlike more advanced European countries with strong central governments, even into this century individual Italian cities and towns taxed the goods that came into them, so that all but local produce was expensive and relatively rare.

And when even salt is a luxury, it's easy to see why, outside of the Italian granary, good wheat was scarce, and breads, especially for the poor, were made from whatever grain was grown locally, sometimes even pounded from seeds gathered wild in the countryside. (Carol Field writes that during World War II a Venetian baker fleshed out his flour with sawdust and used water right from the sea to compensate for his lack of salt).

A cuisine founded on adversity does not always adapt well to prosperity, no more than does one used to a fierce regionalism fare well when suddenly thrust into homogeneous modernity. Just as we are discovering the genius of the many Italian cuisines, much that made them distinctive is fading away, perhaps forever, at least in the cooking of the poor.

This is one good reason to be grateful to Carol Field for searching out artisan bakers all over Italy and patiently learning their methods, and especially for having faith that we might be interested in what are often simple and sometimes difficult breads ("the wetter the dough, the better the bread," said one baker; it can cling to even floured hands with the tenacity of wallpaper paste).

Fortunately, she has a contagious enthusiasm, and her instructions are helpful and clear. If you respect the specific proportions and preparation advice—since it is often these and not the simple ingredients that give each loaf its special distinction—you will find yourself turning out one enticing rustic loaf after another.

Among them . . . *pane tipo* of Altamura, made of the durum flour that gives good pasta its golden color and chewy texture; an olive oil loaf from Liguria, whose hint of oil-inspired sweetness is tempered by a salt-flecked crust; a big crusty wheel of chewy peasant bread from Puglia, honeycombed with tiny holes; a delicate, salt-free traditional Tuscan loaf whose mellow flavor and fine crumb provide the perfect match to that region's rich and flavorful cuisine.

This last is the perfect loaf for making many of the traditional dishes based on (usually stale) bread, something in which Italian cuisine truly glories, and which are often slighted in the cookbooks. What a joy, then, to have in this book a whole chapter devoted to nothing else—garlic bread, *crostini, crostoni,* hearty soups, bread-crumb dumplings, and even a dessert of poached pears and Italian corn bread (in texture more like rye bread than what we know by that name).

There are also breads made with rye, cornmeal, and graham flour; breads flavored with cheese, herbs, pesto, and *olivada;* festive and special breads; sweet breads and savory breads; rolls and breadsticks; pizza and *focaccia;* and tarts, cakes, cookies . . . although this sweeps us far ahead of where I have so far managed to make my way. This is not a book to rush through, any more than Carol Field rushed through the writing of it. I know that because her fondness for her subject lingers on every page.

JANE AND MICHAEL STERN
SQUARE MEALS
(Alfred A. Knopf, 1984, 337 pp., $17.95)

❁

The first thing to say about this subversive volume is that it is a happy, uncomplicated, and almost entirely uncritical celebration of the popular myths that most of us, these past eighty-odd years, have been quite happy to imagine as "American cooking"—a populist celebration of lunch counter blue plate specials, the fancy fixings of ladies' luncheons, school cafeteria tray-slappers, soda fountain fancies, and the exotica of suburban cuisine.

It is subversive because it makes no distinction at all between the food we actually ate and the food we only imagined eating. A substantial part of this book is constructed from the food of magazine articles and recipes printed in those ubiquitous little brochures and leaflets from food companies and appliance manufacturers. The feelings of déjà vu that haunt this book from first page to last are not so much of forgotten mealtime pleasures as of appetite once inspired by advertising copy—not the cooking we ate with our mouths but the cooking we ate with our eyes.

This is an important distinction: it would be a mistake to think that the sum of these dishes equals what Americans have been cooking since the turn of the century. Discounting such ordinary fare as deep-dish apple pie, meat loaf, or fudge, whose recipes can be found in any standard cookbook (a sure measure of true popularity), and regional specialties like Cincinnati chili, the rest of the recipes, which the Sterns have unearthed from such recondite sources as "Madam, Dehydrated Dinner is Served" or *Recipes That Pep Up Meals with Wise Potato Chips*, were, I suspect, treated much the same way we treat their progeny today—tucked in the back of the recipe drawer and forgotten. Very possibly, no one before the Sterns ever had the courage to actually *try* them.

Don't mistake my meaning, however. I think this cheerful obliviousness to the lines between reality and fantasy food is exactly what makes this book valuable. It is really neither culinary history nor a cookbook of honest American fare, though there are bits and pieces here of both. Instead, this book is to our culinary past as our high school yearbook is to our education: a romantic gloss over a still mostly undecipherable but fearsome reality.

Like a yearbook, the high points of what was really a very tedious and awful experience are exaggerated way out of proportion, and the bad points are either omitted or romanticized—the Sterns, while they include some truly awful recipes, offer no simply bad ones—and, consequently, the "reality" of the book has no connection at all with what really happened, only with what, at the time, we all wanted reality to be.

Perhaps the best proof of the truth of this analogy is that this book is also something we wouldn't even have been able to open without agonizing embarrassment if it weren't for the many intervening years (the authors curb this account at the close of the 1950s). And even today . . . I have to warn you that perusing this book may still prove totally mortifying to anyone at all self-conscious about his or her culinary origins. Here are dishes that, to your eternal shame, you once thought really terrific—vulgar, vulgar food you once admired as the height of class.

Still tempted? If so, you'll find the Sterns as affably uncritical company as could be hoped for, and if you wonder why, look at the jacket photo. This is stuff that, at best, they can barely remember from their childhood: it isn't *their* yearbook they've given us, but Mom's or big brother's. "Hey," they say, "you didn't look so bad in those pointy eyeglasses. And baggy pants are back again!" But we know better.

Let's come right out and say it: much of the food lovingly detailed in *Square Meals* is outright garbage, disgusting stuff that any of us would now be ashamed to serve at our tables. If cookbooks were given ratings, this one would receive an X. But that in itself isn't so bad. Every culture has a rich strand of vulgarity in its eating that permeates the popular culture without making it into the official record of the cuisine. Even so, it is far more often consumed than the highly styled recipes of its great chefs: for every dish cooked from *Gourmet* magazine, a hundred times more families have eaten string bean casserole made with Campbell's cream of mushroom soup and topped with canned fried onion rings (an old favorite inexplicably missing from the book).

Classic vulgarity in eating—the gorgings of the poor—is styled in offal: the pig killed, its kidneys are roasted in gobbets of its own fat, the head simmered in stock, the ears stuffed with buttered bread crumbs and deep-fried in batter. The better cuts were put up or sold to the rich, but the remaining parts were cheap and spoiled easily, an actual command to gorge.

Here, where that kind of food goes straight to the dog food factory, our own bad taste is more complexly constructed. Its foundation, however, is simple surrender to the urgings of tongue and gut. Eat as much as you can as fast as you can ("Bet you can't just eat one") is the rule; the cook conforms to it by making lots of bland food that can taste good quickly—salty, sweet, or both . . . and not much else at all.

The next step toward the truly crass requires that the food also be as easy as possible to make. There is no more edifying spectacle in vulgar American cuisine as when greed gets down in the mud and wrestles with sloth—and no recipe succeeds better than one that satiates the first and still indulges the second.

But the point where vulgarity returns to haunt us is when we want to pretend that these dishes—even while meeting those two conditions above—are also utterly refined, just what Mrs. Van Snoot would serve the bridge club if she only knew about it. What hurts is not that we cooked and ate this food, but that we *aspired to do so:* blinded by naïve self-regard, we believed those hucksters, bought back our own vulgarity, and called it class.

The Sterns lead us along this path of terrible self-realization step by subtle step. They know we look back fondly on the number of White Castle burgers we used to scarf away, that we are still ambivalent about Lipton instant onion soup dip, but that only late in the evening, after a lot of drinks, are we prepared to admit that long-forgotten appetite for Meat Loaf Wellington, Ming Dynasty Casserole, or, God save us, Flaming Cabbage Head Weenies with Pu Pu Sauce. Happy memories!

Nabisco Famous Wafer Roll

¶ This recipe is still printed on every box, but it works just as well with other thin sugar cookies. Try it with Pepperidge Farm Molasses Crisps, with a pinch of ginger in the whipped cream. Or, even better, just substitute 1 tablespoon raspberry liqueur for the vanilla in the following.

1 cup heavy cream
⅓ cup confectioners' sugar
½ teaspoon vanilla
20 chocolate wafer cookies

Whip the cream with the sugar and vanilla. Reserve 1 cup and spread each wafer with the remaining cream, stacking them up in fives on wax paper. Chill 15 minutes. Lay stacks on side, end to end, forming a long roll. Spread reserved whipped cream over outside of roll. Cover and chill at least 4 hours. Cut *diagonally*.

Vilma Liacouras Chantiles
THE NEW YORK ETHNIC FOOD
MARKET GUIDE AND COOKBOOK
(Dodd Mead, & Co., 1984, 370 pp., $14.95 paperback)

This is a book about the new American cooking. Not only—obviously—the different foodways of our newest Americans, but a peek, I think, into how you and I may be cooking in the next dozen years if the best aspects of the current culinary ferment catch on and grow. Because here are hands that can pull flavor and variety from a pinch of this and a handful of that, eyes that can instantly size up the freshness of a red snapper or the ripeness of a lichee fruit, and appetite with tenacity enough to demand the absolute best that the pocket can afford. In short, some of our country's best cooks—and almost completely ignored until now.

Most of the markets and shops in this book exist to cater to those tiny ethnic enclaves whose inhabitants, whether by reason of recent arrival here or simple reluctance to change, have least assimilated our homogeneous cuisine. Some are prosperous, but many are poor or almost poor, and the stores that they shop in are sometimes nothing more than indoor stalls, without name or sign, family owned and staffed, and with only the children fluent in English.

New York City is home to countless such stores (not surprising considering that it is home for immigrants from thirty-two European countries alone). Vilma Liacouras Chantiles has, it seems, been in almost every one of them. She has wandered through the city markets where tiny stalls jostle together, elbowed through crowded fish stores, ferreted out obscure and tiny shops with hardly room enough for both her and the proprietor. And from all of them, she brings back a sense of that roughhewn but friendly humanity that those who venture into such places often experience (at least when they have the sense to arrive when trade is slow), finding owners and customers alike genuinely proud of their foods and often willing to share their culinary uses in such English as they command.

This book has many virtues, but the best thing about it is that, for once, we are given a food book as much about people as ingredients. The author generously mixes her own observations with the banter, opinions, asides, and casually tossed-off recipes of those she writes about, and the pages come alive with the vivid presence of an America that most of us hardly know, the poorer elements of our immigrant and ethnic communities. True, included here are such bastions of the middle class as B. Altman's and Zabar's. But the majority are places where Jamaicans, Bulgarians, and Koreans rub shoulders, stores where owners of one ethnicity saw demographic shifts threaten their modest livelihoods and learned a new language and how to handle produce equally as strange so they could serve a different clientele and survive.

" 'My customers are mostly Puerto Ricans and Albanians,' says the Naples-born owner [Raffaele Santelle] as he sells *yautia* roots to a Hispanic shopper. . . .'' Whatever America is, you can find more than a taste of it in that sentence, and there are many others like it in this book: the Israeli, Bulgarian, and Greek customers in Baruir Nercessian's "Oriental-American" grocery in Queens ("Here is grinding poppy seeds and nuts"); Cuzin's Meat Co. on Manhattan's Ninth Avenue: "We have all kinds of customers—Hispanic, Caribbean, blacks, Italians, and other Americans—but we specialize in short ribs for Koreans"; Puzan Fish Market (also on Ninth Avenue), where the owner, Ik Sang Kim, explains, "Spanish-speaking customers like octopus, kingfish, and shrimps; Japanese and Koreans buy tuna, fluke, octopus, tile . . . U.S. Post Office workers pick everything. . . ."

Even these brief glimpses show an ambience quite different from the upscale hush of the specialty food market, where artisan-made foodstuffs are artfully displayed and bright young urban professionals tend counter. Not so in the stores that cater to a genuine ethnic clientele. Here, the flooors are strewn with sawdust and the aisles cramped, the foods exulting in bright-colored, pungent-smelling life. Turtles crawl in their cages, chickens peck and squawk, beans, nuts, grains, spices, seeds spill from burlap bags, and deliverymen stagger through with whole, dressed pigs slung over their shoulders. As we tag along at the author's side, we begin to feel at home, and wonder why we have never come before.

And there's much to marvel at, savor, and enjoy: the *Pagliacci*-singing peperoni vendor in the Arthur Avenue Market (Bronx); the bakery on Atlantic Avenue (Brooklyn) with a huge old brick oven out of which come such Middle-Eastern specialties as *baklava, berraza* (flat pastries topped with sesame seeds and pistachio nuts), and *zahter,* a bread flecked with bits of thyme and sumac; the Hungarian meat market on Second Avenue (Manhattan), with thirty-four varieties of sausage, strung and then smoked over hardwood sawdust in the back kitchen.

I wrote earlier that this book has many virtues, the most obvious being its usefulness to New Yorkers in first finding these shops and then orienting themselves inside. But the wealth of evocative detail will spur the rest of us to explore the ethnic enclaves in our own locality, and give us some understanding of what we will find when we get there and what to do with what we bring home. Because not only are the pages packed with description and useful tips, but most of the recipes (which fill half the book) were contributed by shop owners and customers, and provide an amazingly accessible and tempting set of dishes, a sampling of which I have included below (the comments introducing them, by the way, are mine, not the author's).

These run the gamut from appetizers (Afghan herb filo triangles) through desserts (Southern sweet potato pie), with such stops along the way as a Bermuda-style hoppin John, a Korean version of a Spanish fish soup, and Norwegian *and* Danish meatballs. Best of all is the special section on street snacks, with directions for making such curb-side cuisine as New York egg creams, *falafel, souvlakia, gyro,* and *empanadas.*

Many shops are willing to fill mail orders and some issue catalogues. Whatever exotic national specialties you've been searching for—*farinha de mandioca* and Brazilian black beans to give your *feijoada* that authentic touch, *fenalaar* (Norwegian cured and dried mutton) for your next wilderness trek—or any other hard-to-find ethnic ingredients (German, Hungarian, Spanish, Portuguese, Japanese, West African, or whatever) your chances of finding a source for it here are better than in any other book I know, including those especially compiled for mail-ordering.

But read this book for its cooks; they have a lot to share. Here are Americans whose palates have declined the bland and overprocessed stuff of our common table to keep faith with a humble but richly flavored cooking, a cooking that we are just now beginning to seek out for ourselves.

Sicilian Fish Stew

¼ cup olive oil, or more to taste

3 onions, sliced

5 or 6 fresh tomatoes, thinly sliced (or substitute canned Italian plum tomatoes)

Salt and freshly ground pepper

3 large sprigs fresh basil, chopped

3 pounds salmon, filleted with skin on

Dry white wine

2 sprigs parsley, chopped

Heat the olive oil in a large pot and add the onions and tomatoes, stirring them gently over medium heat until the tomatoes collapse and the onions are translucent, about 15 minutes. Season to taste with salt and pepper. Add the basil and cook a few more minutes, then add the salmon and enough wine (or water) to cover the fish. Lower heat and simmer until the salmon is flaky, about 15 minutes. Serve warm strewn with the parsley.

(Serves 4 to 5)

Gyro

¶ One of the things I miss most about New York are the gyro shops, where huge, too-big-to-be-natural, spicy-seasoned chunks of lamb rotate on vertical spits. The cook slices paper-thin cuts to order and stuffs them into pita bread. Delicious—and far superior to the almost always too-tough *souvlaki* (when that is made with lamb at all). This recipe is the next best thing (you have to do the work yourself).

Ground lamb, estimating ¼ pound per person
Seasonings of: salt and freshly ground pepper, oregano (Greek, if possible), ground allspice, paprika, and fresh or dried basil
Thin slices lamb fat, cut from the breast

Pita bread (1 per person)
With garnishes of: *tzatziki* (yogurt seasoned with cucumber, parsley, dill, garlic, vinegar) or plain yogurt, sliced tomatoes, slivered onions, shredded lettuce, vinegar (optional), and dried oregano

Knead generous amounts of the seasonings into the lamb—it should be very spicy. Wrap in plastic and let rest for several hours in the refrigerator (overnight is best). When ready to broil, shape into thick, hamburger-size patties. Skewer the patties flat together, inserting a very thin slice of the lamb fat between each (to baste the meat while it cooks). When assembled, press the resulting loaf firmly together. Grill over charcoal as far from the coals as possible, turning often to cook evenly on all sides. When done, set on a carving board and remove the skewer without disturbing the loaf. With a very sharp knife, slice the loaf into thin strips, cutting on a bias. Serve with pita bread and garnishes ranged around. (*Note:* Commercial ground lamb is too fatty for this dish; it will set your grill ablaze. Have your butcher grind something leaner.)

Tropical Drink

¶ I spent one hot summer in New York living uptown on East 94th Street in a fifth-floor walk-up, rooming with an aspiring pianist whose practice sessions often degenerated into monomaniacal hour-long repetitions of the same six-note phrase. I would slip off into the humid darkness to seek relief at the Papaya King, whose stand was a short walk away and whose sticky sweet, ice-frosted papaya special seemed a properly exotic accompaniment to Manhattan summer nights. Vilma Liacouras Chantiles might be horrified by my comparing that commercial concoction to the following fruit-packed tropical frappe, but that papaya tang just swept me away (helped perhaps by a tot of dark Haitian rum, my own contribution and the perfect foil to the flavors of papaya and banana).

1 nicely ripe papaya, peeled and seeds removed	Pinch ground cinnamon (optional)
1 banana, peeled	2 to 4 ice cubes
1 cup strawberries, washed and hulled	Fresh mint for garnish

In a blender, whip up the papaya, banana, and strawberries, and the cinnamon if using, until blended. Drop in the ice cubes and continue blending until the ice is crushed. Garnish with mint.

(Serves 2)

ELIZABETH DAVID

AN OMELETTE AND A GLASS OF WINE
(Viking Press, 1985, 318 pp., $17.95)

❋

There are a handful of books that I have used constantly over the years, and one of them is Elizabeth David's *French Provincial Cooking*. It was she, unwittingly, who really started my serious cooking. . . .
—DIANA KENNEDY

Mine, too. It's hard to read this new collection of occasional pieces and essays written over a span of the last thirty-five years without the mind being flooded with now familiar images: simple picnics of bread and cheese beside some tiny tributary of the Seine or gossiping with Norman Douglas at an outdoor café on Capri, drinking that island's thin wine and eating slices of salami produced from his coat pocket.

But another image also intrudes of another woman, and now all of twenty years ago. She is young, just married, a graduate student. Her hair is pulled back in a neat, tight braid; she wears her cleanliness as perfume. Her new kitchen is freshly painted, the trim a bright, light orange, lustrous in semigloss. A Marimekko print makes its calligraphic gesture on the whitewashed brick wall; the treasured single copper saucepan, scoured shiny as a penny, hangs nearby. And, on the table, a chunk of bottom round, bloody in its butcher's paper, a large yellow onion, a handful of mushrooms, a bottle of wine, and *French Provincial Cooking* opened to page 397, *Boeuf à la Bourguignonne*.

Others can rightly claim credit for making French cooking—and other foreign cuisines—part of our popular culinary idiom. But it was Elizabeth David who convinced us that it was all right to care about cooking as a serious thing, because she herself did so with a discrimination as fine and as passionate as any we ourselves had just been learning to make in college over such things as the grave, spare lines of T. S. Eliot.

No one before or after her has quite this same sensual fineness of understanding. It springs, I think, from perfect culinary pitch. Even if you have never tried one of her recipes, you sense it in the clarity of her prose. There is no one near her stature who is less a bully: she commands assent not by pulling rank but by drawing out the logic of a dish by an act of utterly absorptive empathy.

Questioning and watching at the side of a cook or sitting to table, her creative attention surrenders to the claims of the dish; *it*, not her, sets the terms of understanding. She is never oblivious to the people who have made it nor to the surroundings in which she eats. She gives these things their due place in the tapestry, but they are never the meaning of it. This is why, despite the length of her bibliographies, she gives the impression that she has brought the cuisines she writes about into existence with a sustained and furious burst of sensuous imagination. She makes the act of cooking a very special sort of bliss, logical and sensual in a single whole, like composing a sonnet or framing a syllogism.

There is never a hint of the lip-smacking, paunch-stroking gourmandism in vogue before her, with its endless picking of crumbs off the tablecloths of restaurants past. Nor is she eager, as are those who come after her, to help translate each dish into the stuff of the local supermarket, robbing it of the particularity that gives it its dignity. It is her purity of purpose that puts her in a class apart.

But it also makes her a little daunting, which is why, for some of us, as we grow older, her books start to slip further and further to the back of the bookcase. We tap them fondly now and then as we pass them by; they remind us of that youthful self who once thought its passion equal to her own. Our later self has come to know better: it needs the coaxing, the flattering, the entertainment, the spaces to rest in between the recipes, and mostly it wants more sense of shared human frailty in our guide.

It is in that last need especially that Elizabeth David seems most unyielding. It explains, I think, the common frustration felt toward her famous reticence. With her, more than any of the others, we want to find that edge of vulnerability that will let us feel more comfortable in her company.

If she senses that need, she does nothing obvious to meet it: few food writers are so relentlessly antiautobiographical. This is entirely consistent with the disciplined way that she subjugates herself to allow the dishes to speak for themselves. Except in the incidental if often luminous use of herself to build up the texture of understanding, self-revelation serves her no purpose.

Still, I suspect that she is ironically bemused that the same lines her readers vainly parse for clues about her life are vibrant with exposure. Just as the nerves of the most reticent of poets can live visible on every page, so is there the pulse of a sensibility strongly alive on hers. If it fails to register, the fault is in ourselves. Because we know it only from the outside, we have no sense of how vulnerable perfect culinary pitch can render its possessor, how exposed such intensity leaves the tongue to hurt.

Although she never directly says so, again and again, especially in these more personal pages, she conveys how much a carelessly or badly made dish can affect her—in just the same brutal, physical way that an off-key note will shred a musician's ear. Confronted with such a meal, most of us plow on regardless. But she must either suffer real pain . . . or flee.

This susceptibility before food is the very opposite of "exquisite taste," with its connotations of an easily jaded palate, a connoisseurship that can be switched on or off at will. Her palate risks more than mere taste from each thing it savors: flavor can buzz in her mouth like a live wasp. An old Chinese proverb has it, "To eat well requires an adventurous spirit." Such vulnerability as hers hones that platitude to a razor's edge.

At least this is how I read her tenderness before the simple dishes that are almost always her subject, and nowhere more than in the occasional compass of these pages: plain mushrooms wrapped in grape leaves, a gratin of sweet fennel and cream, a fondue made with Guinness stout. Mixed among her accounts of restaurant forays and market foraging in provincial France are essays on pizza, home-baked bread, and potted meats, appreciations of neglected ordinaries such as lemons, tomatoes, mulberries, sardines. Delicately, nicely, she works each food, each flavor, into simple dishes exactly right, leaving each of us not only wiser but with a gently shared sense of physical release. It is this that gives each page its vital tension, her books their sense of purely private quest.

THE COOKING OF
THE SEPHARDIC JEWS

Suzy David, *The Sephardic Kosher Kitchen* (Jonathan David, 1984, 227 pp., $14.95); Viviane Alchech Miner, *From My Grandmother's Kitchen, A Sephardic Cookbook* (Triad, 1984, 184 pp., $8.95 paperback); A Lady, *The Jewish Manual* (NightinGale [Box 322, Cold Spring, NY 10516], 1983, 234 pp., $9.95 paperback).

Jewish cooking is recipe raised to a higher power: a set of definite injunctions, a grid that can be placed over almost any set of alien foodstuffs to give them a name, a hierarchy, a way of preparing them, and, most of all, a familiar face. On first glance, it seems rigid and unadapting; in practice it has proven astoundingly supple and various, joining in complex harmony the many random foods whose flavors, taken each by each, are a history of that people.

Consider the cooking of the Sephardic Jews. Although that name is now applied to all Jews native to the Mediterranean basin, the Hebrew *Sepharadh* means Spain and referred originally to the culturally rich and financially prosperous Jewish population that flourished there under the Moors. However, in 1492, Spain's new Christian rulers decreed that all Jews must accept baptism or be expelled. Some became at least nominal Christians; most fled.

Most also sailed eastward. The Ottoman Empire welcomed them as a buffer population in areas of Europe that it had recently conquered: Bulgaria, Yugoslavia, Romania, Greece. Salonika, then Turkish, now Greek, became their cultural and intellectual center. While never able to restore in full what the Inquisition had destroyed, they did establish a network of communities through the Balkans linked by a common language (Ladino, Castilian Spanish disciplined by Hebrew), culture, and religion, and, finally, a shared nostalgia for the foods, the flavors they had known in Spain.

This is what two of the cookbooks reviewed here have to offer us, a wildly successful marriage of Balkan and Mediterranean cuisines: on the one hand, the eggplant, tomato, lemon, cinnamon, almond, and hot and sweet peppers of Spain; on the other, the fish roe, yogurt, dill, salty cheeses, and pickled vegetables of Bulgaria, plus that sweet-

and-sour savor that seems the common denominator of all Jewish cooking.

A heady mixture, this Sephardic cuisine, but also a surprisingly harmonious one from the evidence. Consider, for example, Suzy David's cold bass in lemon and dill, her zucchini flavored with burnt sugar and garlic, or the sweet-and-sour stuffed grape leaves; Viviane Alchech Miner's cucumber and chicken soup, her eggplant salad with garlic and cheese, or meatballs with garlicky potatoes.

In fact, I can truthfully report that no ethnic cooking has excited my interest recently as much as the Sephardic cooking presented by these two cookbooks, and I would be hard pressed to decide which I like the better. Suzy David's recipes may have a slight edge in appeal, maybe, but Viviane Alchech Miner's are set in a fondly remembering prose. These are both fine books.

But they deceive on one point: the cuisine they share in common is only *one*, not *the*, Sephardic cooking. Not all the Sephardic Jews who fled Spain went east and not all Jews who left went in 1492. Those who claimed conversion to Christianity ("Marranos") found that this did not always render them immune to persecution. Many of these left later, and some eventually arrived in England. Although Jews had been banned from Britain by royal decree since 1290 (and did not get full rights until 1858), Sephardic Jews had been living openly in that country since the mid-seventeenth century, and their presence had attracted a fellow community of Ashkenazic (Eastern European) Jews.

This brings us to *The Jewish Manual*. First published in 1846, it is the earliest known Jewish cookbook written in English, a charmingly written guide to help the middle-class Jewish housewife prepare proper "British" cooking while still remaining faithful to the precepts of her religion. The anonymous author has since been almost positively identified as Judith Montefiore, herself of Ashkenazic descent (a Cohen) but married into the most prominent Sephardic family in England. And while there is a definite Eastern European presence in the book, the predominant flavor is, I think, Sephardic, possibly because at the time the Sephardic Jewish culture was considered the higher of the two.

So, while many of these recipes are interesting in their own right, the book is truly fascinating for its picture of Sephardic cooking melding itself into a much less likely culinary tradition than that of the Ottoman Empire—that of Victorian England. I don't so much mean the presence of obviously Spanish/Portuguese recipes (the *sopa d'oro*, *impanado*, or *eschobeche*) as the use of ingredients such as almonds, lemon, and cinnamon (but no garlic!) to enhance the blander British fare.

Sometimes this is done for obviously necessary reasons, as in the various butterless sauces devised to serve with roast meat, but in other instances it is clearly palate, not precept, at work, as in the "egg marmalade" that is really a lemon curd enhanced with almonds, or the standard veal broth ("white soup") given an un-English savor with bits of chorizo. Chorizo ("a sausage peculiar to the Jewish kitchen"— and surely a kosher version of the all-pork Iberian model) is used throughout the book, including in a "chorissa omelet," in reality a *frittata*.

The connections between British Sephardic cooking and that of the Balkans are harder to make, though they are there in the simpler, more traditional recipes, the chicken and rice, the fritters cooked in olive oil, the almond dolce, and the pear syrup. But the point, of course, is that Sephardic cooking will suffer no simple definition; its people are too diversely scattered and history too uncertain for that.

So, in fact, do the authors of two contemporary cookbooks disprove their titles with their own lives. Suzy David spent her childhood in Sofia, Bulgaria, but fled to Israel in 1943. Viviane Alchech Miner's maternal grandfather left Varna, Bulgaria, at the turn of the century; her grandmother had left Constanţa, Romania, even earlier. They met and married in Geneva, Switzerland. And so there is a special poignancy to her family in that city welcoming honored guests in the "centuries-old Sephardic tradition" of a spoonful of homemade jam in a crystal bowl and a small glass of water, thus bringing to Switzerland a custom they had at some point learned from the Greeks, along with the recipes for plum and for rose petal conserve.

The start, then, to another chapter . . . for this is a story far from finished. When it is, what a cookbook that will be! And, in the interim, here are three of its most splendid chapters.

Alice B. Toklas

THE ALICE B. TOKLAS COOK BOOK

(Harper & Row, 1984, 188 pp., $14.95)

❁

> More than an abundant collection of excellent and tempting rec-
> ipes; it is also a way of life. . . . shrewd worldly comment, rem-
> iniscences, personalities, anecdotes. . . .
> —*The New York Herald Tribune*

I came along too late for Gertrude Stein and her circle—much too
late, of course, for fantasies of being invited into it—but even too
late to grasp what all the fuss was about or to feel anything of the
magic that, for some at least, has lingered down through the years.

For those who do feel those things, this book evokes special emo-
tions, tenderly expressed by M. F. K. Fisher in the foreword of this
new edition. But if you, like me, pick it up with only a few scattered
impressions about Gertrude Stein and Alice B. Toklas, you may well
begin reading with puzzlement and soon sink into total disgruntle-
ment.

Because, while it would be wrong to say that this is a terribly
overrated cookbook, it is very much a wrongly reviewed one. Alice
B. Toklas does not write to flip polished nuggets of anecdote at her
audience; she is not Dick Cavett. She portrays her life and her cooking
as it impressed her, not as others pressed her to tell. Thus she devotes
a whole chapter to her servant problem but hardly a page to Picasso—
and that mostly to tell how she once concocted an artistic fish dish
for him out of chopped herbs, truffles, and hard-boiled egg. (The
master declared it authentic—authentic Matisse.)

There is something very British about this sort of resolute self-
possession that makes the book very disconcerting, an effect empha-
sized further by the strangely appropriate illustrations by Sir Francis
Rose. I mean the tidy measures of the prose with its emotional in-
sularity, the insistence on little refinements, the sudden bursts of
eccentricity, the occasional sharp insight with its prick of common
sense. Although this is a book about expatriate Americans living a
notorious companionship, there is no relishing wink of scandal, nor
even any whisper of the brash, innocent egoism of Gertrude Stein's
modernist prose.

And then there are the recipes. I've never seen the original American edition, but I well remember the first paperback, published in the sixties and notorious with a certain element for its hash fudge brownie recipe. It is a measure of the misconceptions about this book that that confection is (1) neither her recipe, (2) nor a brownie, (3) nor even fudge. It is a kind of Middle Eastern sweetmeat, molded of pulverized spices and herbs (including, of course, hashish), plus figs, dates, and nuts.

This recipe, although contributed by a friend, does represent a quality that characterizes many of her own dishes as described in the book; they do not, contrary to the reviews, make you want to rush into the kitchen and try them out. Make no mistake: this book reveals that Alice B. Toklas deserved the praise lavished on her cooking. It is full of insights well worth gleaning and recipes polished to a mellow shine. But too many of them are simply not recipes we much cook from anymore. They require too much labor and too many calories for their effects; they are too redolent of truffles and pheasants and butter and heavy cream—and of Jeanne or Caroline or Margit endlessly sieving, mincing, whipping . . . and plotting to quit.

No, to enjoy this book you must find your pleasure in the company of Alice B. Toklas—in a woman who knew exactly who she was. It is this that gives the book its measure of wild charm and also draws its limits, for she was a person of intense domesticity who, having established her realm, felt totally independent within it.

While the gaze she directs at the famous people who grace their table is alert, curious, even sensitive, it is also finally enigmatic, for they have no real impact on her perfect sense of self. She never wrestles with them for something in the way we think we should treat famous folk, emerging from their presence with a trophy, a kiss or wound or autograph. The historic events—such as the German occupation of France—are treated the same way. So is Gertrude Stein herself. There is never one false note in the impeccable ordinariness with which she surrounds that liaison to ever suggest she was ever surprised, frightened, or intoxicated by what happened to her, by the sui generis nature of her life.

This, I think, is one reason why Gertrude Stein loved and treasured her, and why we can, too—that she was at once so unique and, in her way, so worthy, and so uninterested in knowing about it from anyone else.

JACQUELINE HIGUERA MCMAHAN
CALIFORNIA RANCHO COOKING
(The Olive Press [P.O. Box 194, Lake Hughes, CA 93532], 1983,
248 pp., $14.95 [plus $1.50 postage])

Sometime in October 1833, even as the cold weather closed in around them, a beaver trapper named Joe Walker and the survivors of his party stumbled half starved out of the snow-filled gulches of the high Sierra and down into the San Joaquin Valley. There they found herds of branded horses, fat longhorns, and, finally, Indians who spoke the word *español* and pointed westward. They continued on until one night at camp they were puzzled by an insistent, distant rumble. Some thought it might be an earthquake, rumor of which had preceded them, but Joe Walker knew better. He had brought his men to within sound of the Pacific.

America had discovered the way over the mountains to California. The trappers spent that winter at the San Juan Bautista mission, welcomed by the Franciscan friars. Later, they continued south to the Santa Clara valley and Monterey, wondering at the Eden they had discovered. Here in this fertile land, whole herds of horses and cattle grew fat and numerous almost without tending. And life was all a man could ask—spent entirely outdoors on horseback, the food highly spiced and plentiful (if mostly beef and beans), with plenty of partying and bull-and-bear baiting, and women "well formed, with languishing eyes and soft voice."

It was a fateful collision of cultures. The trappers had stumbled onto a fragile civilization closer to the sixteenth century than to their own. Cut off from all but tenuous connection with Mexico, the *Californios* lived self-contained lives, money so casually regarded that a bowl of silver coins was left out for visitors to take as they needed (until too many Americans took the whole bowl). Accustomed to making agreements by a word, a glass of wine, and an embrace, generous in the illusion that the wealth of the land was inexhaustible and that these newcomers shared their vision of it, the rancho culture faced certain doom.

Among the ranchos of the Santa Clara when Joe Walker visited that area was Los Tularcitos, founded in 1821 by Jacqueline Higuera McMahan's great-great-grandfather. By the birth of her grandfather, the rancho was in decline; by his death it was entirely gone. All that remains now is the ranch house (part of a city park), a grove of olive trees, and the memories that live in this book.

Memories and recipes. . . . One particular quality that makes this book so wonderful is that the author is sharing a cooking that is a living reality for her, rich in association, familiar in her kitchen. Thus, each dish pulls with it a tangle of history, anecdote, proverb, useful hints and much encouragement, just as if we were standing at her elbow as she rolled out her tortillas—or even at the side of Aunt Nicolassa . . . or before her, Aunt Emma, whose flour tortillas were so famously delicate that she rationed them out one by one from her lap, never letting them mingle on the dining table with the *other* tortillas.

You see how easy it is to slip away into this universe—the family so lovingly evoked, the author such delightful company. She is also a fine cook. I'm no authority on Californio cuisine, but I trust a cook who tells me not to underestimate a dish (in this instance, red tortillas) "because of the simplicity of the ingredients." This is an admonition that could be set before almost all of her recipes, which are universally unfussy, simple, and good.

Rancho cooking was generous more than various, since staples were few, but within its range it is capable of offering much pleasure to the eater and of teaching new skills to the cook. Jacqueline Higuera McMahan is equal to the task, informative in many large and small ways, whether in choosing chili peppers, filling enchiladas, or barbecuing a bull's head. She will also help you discern the many subtle differences between Tex-Mex and Californio cuisine, which even in her own state can be casually lumped together as one.

So, expectedly, here are excellent recipes for chunky, spicy *salsas*, pit barbecue, green (sweet) corn tamales, eggplant enchiladas, chilies in walnut sauce, *carne con chile*, a super mushroom-chili burrito. But since her family has a history of knowing a good dish when they see it, you'll also find an Argentinean green steak sauce, a Chilean meat pie, Mr. Piazzi's pasta with spinach, plus seafood dishes, a charming chapter on picnics, another on desserts. Good food, good company—and no need to wait for an invitation. As the old Spanish proverb has it, "Better to arrive on time than to be invited." *Buen provecho!*

Among the many good recipes in the book is this excellent hot *salsa* recipe, which I have slightly adapted and use with great abandon. Besides being an excellent dip to serve with toasted tortilla chips or fresh vegetables, it can be spread thickly on a crusty French or Italian roll for a great summer lunch. Best of all, though, is to have it as a topping on a bowl of freshly made succotash (see page 137): chili works synergistic wonders on corn and beans. The secret to the *salsa* is the roasting of the peppers, which I do in summer right on the grill over coals of mesquite, before tossing on the beef or chicken.

A Salsa *of Roasted Chili Peppers*

3 to 8 serrano chili peppers or some other hot green chili like jalapeño
1 pound ripe tomatoes
1 bunch scallions, chopped
1 onion, chopped

2 cloves garlic, minced
2 teaspoons olive oil
1 tablespoon red wine vinegar
1 to 2 tablespoons chopped cilantro
Salt to taste

Roast the peppers over a grill or on a gas flame until they are blackened all over. Wrap in foil for 15 minutes or until cool, then scrape away the charred skin under cold running water, remove stem and seeds, and mince the flesh. Peel, seed, and roughly chop the tomatoes, reserving all liquid in a bowl. Mix with the bits of pepper flesh and all the other ingredients. Let the mixture mellow for an hour or so before serving. It should be eaten within a few days of its making. (*Note:* I must confess that I don't take my *salsa* too hot, but I love that roasted pepper flavor. So I grill a sweet red pepper and add that to the mixture as well. Not authentic, maybe, but real good.)

MARY RANDOLPH
THE VIRGINIA HOUSE-WIFE
a facsimile of the 1824 edition, with excerpts from later editions
and historical notes and commentaries by Karen Hess
(University of South Carolina Press, 1984, 370 pp., $14.95)

What are we to do with Mary Randolph? Even *new* cookbooks produced these days lead such short useful lives, no matter how good.
For cooks now in their twenties, "grandma's" cooking means the fare
of the 1940s; Mother's (and by then, maybe Dad's, too) was taken
from cookbooks of the 1960s. How quaint they now seem: Clementine
Paddleford, Sheila Hibben, June Platt, Sylvia Vaughn Thompson.
No one will know these names in ten years; few who recognize them
now still regularly consult their books. It might have been better to
try to resurrect our interest in *them* while that might still be possible,
the cooking of Mary Randolph seeming beyond all hope of recall.

Nonetheless, this attractive edition is meant to be used—and by
home cooks, too, not just scholars. Karen Hess, the editor, is this
country's culinary conscience and she has been using her brilliant
critical editions of American classic cookbooks—first Martha Washington's *Booke of Cookery* and now this volume (may their tribe increase!)—to reacquaint us all with the lost richness—genius, really—
of our culinary heritage. This would be a sad effort if it were a hopeless
lament, but her notes are full of enthusiasm and challenge: a call to
arms, not a lulling analysis of *temps* long *perdu*.

There is no doubt that Mary Randolph's book has a long and popular
history. It was *the* American cookbook for most of the last century
and, for the South, even into this one. This reputation—as we shall
see—was well deserved. (That its virtues were recognized at the time
can be seen in the Southern legend that she went through three
fortunes testing the recipes.)

But what makes Mary Randolph important to us is not only the
quality of her cooking, but also her good luck. She was the right
woman at the right time to take advantage of the moment when
America's cuisine reached first maturity. It was a time of abundance;
game and fish were plentiful, farm produce profuse and cheap. She

doesn't write of chickens but in the plural; her smallest unit of pig is the joint. She knows forty vegetables and seventeen aromatic herbs.

At that same time, this nation was beginning to develop beyond the English cooking that is our culinary foundation. Not only were we taking dishes and flavors from other cuisines—Spanish, French, Italian, Indian, Creole, African—but we were learning to meld them into something uniquely our own. What is so fascinating about Mary Randolph is watching her inspired but unselfconscious palate pulling all this—the abundance of good things, the enticingly different ways of preparation—into an imaginative but sensible home cooking.

Here again Mary Randolph was fortunate, if in a way she herself might not have appreciated. Although she and her husband were both of the Virginia elite, they suffered financial problems that forced them to give up Moldavia, their stately Richmond home, and ultimately open a boarding house. If it were not for these reverses, she might never have written a cookbook at all. Or, if she had, it might have focused on a richer, more patrician cuisine.

Instead, a surprising number of her recipes are accessible to us, and the taste that informs them even more so. "Great care must be taken," she says about the cooking of asparagus, "to watch the exact time of their becoming tender; take them just at that instant, and they will have their true flavour and colour; a minute or two more boiling destroys both."

Despite her generous use of both sweet milk and butter, her recipe for mashed potatoes calls for only a tablespoon of both: "do not make them too moist"—which is exactly right if it is the taste of potato you love. "The great excellence of a beef steak," she comments, "lies in having it immediately from the gridiron." How much better American cooking would be if *that* single rule were followed!

I could go on and on here, for this is a book of many pleasant surprises: see her recipe for gazpacho, for example, or polenta, oyster loaves, or the "nice twelve o'clock luncheon." But, ultimately, what makes the book rewarding comes less from the many attractive recipes as from the astonishing, perhaps even disturbing, insight it gives us into our past.

I don't know about you, but the general images I have for the cooking of the last century in this country are two: on the one hand, a "home-spun" frontier cuisine of at best limited, rough, and honest fare (mostly pork, corn, and whiskey); on the other, the vulgar, ostentatious but naïve gorgings of such as Diamond Jim Brady, who once swore he would eat a Turkish towel if it were dipped in the right sauce.

Mary Randolph gives the lie to this condescending fiction: her cooking is profoundly sensual *and* moral. Her recipes are economical, clear, direct, and amazingly (given the kitchen equipment at her disposal) uncomplicated, and yet they summon the very best out of the ingredients at hand with an open and uninhibited appetite.

In fact, what she offers us is an almost utopian cuisine, where excellent, fresh, seasonal food is worked to simple perfection—without resort to convenience foods or modern culinary equipment. And what Karen Hess is arguing, from the persuasive force of Mary Randolph's compelling example, is that what that lady could do a hundred years ago, surely we can do, too, with all that is at our disposal today. And in such company, no one would wish anything else.

But when I put aside the pleasure of Mary Randolph's inspiration to reach out for her hand as an actual guide, I feel her suddenly whirl away from me back down the corridors of time—past not only the good cooks named above but also Mary Lincoln, Maria Parloa, and the Shaker and Creole cooks whose palates were also honest and true.

We can admire, even envy, where we cannot yet hope to emulate. The easy balance of sensual and moral that gives her cooking its surety is for us a much more slippery thing—as evidenced by the fact that few modern cooks convince us they hold it for long. They quickly seem stuffy or flabby or fake, and we put their books, their examples aside. Mary Randolph can't, won't reform us. But we can still take her as a refreshment and reason to hope. Such a balance did once exist and through her we learn how fine a thing it was. Without ever intending it, Mary Randolph teaches us to see the past (and ourselves, too) with new and astonished eyes.

PUMPKIN PUDDING [PIE].   Stew a fine sweet pumpkin till soft and dry, rub it through a sieve, mix the pulp of the pumpkin with six eggs [beaten until] quite light, a quarter pound of butter, half a pint of new milk, some pounded ginger and nutmeg, a wine glass [2 ounces] of brandy, and sugar to your taste. Should it be too liquid, stew it a little dryer; put a paste round the edges and in the bottom of a shallow dish or plate, pour in the mixture, cut some thin bits of paste, twist them up and lay them across the top and bake it nicely.

Bibliography

✾

Artusi, Pellegrino. *Italian Cook Book*. Translated by Olga Ragusa. New York: S. F. Vanni, 1945.

Bailey, Pearl. *Pearl's Kitchen*. New York: Harcourt Brace Jovanovich, 1973.

Barr, Ann and Paul Levy. *The Official Foodie Handbook*. London: Ebury Press, 1984.

Beard, James. *Delights and Prejudices*. New York: Atheneum, 1964.

———. *The New James Beard*. New York: Knopf, 1981.

Blot, Pierre. *Hand-Book of Practical Cookery for Ladies and Professional Cooks*, New York: Appleton, 1969. (Facsimile edition. New York: Arno, 1973.)

Boni, Ada. *Italian Regional Cooking*. New York: Dutton, 1969.

Bowen, Elizabeth. *The House in Paris*. New York: Knopf, 1963.

Bradley, Richard. *The Country Housewife and Lady's Director* (a facsimile of the 1736 edition with an introduction, notes, glossary, and bibliography by Caroline Davidson). London: Prospect Books, 1980.

Bremer, Frederica. *The Narrative of a Winter Residence and Summer Travel in Greece and Its Islands*. London, 1863.

Brugiere, Sarah van Buren. *Good Living*. New York, 1890.

Bugialli, Giuliano. *The Fine Art of Italian Cooking*. New York: Quadrangle/New York Times, 1977.

Bunyard, Edward A. *The Anatomy of Dessert*. New York: Dutton, 1934.

Chamberlain, Lesley. *The Food and Cooking of Russia*. London: Allen Lane, 1982.

Chantiles, Vilma Liacouras. *The New York Ethnic Food Market Guide & Cookbook*. New York: Dodd, Mead, 1984.

Child, Julia, and Simon Beck. *Mastering the Art of French Cooking.* Vol. 2. New York: Knopf, 1970.

Claiborne, Craig. *Craig Claiborne's Favorites.* Vol. 2. New York: Quadrangle/The New York Times, 1976.

Condon, Richard. "Harry's Bar of Venice," *Gourmet* 42, no. 2 (1982).

Courtine, Robert. *Real French Cooking.* London: Faber and Faber, 1956.

————. *The Hundred Glories of French Cooking.* New York: Farrar Straus Giroux, 1973.

David, Elizabeth. *French Provincial Cooking.* London: Penguin, 1967.

————. *Italian Food.* London: Penguin, 1963.

————. *Mediterranean Food.* London: Penguin, 1955.

————. *An Omelette and a Glass of Wine.* London: A Jill Norman Book, Robert Hale, 1984.

————. *Summer Cooking.* London: Penguin, 1965.

David, Suzy. *The Sephardic Kosher Kitchen.* Middle Village, N.Y.: Jonathan David, 1984.

Davidson, Lionel. "The Breton Fart." In *Writer's Favorite Recipes,* compiled by Gillian Vincent and the National Book League of Great Britain. New York: St. Martins, 1979.

De Groot, Roy Andries. *Auberge of the Flowering Hearth.* New York: Bobbs Merrill, 1973.

Der Haroutunian, Arto. *Middle Eastern Cookery.* London: Century, 1982.

Famularo, Joe, and Louise Imperiale. *The Festive Famularo Kitchen.* New York: Atheneum, 1977.

Farmer, Fannie Merritt. *The Boston Cooking-School Cook Book.* Boston: Little, Brown, 1896.

Field, Carol. *The Italian Baker.* New York: Harper & Row, 1985.

Finn, Molly. *Summer Feasts.* New York: Simon & Schuster, 1985.

Fisher, M. F. K. *The Art of Eating.* New York: World, 1954.

———. "I was Really Very Hungry." In *As They Were.* New York: Knopf, 1982.

———. *With Bold Knife and Fork.* New York: Putnam, 1969.

Forbes, Leslie. *A Taste of Tuscany.* Boston: Little, Brown, 1985.

Ghedini, Francesco. *Northern Italian Cooking.* New York: Dutton, 1973.

Giobbi, Edward. *Italian Family Cooking.* New York: Random House, 1971.

Grass, Günter. *The Flounder.* Translated by Ralph Manheim. New York: Harcourt Brace Jovanovich, 1978.

Greene, Bert. *Bert Greene's Kitchen Bouquets.* Chicago: Contemporary Books, 1973.

Grigson, Jane. *The Art of Charcuterie.* New York: Knopf, 1967, 1968.

———. *Food with the Famous.* London: Michael Joseph, 1979.

———. *Jane Grigson's Vegetable Book.* New York: Atheneum, 1979.

———. *The Mushroom Feast.* New York: Knopf, 1975.

———, ed. *The World Atlas of Food.* New York: Simon & Schuster, 1974.

Harland, Marion. *Common Sense in the Household, A Manual of Practical Housewifery.* New York: Charles Scribner's Sons, 1883.

Hartley, Dorothy. *Food in England.* London: MacDonald & Jane's, 1979.

Hazan, Marcella. *The Classic Italian Cook Book.* New York: Knopf, 1977.

Herter, George Leonard. *The Bull Cook and Authentic Historical Recipes and Practices.* Waseca, Minn.: Herter's, 1960.

Hess, John L. and Karen. *The Taste of America.* New York: Viking/Grossman, 1977.

The Home Comfort Cook Book. The Wrought Iron Range Company, 1937.

Johnston, Mireille. *The Cuisine of the Sun*. New York: Random House, 1976.

Jones, Evan. *American Food, The Gastronomic Story*. New York: Dutton, 1975.

Jouveau, René. *La Cuisine Provençale*. Berne: Éditions du Message, 1962.

Kennedy, Diana. *Nothing Fancy*. New York: Dial, 1984.

Kent, Louise Andrews. *Mrs. Appleyard's Kitchen*. Boston: Houghton Mifflin, 1942.

Keys, Ancel and Margaret. *The Benevolent Bean*. New York: Noonday, 1972.

————. *How to Eat Well and Stay Well the Mediterranean Way*. New York: Doubleday, 1975.

Klein, Maggie Blyth. *The Feast of the Olive*. Berkeley: Aris, 1983.

A Lady. *The Jewish Manual* (facsimile edition of 1846 edition, with introduction by Chaim Raphael). Cold Spring, N.Y.: NightinGale, 1983.

Lamb, Venice. *The Home Book of Turkish Cooking*. London: Faber, 1969.

Land, Mary. *Louisiana Cookery*. Baton Rouge: University of Louisiana Press, 1954.

Lane, Margaret. *The Beatrix Potter Country Cookery Book*. London: Frederick Warne, 1981.

Lawrence, D. H. *Sea and Sardinia*. In *D. H. Lawrence in Italy*. New York: Penguin, 1985.

Leyel, Mrs. C. F., and Miss Olga Harley. *The Gentle Art of Cookery*. With an Introduction by Elizabeth David. London: Chatto & Windus/The Hogarth Press, 1983. (First published in 1925.)

Lincoln, Mary. *Mrs. Lincoln's Boston Cook Book*. Boston: Roberts, 1883.

London, Sheryl. *Eggplant & Squash*. New York: Atheneum, 1976.

Lutes, Della T. *The Country Kitchen*. Boston: Little, Brown, 1936.

McCully, Helen, and Jacques Pépin. *The Other Half of the Egg*. New York: Barrow, 1967.

McMahan, Jacqueline Higuera. *California Rancho Cooking*. Lake Hughes, Calif.: The Olive Press, 1983.

Macmiadhacháin, Anna, Mary Reynolds, Claudia Roden, and Helge Rubenstein. *The Mediterranean Cookbook*. Secaucus, N.J.: Chartwell, 1979.

Mariani, John. *The Dictionary of American Food & Drink*. New Haven: Ticknor & Fields, 1983.

Mark, Theonie. *Greek Islands Cooking*. Boston: Little, Brown, 1974.

Médecin, Jacques. *Cuisine Niçoise*. London: Penguin, 1983.

Miner, Viviane Alchech, with Linda Krinn. *From My Grandmother's Kitchen, A Sephardic Cookbook*. Gainesville, Fla.: Triad, 1984.

Morash, Marian. *The Victory Garden Cookbook*. New York: Knopf, 1982.

Muir, Edwin. *The Autobiography of Edwin Muir*. London: Hogarth, 1954.

Nelson, Richard. *Richard Nelson's American Cooking*. New York: New American Library, 1983.

Olney, Richard. *Simple French Food*. New York: Atheneum, 1974.

Orwell, George. *Down and Out in Paris and London*. London: Gollancz, 1933.

Parloa, Maria. *Miss Parloa's New Cook Book and Marketing Guide*. Boston: Estes & Lauriat, 1880.

The Picayune Creole Cook Book. 2d ed. (1901). New York: Dover, 1971.

Platt, June. *June Platt's New England Cook Book*. New York: Atheneum, 1971.

Price, Pamela Vandyke. *Eating and Drinking in France Today*. New York: Scribners, 1974.

Quayle, Eric. *Old Cook Books*. An Illustrated History. New York: Dutton, 1978.

Randolph, Mary. *The Virginia House-Wife*. (Facsimile of the first edition, 1824, with additional material from the editions of 1825 and 1828 to present a complete text, with historical notes and commentaries by Karen Hess.) Columbia, S.C.: University of South Carolina, 1984.

Romagnoli, Margaret and G. Franco. "Bon Appétit Cooking Class." *Bon Appétit* (August 1981).

Romer, Elizabeth. *The Tuscan Year*. New York: Atheneum, 1984.

Root, Waverley. *The Best of Italian Cooking*. New York: Grosset & Dunlap, 1974.

———. *The Food of France*. New York: Random House, 1958.

———. *The Food of Italy*. New York: Atheneum, 1971.

Rorer, Sarah Tyson. *Mrs. Rorer's New Cook Book*. Philadelphia: Arnold, 1902.

St. Botolph Society. *The Cocktail Book*. Boston: Page, 1925.

Salaman, Rena. *Greek Food*. London: Fontana, 1983.

Scott, Maria Luisa, and Jack Denton Scott. *The Great Potato Cookbook*. New York: Bantam, 1980.

Sharman, Fay. *The Taste of France*. Boston: Houghton Mifflin, 1982.

Shenton, James P., Angelo M. Pellegrini, Dale Brown, Israel Shenker, and Peter Wood, and the Editors of Time-Life Books. *American Cooking: The Melting Pot*. New York: Time-Life Books, 1972.

Simon, André L. *A Concise Encyclopedia of Gastronomy*. Woodstock, N.Y.: The Overlook Press, 1981. (Original copyright 1952.)

Sokolov, Raymond. *Fading Feast*. New York: Farrar Straus Giroux, 1981.

Stern, Jane and Michael. *Roadfood and Goodfood*. New York: Knopf, 1986.

————. *Square Meals*. New York: Knopf, 1984.

Toklas, Alice B. *The Alice B. Toklas Cook Book*. New York: Harper & Row, 1984.

Tropp, Barbara. *The Modern Art of Chinese Cooking*. New York: Morrow, 1982.

Ungerer, Miriam. *Good Cheap Food*. New York: Viking, 1973.

Uvezian, Sonia. *The Cuisine of Armenia*. New York: Harper & Row, 1974.

Viazzi, Alfredo. *Cucina e Nostalgia*. New York: Random House, 1983.

Waldo, Myra. *The International Encyclopedia of Cooking*. Vol. 2, Glossary. New York: Macmillan, 1967.

Washington, Martha. *Martha Washington's Booke of Cookery* (with introduction and commentary by Karen Hess). New York: Columbia University Press, 1981.

Wells, Patricia. *The Food Lover's Guide to Paris*. New York: Workman, 1984.

White, Florence. *Good Things in England*. London: Jonathan Cape, 1968.

Willan, Anne. *French Regional Cooking*. New York: William Morrow, 1981.

Wolcott, Imogene. *The New England Yankee Cook Book*. New York: Coward-McCann, 1939.

Work Projects Administration, Writers' Program. *New Orleans City Guide*. Boston: Houghton Mifflin, 1938.

Work Projects Administration, Writers' Program. *The North Carolina Guide*. Chapel Hill: University of North Carolina, 1955.

Work Projects Administration, Writers' Program. *South Carolina, A Guide to the Palmetto State*. New York: Oxford, 1941.

Index